WHAT'S COOKING

AGRICULTURE AND FOOD SERIES

A strong food and agriculture system is fundamental to economic growth, poverty reduction, environmental sustainability, and human health. The Agriculture and Food Series is intended to prompt public discussion and inform policies that will deliver higher incomes, reduce hunger, improve sustainability, and generate better health and nutrition from the food we grow and eat. It expands on the former Agriculture and Rural Development series by considering issues from farm to fork, in both rural and urban settings. Titles in this series undergo internal and external review under the management of the World Bank's Agriculture and Food Global Practice.

Titles in this series

WHAT'S COOKING: DIGITAL TRANSFORMATION OF THE AGRIFOOD SYSTEM

Kateryna Schroeder, Julian Lampietti, and Ghada Elabed

 WORLD BANK GROUP

CONTENTS

Figures

Maps

Photo

Tables

As a source of jobs and economic opportunities for hundreds of millions of people and nourishment for all, the agriculture and food system is critical to achieving the Sustainable Development Goals (SDGs).

But the agriculture and food system is not currently fit for this purpose. Poverty endures in rural areas. The way food is produced and consumed is associated with many health issues, including undernutrition, foodborne illnesses, and diet-related chronic diseases. The agrifood system also puts huge stress on the environment by driving large-scale land conversion, overtaxing natural resources, and generating up to 29 percent of global greenhouse gases. While the agrifood system is a driver of climate change, however, it is also part of the solution. A more sustainable agrifood system that helps restore landscapes and generates ecosystem services, including carbon sequestration, is possible.

This will require a fundamental shift in how the agrifood system operates. Digital technologies can help accelerate that shift by bringing down transaction costs and addressing pervasive information asymmetries. The digital revolution—and the data it generates—are key to building an agriculture and food system that is efficient, environmentally sustainable, equitable, and able to link the world's 570 million farms with 8 billion consumers.

Digital technologies promise to transform the agrifood system in unprecedented ways. Unlike past technological revolutions in agriculture, which began on farms, the digital agriculture revolution is being sparked at multiple points along the agrifood value chain. The change is driven by the ability to collect, use, and analyze machine-readable data about practically every aspect of the value chain, and by the emergence of digital platforms disrupting business models in the agrifood system. Ultimately, digital technology could help lower the costs of organizing agrifood chains, increase the amount of available usable information related to the agrifood system, and ensure equitable access to this information by all stakeholders.

How can we ensure that digital technology delivers on its promise for agriculture and food?

What's Cooking: Digital Transformation of the Agrifood System investigates how digital technologies can accelerate the transformation of the agrifood system, including by increasing efficiency on the farm; improving farmers' access to output, input, and financial markets; improving quality control and traceability; and increasing efficiency in the design and delivery of agriculture policies. It also analyzes the role of digital agriculture in improving equity and environmental sustainability in food systems and highlights the risks that could emerge along the way, including risks associated with data governance, inadequate competition within and between digital platforms, and the potential deepening of the digital divide. With these in mind, it identifies public policy entry points to spur this digital transformation while minimizing the risks.

More important, the report aims to ignite a discussion around these emerging trends in digital agriculture and lead to change. With change comes opportunity for positive transformation and the opportunity to steer the agrifood system in a direction that will deliver the triple benefits of healthy people, a healthy planet, and healthy economies.

Mari E. Pangestu
Managing Director
Development Policy and Partnerships
The World Bank

ACKNOWLEDGMENTS

This report was prepared by a team led by Kateryna Schroeder (Agriculture Economist and Task Team Lead), Ghada Elabed (Senior Agriculture Economist and co-Task Team Lead), and Maria Claudia Pachon (Senior Digital Development Specialist and co-Task Team Lead), under the overall guidance of Julian Lampietti, Practice Manager. The team comprised Hanane Ahmed, Mekbib Haile, Eva Hasiner, Alexandra Horst, Marie-Agnes Jouanjean, Armine Juergenliemk, Laura Ralston, and David Treguer. The team expresses its gratitude to Martien Van Nieuwkoop (Global Director, Agriculture and Food Global Practice) and Boutheina Guermazi (Director, Digital Development) for providing strategic guidance and serving as invaluable sources of encouragement.

A series of background papers used in the study were prepared by Derek Baker (Professor of Agribusiness and Value Chains, University of New England), Elinor Benami (Assistant Professor of Agricultural and Applied Economics, Virginia Polytechnic Institute and State University), Regina Birner (Professor and Chair of Social and Institutional Change in Agricultural Development, University of Hohenheim), Michael Carter (Distinguished Professor of Agricultural and Resource Economics, University of California, Davis), Thomas Daum (Research Fellow, University of Hohenheim), Madhu Khanna (Agricultural and Consumer Economics Distinguished Professor, University of Illinois at Urbana-Champaign), Don Larson (Independent Consultant), John Nash (Independent Consultant), Valeria Pesce (Independent Consultant), Carl Pray (Distinguished Professor of Agricultural, Food and Resource

Economics, Rutgers University), Caroline Pulver (Independent Consultant), and Ashley Rootsey (Innovation Manager, Food Agility Cooperative Research Centre).

Chapter 5 was prepared by Marie-Agnes Jouanjean and Francesca Casalini of the Organisation for Economic Co-operation and Development (OECD) with inputs from Kateryna Schroeder (World Bank). The team is also thankful to Emily Gray of OECD for assisting with the clearance process.

Katie Freeman provided the box on the digital technologies for sustainable intensification in Uruguay. Marina Kayumova provided the box on measuring good regulatory practices for access to digital technologies in rural areas. Michael Norton conducted spatial analysis. The International Center for Tropical Agriculture and the Food and Agriculture Organization of the United Nations provided support in developing the Digital Agriculture Profiling tool. Ina Ajazi, Elizabeth Ash, Rebecca Chamberlin, John Dearborn, John Downes, Kyle Farrell, Aolin Gong, Sinan Hatik, Randolph Kent, Dong Ku Lee, James Lee, Joseph Massad, Yulia Mitusova, Sheva Tabatabainejad, Olga Thomas, Fang Zhang, and Jenny Zhang provided invaluable research support.

The team is grateful to Rabah Arezki, Thomas Bauer, Regina Birner, Christopher Brett, Diego Arias Carballo, Peter Cook, Thomas Daum, Marianne Fay, Madhur Gautam, Georges Houngbonon, Alan Johnson, Marc Lixi, Oksana Nagayets, Carl Pray, Parmesh Shah, Adam Struve, William Sutton, and Hans Timmer for the thoughtful guidance and comments on the report.

The team thanks World Bank communications experts Flore Martinant de Preneuf and Xenia Zia Morales for their continuous support; Funda Canli, Teguest Demissie, and Rosalie Trinidad for the administrative assistance; and Joe Brinley, Joe Caponio, Mike Crumplar, and Bruce Ross-Larson at Communications Development for editorial support. The World Bank's Formal Publishing program coordinated the design, copyediting, typesetting, printing, and dissemination of the book.

This publication was made possible by the generous support of the members of the Digital Development Partnership—the World Bank's program helping developing countries leverage innovation and technology to solve their most pressing challenges. For more information, please visit https://www.worldbank.org/en/programs/digital-development-partnership.

ABOUT THE AUTHORS

Ghada Elabed is a Senior Agriculture Economist at the global engagement unit in the Agriculture and Food Global Practice. Ghada works in both analytical and operational projects spanning the areas of climate-smart agriculture, agriculture policy, digital agriculture, and the agriculture and energy nexus. Before joining the World Bank Group, Ghada worked as a researcher at Mathematica Policy Research. Ghada earned a PhD in agricultural and resource economics from the University of California, Davis; an MS in environmental economics from École Polytechnique, France; and a BS in agronomy from AgrosParisTech, France.

Julian Lampietti is the Global Engagement Manager in the Agriculture and Food Global Practice. His responsibilities include strategic planning, donor outreach, and oversight for global knowledge and advisory programs. Previously, he managed the Agriculture and Food program in the Middle East, North Africa, Eastern Europe, and Central Asia. Julian was formerly based in Buenos Aires, Argentina, and he has published books and journal articles on a broad range of topics, including poverty, economics, agriculture, food security, logistics, and energy. He holds a PhD in public policy from the University of North Carolina at Chapel Hill and a master's degree in natural resources economics from Duke University.

Kateryna Schroeder is an Agriculture Economist in the Europe and Central Asia unit of the Agriculture and Food Global Practice. In her work she focuses on digital agriculture, agricultural and trade policy analysis, and food security.

Before joining the World Bank Group, Kateryna worked as a researcher at the Food and Agricultural Policy Institute and as a frequent consultant with the Food and Agriculture Organization of the United Nations on issues related to food security, nutrition, and trade. She holds a PhD in agricultural and applied economics from the University of Missouri.

ABBREVIATIONS

ADI	Agriculture Digitalization Index
CAP	Common Agricultural Policy (European Union)
DLT	distributed ledger technology
EBA	Enabling the Business of Agriculture
EEE	efficiency, equity, and environmental sustainability
eNAM	Electronic National Agricultural Market (India)
EU	European Union
GDP	gross domestic product
GHG	greenhouse gas
GPS	global positioning system
GSM	Global System for Mobile communications
IACS	integrated administration and control system
IBLI	Index-based Livestock Insurance program (Kenya)
ICT	information and communication technology
IoT	internet of things
LPIS	Land Parcel Identification System
MFD	Maximizing Finance for Development
NASTP	National Agricultural Science and Technology Park (China)
OECD	Organisation for Economic Co-operation and Development
PPP	progress, policy and enabling environment, and potential impact and replicability
PRTC	policy-related transaction cost
QR	quick response (matrix bar) code
R&D	research and development

SAR	special administrative region
SMS	short message service (text)
TFP	total factor productivity
VRT	variable rate technology/technologies

All dollar amounts are US dollars unless otherwise indicated.

A FRAMEWORK TO GUIDE THE PUBLIC POLICY RESPONSE AIMED AT MAXIMIZING THE EFFICIENCY, EQUITY, AND ENVIRONMENTAL SUSTAINABILITY OF THE DIGITAL TRANSFORMATION

The world's agrifood system has the potential to help reduce poverty, improve nutrition, and provide vast environmental benefits. But it is off course in achieving these aspirational goals. The global food supply is plentiful, yet undernourishment has been rising since 2014. Poverty rates are also on the rise, with most of the world's poor living in rural areas. Foodborne diseases continue taking a toll on human life and public budgets. And agriculture remains a major contributor to negative environmental outcomes.

Why are the promises unmet, and why is the world off course? High transaction costs and information asymmetries have a lot to do with it. All of us, 7.7 billion and counting, are part of agricultural markets, and most of us make decisions every day about the food we consume. Agricultural goods are produced on 570 million farms, mostly small and run by families in developing countries. Food systems are local, but also global, linked through trade and sophisticated financial and insurance markets. These markets rely on transactions and information that influence the decisions farmers make about inputs, land, labor, capital, and outputs—and the choices consumers make about the attributes of the food they consume, including prices, production practices, and environmental impacts. The contrast between food surpluses on farms and food shortages in stores during the COVID-19 lockdowns highlights the high transaction costs and information asymmetries that plague the agriculture and food system.

The goal of this report is twofold. First, it examines the pathways through which digital technologies can accelerate the transformation of the agrifood system. Second, it outlines the role public policy and investment can play in maximizing the positive and minimizing the negative impact of digital technologies on this transformation. The report investigates how digital technologies can improve the allocation of physical, natural, and human capital on the farm and reduce transaction costs off the farm, gaining efficiency. It also analyzes the role of digital agriculture in improving equity and environmental sustainability in food systems and highlights the risks that could emerge along the way. The role of governments in this process is to increase the space for private sector activity, improving the policy and regulatory environment and using public investments to crowd in private sector investment. In creating incentives to prompt private economic agents to maximize societal benefits, the public sector must also mitigate the potential (sometimes unknown) risks arising from digital agriculture.

DIGITAL TECHNOLOGIES OFFER HUGE OPPORTUNITIES

Digital technologies and networks—rapidly developed and deployed—can transform the agrifood system by overcoming the long-standing transaction costs and information asymmetries. The digital agriculture revolution builds on earlier revolutions but is profoundly different. Rather than spreading sequentially from on-farm innovations, it is emanating simultaneously from multiple entry points along the food chain (figure ES.1). Making this possible is the ability to collect, use, and analyze massive amounts of machine-readable data about practically every aspect of the value chain, and the emergence of digital platforms disrupting business models in the agrifood system. In 2014, 190,000 data points were produced per farm, per day, and experts predict that by 2050 each farm will produce around 4.1 million data points daily. Extrapolating across the agrifood system, the number of data points flowing across different stakeholders is countless. This massive set of decisions and transactions offers the possibility for small-scale, flexible organizational and production systems to flourish and nimbly navigate a changing operating environment, contributing to healthy people, a healthy economy, and a healthy planet.

On the farm, emerging digital technologies can increase farmers' technical efficiency. Emerging, although limited, evidence shows that improved access to information has positive impacts on farmers' technology adoption, while studies on precision agriculture show a largely positive impact on farmers' profitability. For example, some technologies are significantly improving farmers' access to information about the range of productivity-increasing technologies and about how best to use them. Faster access to more information has a largely positive impact on farmers' profitability. Also increasing productivity are geo-enabled digital technologies that support farmers' decision-making through the acquisition and leveraging of granular data about their fields and animals in combination with timely, accurate, and location-specific weather and agronomic data.

Off the farm, digital technologies can increase farmers' access to upstream and downstream markets by drastically lowering information-related transaction costs. That could allow them to tap into a larger, thicker set of markets through improved price discovery, buyer-seller matching, lower transport

FIGURE ES.1 Digital Technologies Allow Information to Flow More Easily across the Food System

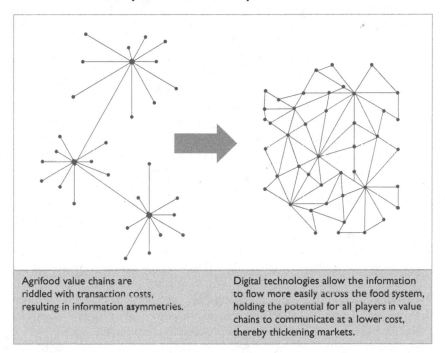

| Agrifood value chains are riddled with transaction costs, resulting in information asymmetries. | Digital technologies allow the information to flow more easily across the food system, holding the potential for all players in value chains to communicate at a lower cost, thereby thickening markets. |

Source: World Bank.

costs, and digitally enabled collective action to increase farmers' inclusion and bargaining power in agrifood value chains. Already farmers are seeing new incentives for quality improvement, changes in the way they allocate resources, and higher incomes and profits.

Digital technologies, such as distributed ledger technology, can transform quality control and traceability. Decentralized tracing of food throughout the supply chain creates opportunities for safer, more sustainable food. Safer sourcing is important because some 600 million people fall ill after eating contaminated food each year, costing low- and middle-income countries $110 billion in lost productivity and medical expenses. Knowing where food comes from and how it was produced allows consumers to make more informed decisions about the impacts of the food they consume on their health and the planet's health. More sustainably sourced food also earns a price premium from environment-and-health-conscious consumers who can afford it. This price signal, when transmitted to various actors along the value chain, could encourage safe production practices.

Digital technologies, such as mobile money and remote sensing for insurance, can remake rural finance markets. Mobile money reduces the cost of depositing and withdrawing savings in formal institutions and enables farmers in need to access friends' and family's savings. Remote-sensing data and advanced computing capacity improve yield estimates, reducing the design risk that plagued first-generation index insurance contracts. Remote-sensing data also reduce the costs of monitoring traditional insurance contracts. Digital credit scoring, using nontraditional data to predict individual default risk and determine credit terms, promises to reduce the costs associated with processing loans and to deepen the penetration of credit markets. But more work is needed to improve the ability of digital credit scoring to predict default risks.

Digital technologies can increase efficiency in the design and delivery of agricultural policies. Both the political economy and the policy-related trans-action costs shape a country's portfolio of policy instruments, including those influencing the adoption of digital technologies, often leading to second-best policy instruments. Governments incur these costs gathering information, planning and designing policies, collecting revenue, and implementing and monitoring the policies. Digital technologies have the power to lower many of these costs and increase the gains for farmers and consumers. Properly directed, they may also help to deliver more efficient, equitable, and environ-mentally sustainable outcomes for the agrifood system.

The environmental impacts of digital technology on the food system are expected to be mostly positive. They will stem from the direct, enabling, and behavioral effects of digital technologies, but the empirical evidence on these effects is still scarce. The direct effects arise from changes to production and dis-tribution processes that have a direct impact on the use of natural resources and on greenhouse gas emissions. Yet precision technologies apply water, fertilizers, herbicides, and pesticides only when and where they are needed, limiting the harm to soil and water resources caused by excessive or inadequate applications. Enabling effects are attributable to the enhanced scope for environmental mon-itoring of agricultural production systems. For example, blockchain-enabled traceability could reduce food losses in food systems by up to 30 million tons annually if it were to monitor information in half of the world's supply chains. Behavioral effects result from transforming the behavior and attitudes of food consumers and producers, increasing the environmental sustainability of the agrifood system. Digital technologies can generate data on how inputs harm the environment and communicate that data to promote systemic changes in the input industry's values and behavior. They can also disseminate information to producers and consumers about ways of improving environmental sustain-ability, particularly about reducing food waste, in downstream markets.

The danger of digital technologies, despite their potential benefits, is that they may also encourage a rebound effect. Precision agriculture technologies could lead to less pollution per unit of input or output by increasing the effi-ciency of using such natural resources as water and land. But since they increase total resource use or increase yield per acre, their total effect on pollution is unclear. Precision farming may accelerate the depletion of natural resources in the rebound effect well known to energy economists, where efficiency gains led to increased machinery use, and thus to increased energy use and greenhouse gas emissions. In agricultural water management, the rebound effect is increasingly discussed in connection with the risk of rising water withdrawals and uses. Precision agriculture could also lead to higher marginal abatement costs. Because precision technologies make inputs more productive at the margin, the opportunity cost in forgone profits of not using them is higher as well. The impact of digital agriculture on biodiversity is also ambiguous.

THE RISKS OF A DIGITAL DIVIDE REMAIN SIGNIFICANT

Digital technologies can do much to narrow the economic, spatial, and social divides in rural areas. They can narrow economic divides by changing economies of scale on farms and facilitating easier access to markets. They can narrow spatial divides and lessen the disadvantages of remoteness by lowering hurdles to information, markets, and services. And they can narrow social divides by creating opportunities to integrate disadvantaged groups into society, for example, by changing social interaction through digital means.

But the same economic, spatial, and social divides risk widening a digital divide. Small, isolated communities are less likely to enjoy quality broadband coverage. Income and human capital determine the types of devices and services that farms and households can afford or will adopt. Farmers in developing countries and smallholders may lack the skills and knowledge to reap the benefits of digital applications. Consequently, the benefits might accrue disproportionately to farmers positioned to take advantage of such opportunities. In addition, digital technologies increase the demand for skilled labor while decreasing it for unskilled labor, so they can exacerbate and perpetuate labor market inequalities and further widen the gender gap in rural areas. Women and girls face barriers to digital inclusion that reflect their inequalities in access to education, careers, and other opportunities.

DATA GOVERNANCE AND COMPETITION ARE MAJOR CONCERNS

Data-related technical, social, and legal challenges must be addressed for the digital transformation of the food system. The challenges relate to data ownership, data protection, and data veracity and validation. Laws addressing the ownership of data from digital agriculture are frequently either missing or inadequate. Nor is portability, a prerequisite for data access, guaranteed by legislation. In practice, the definitions of ownership, access, and control rights are now left to contractual agreements, which are not perfect safeguards of farmers' rights over their data. Data protection is also a challenge, and current data-sharing practices inadequately protect farmers' data. Since digital technologies collect new types and large amounts of geotagged farm data, it is difficult to separate personal data (protected by data privacy law) from nonpersonal data (not protected). An additional data protection challenge is the global nature of food chains and the heterogeneous data protection regimes across countries. And data-driven agrifood chains can be weakened by incorrect or intentionally manipulated data.

There is growing concern that digital technologies will increase market power and concentrate the gains from trade in the hands of few. By quickly transferring high volumes of data, digital technologies could increase power and vertical consolidation in the entire food supply chain, with harmful effects. And agricultural data could make farmers' decisions more transparent than those of other value chain actors since farmers using digital technologies tend to share disproportionally more of their data, which further reduces their bargaining power. The increasing returns to scale of data-driven digital platforms also lead to market concentration and create barriers to entry for smaller firms. Indeed, platform incumbents are increasingly able to invest in sophisticated algorithms that exploit producer and consumer data to earn large profits and impede the entry of smaller firms.

REALIZING THE POTENTIAL OF DIGITAL TECHNOLOGIES TO TRANSFORM THE FOOD SYSTEM WILL REQUIRE CAREFULLY CRAFTED PUBLIC POLICIES AND INVESTMENTS

Public policy must focus on the enabling environment and complementary investments that steer and accelerate the digital transformation of the agrifood system. The creation and use of digital agricultural technologies are fundamentally private sector activities for digital developers and agricultural producers. But investments in digital agriculture may be clouded by market and policy failures in physical or digital markets, by the lack of public-good providers, or by the limited knowledge of available technologies. In such cases, the entry point for public policy is to influence the incentives and decisions of private agents with the goal of maximizing society's efficiency gains and the equity and environmental sustainability impacts from adopting digital agriculture. In creating incentives to prompt behavior among private economic agents that maximizes societal benefits, the public sector must also take care to mitigate the potential risks (sometimes unknown) arising from digital agriculture.

Three foundational enablers can maximize the gains of digital agriculture: digital infrastructure, nondigital enablers, and governmental capacity to foster digital innovation. To increase the availability of digital infrastructure in rural and remote areas and enable good quality and predictable rural connectivity, the public sector needs to put in place enabling policies for telecommunications infrastructure. It also needs to undertake complementary nondigital investments in rural roads, electricity, and logistics to power digital devices and connect digital markets. And to improve the efficiency and monitoring of agricultural policies, ministries of agriculture need to digitize the activities of public agricultural bodies, invest in management information systems and modern data infrastructure, and build the digital skills of public sector workers to support change.

"No regrets" policy actions are key to maximizing the benefits of quickly transforming the food system. To spur the system's transformation, the public and private sectors need to jointly form an innovation ecosystem for digital agriculture. The government's role is to provide supportive public policy interventions that deliver public goods and to create an enabling policy and regulatory environment that fosters open datasets, digital platforms, digital entrepreneurship, digital payment systems, and digital skills. Key areas of focus should be to accomplish the following:

- *Strengthen access to foundational data and promote data sharing.* Strengthening access to foundational data would lower the cost of innovation and could be achieved by digitizing existing public agriculture records, developing digital farmer registries, and investing in global databases for core agricultural data on soil quality, weather conditions, market prices, and pest and disease surveillance. Promoting data portability and interoperability and adopting FAIR data principles in data management—which make data *findable, accessible, interoperable*, and *reusable*—would ensure the wide use of data.
- *Safeguard farmers' data privacy, security, and ownership.* The legal and regulatory framework should address any risks associated with data use. Efforts to ensure appropriate data privacy should be based on four underlying principles. First, collecting data should be transparent (individuals should know if someone is collecting their data). Second, individuals should know, and have a voice in, how their data are being used. Third, the models for data sharing should work for both the suppliers of the data (individuals) and the users of the data (enterprises). Data governance arrangements should build the confidence and trust of users of digital technologies, such as farmers and agribusinesses, and facilitate development of digital applications that can benefit them, such as improving access to finance. Fourth, digital technology providers should be accountable for how they use farmers' data.
- *Review regulations that may constrain the adoption of technologies that enable precision agriculture.* New technologies in some digital agriculture applications require a new legal framework in areas that may at first seem to be not very relevant for agriculture, such as the use of the so-called internet of things, unmanned aerial vehicles (drones), and global positioning systems to collect data for precision agriculture. Data collection raises issues of privacy and data ownership. It also creates the need to address safety and security concerns arising from the potential use of drones as weapons and the harm to bystanders from crashes. Getting the rules right could do much to promote the development of precision agriculture.
- *Enable competition in digital markets.* Given the tendency toward market concentration in digital markets, the policies for taxation, competition, and data sharing need to be adjusted. Policy and regulatory frameworks need to be adapted to provide for competitive markets in the digital era and broadened to consider consumer privacy, personal data protection, consumer choice, market structure, switching costs, and lock-in effects. Both antitrust

regulation and taxation policies remain as key instruments for sharing the economic gains from digital data and ensuring a more competitive environment. Additional approaches could be remunerating individuals who are sharing data with platforms through personal data markets or data trusts. Collective data ownership or digital data funds can be put in place as a basis for a new "digital data commons." In some cases, to spur competition, governments can invest in their own digital transaction platforms, or they can provide seed financing for platforms.

- *Support development of digital payment systems.* Digital payment systems are essential for transactions in the virtual world. But they are successful only when both parties to a transaction have enough interest and trust to use this form of payment. Consumer protection frameworks, robust digital networks, and banking and telecom policies that support digital financial services are all important components of a functioning digital payment system.

- *Support digital entrepreneurship ecosystems.* Digital entrepreneurship is a key driver behind the increased supply of digital solutions in the agrifood system, but it depends on the quality of the surrounding ecosystems. Governments can support such ecosystems by adopting e-agriculture strategies and ag-tech start-up policies, supporting regional and market aggregation of digital entrepreneurial initiatives, investing in mentoring and business advisory programs for enterprise development, and providing seed financing for start-ups, where feasible. In addition, regulatory sandboxes can provide entrepreneurs with a safe space to test new digital technologies that are not covered by existing regulatory frameworks, while ensuring that appropriate safeguards are in place.

- *Invest in transformational research and development.* Digital solutions in agriculture rely on a large body of research, often funded by the public sector. Redirecting state support to fund more research and development (R&D) would improve the enabling environment for digital entrepreneurship. In addition, the private and public sectors need to cooperate closely in R&D in agriculture, and public funding of research centers should be driven largely by the commercial applicability of the research.

Complementary policies are needed to share the benefits equitably, particularly those for skill development. Maximizing the equity impacts from digital agriculture may not be fully internalized by private economic agents; in such instances, the role of the government is to ensure the equitable distribution of digital benefits. Governments can increase the access to and use of digital technologies by marginalized groups. Public policy entry points include investing in digital skills, developing relevant customized digital tools of appropriate design and in relevant languages targeted to disadvantaged groups, and reducing the cost of digital technology adoption through targeted subsidies, where applicable.

Other policies can harness the digital revolution to generate improvements in environmental sustainability. To increase the environmental sustainability of the agrifood system through digital technologies, governments can incentivize use of digital technologies for environmental sustainability by agricultural producers, support increased capacity for environmental monitoring, and shift attitudes about the environmental impacts of the agrifood system. They should nudge producers and consumers in the direction of more environmentally sustainable choices. Possible actions include strengthening digital environmental monitoring, encouraging the use of digital technologies for environmental sustainability, and applying e-education and information dissemination to influence behavior. Other promising solutions include results-based policies, which reward producers directly for specific environmental outcomes and leave producers free to choose the best means to achieve them, given their circumstances.

To identify the most appropriate and effective policies and entry points to spur digital innovation in the agrifood system, governments need clear objectives. In formulating policies for the digital development of the agricultural sector, governments need to prioritize interventions in areas where the gaps are largest, while also anticipating and addressing risks and second-order effects of the interventions. The approach needs to be comprehensive. For example, the ability of digital technologies to reduce transaction costs in the agrifood system can increase market efficiency and competition. But if digital technologies reduce some frictions but not others, they can distort market outcomes, widening the digital divide. Finally, the digital development of the agrifood system is a means to the societal gains of efficiency, equity, and environmental sustainability—not a goal. (The report's digital agriculture profiling tool introduces an assessment framework to evaluate the state of a country's agricultural and digital development and identify public policy entry points to maximize the efficiency, equity, and environmental sustainability of digital transformations in agriculture.)

The coronavirus pandemic hit most countries in early 2020, at a time when the food system was already overdue for a major disruptive change. By accelerating the move to digital technologies, physical lockdown measures could provide an unexpected opportunity to build the system back better. Indeed, ensuring that the policy environment is conducive to digital solutions for agriculture will help shift the global agrifood system toward more efficiency, equity, and environmental sustainability—and contribute to achieving the Sustainable Development Goals to the fullest.

PLAN OF THE REPORT

Figure ES.2 presents the report's organization. The report first establishes a framework for analyzing the ability of digital technologies to improve efficiency, equity, and environmental sustainability in the agrifood system. The report then dives deeper into analysis, examining how digital technologies can lower barriers to on-farm efficiency and reduce transaction costs, exploring how digital technologies can transform rural finance, and investigating how digital technologies can address policy-related transaction costs. Finally, the report addresses policy implications for data use in agriculture and identifies public policy entry points for unleashing the power of digital technologies in agriculture.

FIGURE ES.2 The Structure of the Report

Framework

Chapter 1

Highlights the potential of digital technologies to transform the agrifood system

Chapter 2

Sets out a framework for analyzing the pathways for digital technologies to enhance efficiency, equity, and environmental sustainability (EEE) in the agrifood system

Analysis

Chapter 3

Examines how digital technologies can lower barriers to on-farm technical efficiency and reduce transaction costs to improve farmers' access to input and output markets

Chapter 4

Explores how mobile money, digital credit scoring, and remote sensing can lower transaction costs to improve farmers' access to credit, insurance, and savings

Chapter 5

Analyzes how digital technologies can redefine the scope of agricultural policies in agriculture and improve the EEE in the food system by addressing policy-related transaction costs

Policy

Chapter 6

Discusses the benefits and challenges of data use in agriculture

Chapter 7

Identifies public policy entry points for unleashing the power of digital technologies in agriculture

PART ONE

Setting the Stage

CHAPTER ONE

The Agrifood System's Digital Promise

KEY MESSAGES AND INTRODUCTION

- Agriculture and food are key for achieving the Sustainable Development Goals.
- The modern agrifood system is plagued with multiple inefficiencies, limiting its potential for contributing to a healthy economy, healthy people, and a healthy planet.
- Digital technologies promise to transform the agrifood system in ways not previously seen by drastically lowering information asymmetries and transaction costs in the system.

Delivering the agrifood system's potential for a healthy economy, healthy people, and a healthy planet is one of the most vexing challenges of our time. The agrifood system is severely off course in helping us achieve the Sustainable Development Goals related to hunger, poverty, health, land use, and climate change. Despite its providing food for a world population that has more than doubled over the past 50 years and producing plenty of food globally, the number of undernourished people has been rising since 2014. One in five children under the age of five is stunted, producing lifelong negative consequences for productivity. Some 2 billion people are overweight or obese, resulting in noncommunicable diseases of dietary origin that compromise resistance to new diseases such as COVID-19. Agriculture contributes 24 percent of greenhouse gas emissions, consumes 70 percent of freshwater, and has caused the loss of 60 percent of vertebrate biodiversity since the 1970s (Herrero Acosta et al. 2019).

The cost of these negative externalities is $12 trillion, according to the Food and Land Use Coalition, outweighing a market value of $10 trillion (Pharo et al. 2019). An additional 100 million people are under threat of poverty during 2020 alone because of the COVID-19 pandemic and its associated economic crisis, according to the World Bank's *Poverty and Shared Prosperity 2020* report, pushing us further from our goals by shrinking incomes and creating food and nutrition access challenges that may result in large-scale famine (World Bank 2020a; FSIN 2020). Such close interconnectedness of the agrifood system with economic, health, and environmental outcomes serves as both a challenge and a promise of its contribution to reaching the Sustainable Development Goals.

UNHEALTHY ECONOMY

Poverty is especially entrenched in rural areas, where households and communities often depend on agriculture as a primary source of both food and income (Haggblade, Hazell, and Dorosh 2007). More than 44 percent of the global population lives in rural areas (FAO 2020). In the least-developed parts of the world, the population remains predominantly rural (about two-thirds of just over a billion people). In addition, farming often takes place in remote rural areas, and the disadvantages of remoteness include the high costs of accessing information, services, and markets. Distances to schools, banks, hospitals, and stores are on average greater for rural households than households in cities or peri-urban communities. This remoteness stunts economic growth (Christiaensen, Demery, and Paternostro 2003; Das, Ghate, and Robertson 2015). While poverty rates in rural areas declined considerably over the past decades, it is too early to declare success, since 78 percent of the world's poor people live in rural areas and rely on agriculture for their livelihood (GAFSP 2014).

Increased productivity gains for farmers, rural communities, and poor food-purchasing households are key to reducing poverty in rural areas. Poor households tend to spend a large share of their income on food (Cirera and Masset 2010; Ivanic and Martin 2008). So low food prices can help families escape poverty (Ravallion 1990; Barrett and Dorosh 1996). Affordability and food access are also linked to child nutrition outcomes that also have long-run economic effects. Ironically, however, low food prices can increase poverty for net-producing households and communities, lowering their incomes (Aksoy and Isik-Dikmelik 2008). The key to breaking the cycle of "the more you produce, the lower the price" is productivity. Land and family labor are the chief assets of most smallholder farmers, so technologies that boost land and labor productivity provide a direct path out of poverty (Larson, Muraoka, and Otsuka 2016). For example, during Asia's Green Revolution, a 1 percent increase in agricultural productivity reduced poverty by an estimated 1.9 percent over time. And boosting agricultural productivity in poor and even middle-income countries has been shown to spill over into economywide economic growth as well (Irz et al. 2001; Anríquez and López 2007; de Janvry and Sadoulet 2010; Christiaensen, Demery, and Kuhl 2011).

UNHEALTHY PEOPLE

Agriculture and public health are linked in many ways. Agriculture is essential for good health, producing the world's food, fiber, and medicinal plants, and it is also associated with many of the world's major health problems, including undernutrition, foodborne diseases, and diet-related chronic diseases. According to the latest Food and Agriculture Organization's *State of Food Security and Nutrition in the World* report (2020), the burden of malnutrition in all its forms continues, and the number of undernourished people has been increasing in recent years (FAO et al. 2020). There has been some progress reducing child stunting and low birth weight, but the pace is still too slow. The childhood overweight rate is not improving, and adult obesity is on the rise in all regions. In addition, zoonotic diseases—such as West Nile virus and most recently COVID-19—also point to strong links between agriculture and human health. Poor management of livestock, unsafe food handling, ecosystem degradation, and encroachments on wildlife habitats are responsible for a growing number of illnesses. As a result, about $110 billion in productivity and medical expenses are lost annually in low- and middle-income countries because of foodborne diseases.

UNHEALTHY PLANET

The agrifood system has enormous environmental impacts. Large-scale agricultural intensification, unsustainable farm practices, and food loss and waste along value chains have had severe environmental impacts, including massive deforestation, soil degradation, groundwater depletion, and greenhouse gas emissions, all exacerbated by climate change. With growing populations and growing demand for food, the amount of land devoted to agriculture grew steadily until 2000, slowed only by mechanical and biological innovations that boosted land productivity (Stevenson et al. 2013). Forests occupy 30 percent of all land, and they come under pressure as land is cleared for agriculture by commercial farms and by the shifting cultivation practices of smallholders (Busch and Ferretti-Gallon 2017). On farmed land, soil fertility is not always well managed, and nutrients are depleted, with the long-term consequences of reducing agricultural productivity and increasing poverty, reducing biodiversity, and increasing greenhouse gas emissions (Lal 2004; Larson and Gurara 2013). Agriculture is itself a significant source of greenhouse gas emissions, and also a sector replete with low-cost mitigation opportunities (Larson, Dinar, and Frisbie 2011). The annual cost of land degradation is about $300 billion, and agricultural pollution is on the rise (Nkonya, Mirzabaev, and von Braun 2016). Further, food that is harvested but then allowed to spoil or otherwise wasted occupies land equal in size to China, consumes about 25 percent of all water used in agriculture, and accounts for about 8 percent of global greenhouse gas emissions (FAO 2013).

Worldwide, agriculture is the largest consumer of fresh water, accounting for upwards of 70 percent of annual withdrawals (Gleick 2003). Though land-preserving, intensive agriculture technologies, accelerated by the Green Revolution, have had negative consequences for soil and water resources (Foley et al. 2005; Pingali 2012). Poorly managed irrigation systems can lead to salinized soils and silting and divert water needed to sustain environmental services.

The interconnectedness of the agrifood system with the economy, health, and the environment takes place in the context of the system's vast complexity, high transaction costs, and pervasive information asymmetries. The system involves many actors exchanging vast amounts of information (table 1.1). All 7.7 billion humans participate in agricultural markets, and most of us make

TABLE 1.1 The Global Food System Is Large and Complex, with Many Actors

Upstream				Downstream		
Sector	Volume (US$, billions)	Enterprises (number)		Sector	Volume (US$, billions)	Enterprises (number)
Seed	56	7,500		Food logistics	300	50,000
Fertilizer/ agrochemicals	215	10,500		Meat processing	714	24,000
Machinery	124	5,000		Fruit and vegetable processing	290	32,000
Animal health	34.5	32,000	570 million farms worldwide	Dairy processing	618	20,000
Crop insurance	30	2,000		Bakery	419	117,000
Finance	80	34,500		Candy/ chocolate processing	143	13,500
Feed and feed additives	400	11,000		Beverage processing	586	112,000
Retail	—	Millions		Retail	—	Millions
Total	**—**	**Millions**		**Total**	**—**	**Millions**

Sources: FAOSTAT 2020; Grand View Research 2019, 2020; IBISWorld 2019a, 2019b, 2019c, 2019d, 2020a, 2020b, 2020c, 2020d, 2020e, 2020f, 2020g, 2020h, 2020i, 2020j, 2020k, 2020l, 2020m; IFIF n.d.; Marketline 2018; Mehra 2020; Mordor Intelligence 2019; Porth and Tang 2015; Statista Research Department 2015; Technavio 2020; UNIDO 2018; Varangis 2020; Zion Market Research 2017.

Note: — = not available.

frequent decisions about the food we consume. Most own clothes or use other products that originate in agriculture as well. Agricultural goods are produced on 570 million farms, most of them small, run by families, and located in developing countries (Lowder, Skoet, and Raney 2016; Graeub et al. 2016). Food systems are local, an essential feature in communities, but also global, linked through trade and sophisticated financial and insurance markets. Information and transactions are everywhere, from the decisions farmers make about inputs, land, labor, capital, natural resource management, and outputs, to the choices consumers make about the attributes of the food they consume, including food prices, nutrition, production practices, and environmental impacts.

HOW CAN DIGITAL TECHNOLOGIES HELP ACHIEVE A HEALTHY ECONOMY, HEALTHY PEOPLE, AND A HEALTHY PLANET?

The possibilities of what effective operation of the food system can do are endless—reduced poverty, improved nutrition, vast carbon sequestration, and massive environmental benefits. But the complexity of the agrifood system is vexing. Every decision and transaction in one direction almost invariably produces an equivalent shift in another. Consider rising food prices. They are good for net food producer farmers (many of whom are poor), while they are bad for net food consumers (especially those who are close to the poverty line). These same rising food prices have positive and negative effects on nutrition, where both low and high prices are blamed for problems of obesity and undernutrition. Rising food prices encourage investment in land, labor, and technology, while they also encourage deforestation and environmental degradation. Digital technologies, with their rapid development and deployment, can overcome long-standing market and policy failures and accelerate food system transformation if an enabling environment and complementary investments are put in place.

Technology has long been recognized as a driver of higher on-farm productivity associated with agricultural transformation. The World Bank report *Harvesting Prosperity* posits that the transition from poverty has been achieved through increased agricultural productivity, with higher productivity providing food, labor, and savings to support urbanization and industrialization (World Bank 2020b). While the expansion of markets, finance, and trade are recognized as having contributed to productivity growth in agriculture, technological innovations have been at the heart of the increases in agricultural productivity associated with agricultural transformation. In the 17th to 19th centuries, a progression of innovations, emanating from Great Britain, led to improved soil fertility management, more effective breeding practices, and better plows and powered machines. In the latter part of the 20th century, the creation of new grain varieties brought about a Green Revolution that sparked economic growth in developing countries and dramatic declines in global poverty and hunger (figure 1.1).

Digital technologies promise to accelerate transformation of the agrifood system in ways not previously seen. The earlier revolutions increased agricultural productivity, increased food supply, reduced real food prices, shifted resources out of labor and into capital, paved the way for urbanization and the Industrial Revolution, and led to the corporatization of agribusiness (Thompson 1968; Pingali 2012). The digital agriculture revolution builds on the outcomes of the preceding revolutions, but the new revolution is profoundly different in that it is simultaneously emanating from multiple links along the food value

FIGURE 1.1 Digital Agriculture and Past Revolutions

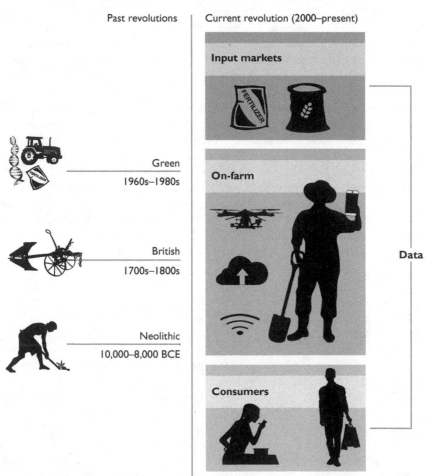

Source: World Bank.

WHAT'S COOKING: DIGITAL TRANSFORMATION OF THE AGRIFOOD SYSTEM

chain, rather than spreading sequentially from innovations adopted on farms. For example, both the British and Green Revolutions originated on the farm before spilling over to rural communities and to firms up and down the value chain. The digital agriculture revolution, by contrast, is bringing change on multiple fronts at accelerated rates. The change is driven by the ability to collect, use, and analyze massive amounts of machine-readable data about practically every aspect of the value chain (box 1.1), and by the emergence of digital platforms disrupting business models in the agrifood system. For instance, in 2014,

---

BOX 1.1 The Digital Revolution Is Different from Other Technological Revolutions because of the Characteristics of Digital Information and Digital Goods

The characteristics of digital information and digital goods (Varian 2000; Belleflamme 2016) distinguish them from other types of economic goods and services and determine the pathways through which they transform the agrifood system. These characteristics also influence how enterprises market and price digital information and digital goods, the circumstances under which farmers adopt them, and the public policy entry points for enabling their use. These characteristics may often depend on the type of digital device available or used. This report differentiates between two types of digital devices or tools: devices *embodied* in agricultural machinery and equipment (such as precision farming tools) and *disembodied* devices (such as smartphones or tablets).

Two characteristics of digital information and digital goods drive the digital revolution in the agrifood system: their device agnosticism, particularly toward disembodied devices, and their nearly zero marginal costs of replication, storage, and transmission. Several other characteristics—their nonrivalry, nonexcludability, infinite durability, and their status as *experience goods*, the qualities of which cannot be determined before purchase—derive from the first two characteristics and determine the economic and social incentives for their development and are discussed in this chapter.

Device agnosticism: Digital information and digital goods are device dependent, but they are often device agnostic when it comes to disembodied devices, allowing even simple devices to perform multiple tasks. Digital technologies are associated with physical electronic devices that combine digital data and software to process, share, or store digital information. This means that the creation and use of digital information and digital goods at a given time depends on past investments in such digital devices. Disembodied digital devices often are not task specific and can be used to manage multiple tasks when acquired and can adapt to new tasks later— primarily by installing new software. A key to the remarkable growth in accessible digital goods and services has been the rapid growth of fairly inexpensive handheld devices that can process ever-increasing amounts of digital data independently and can access greater stores of digital information and processing power through ever-expanding networks. For embodied devices, however, software is often device dependent. For such devices there should be sufficient market incentives for private

(Continued)

companies to invest in the respective hardware and software: for example, in both sensors and crop models.

Nearly zero marginal costs of replication, storage, and transmission: Digital data, and many digital goods, have nearly zero marginal costs of replication, storage, and transmission, fundamentally changing how information is acquired. The costs to generate, replicate, store, and transmit digital data on digital devices are nearly zero, provided data interoperability is in place. For example, smartphones can easily capture both data about soil moisture from sensors mounted on sowing machines and data on location. Digital goods employed to facilitate transactions often capture and transmit data as well, lessening the costs of confirming transactions and building datasets, including large datasets about firms, farmers, and farms. As a result, vast amounts of data can be generated rapidly. In addition, digital technologies can process digital data quickly, sorting through large stores of digital information to answer queries with ever-increasing precision. And because digital data are transported swiftly and inexpensively over electronic networks, geographic distance does not greatly affect the cost of acquiring the data. What matters is having access to the digital infrastructure and platforms that carry digital goods and services, such as cell phone towers, satellite coverage, and internet access.

an average of 190,000 data points were produced per farm, per day, and by 2050, experts predict that each farm will produce around 4.1 million data points daily (Meola 2016). Extrapolating across the agrifood system, the number of data points flowing across different stakeholders is countless. Similar processes are ongoing in other sectors of the economy. As a result, digital transformation may redefine structural transformation. The agricultural sector could register value addition and increase its productivity through digitalization without necessarily industrializing in the traditional sense (UNCTAD 2019).

By lowering the costs of linking farmers to the millions of upstream and downstream markets, by better targeting poor and vulnerable farmers with digitized support services, and by better monitoring environmental impacts, digital technologies can tackle multiple inefficiencies prevalent in the agrifood system. Digital agriculture can improve the data-intensive process of farm decision-making for resource allocation and management by processing and analyzing more precise data faster and by providing advice tailored to the farm. Digital agriculture increases the transparency of agricultural value chains through improved access to information and product traceability, all leading to better choices and more efficient transactions for both producers and consumers. Digital agriculture thus alters the traditional pathways and optimizes the current agrifood system to increase its contribution to a healthy economy, healthy people, and a healthy planet.

The COVID-19 pandemic has disrupted well-established food supply chains, exposing the fragility of the food system, but has also brought an opportunity to build a better, more resilient agrifood system. Restrictions on labor and the interruption of transport, processing, retailing, and input distribution have impaired food production and distribution, threatening food and nutrition security, particularly for the poor. The breakdown of supply chains due to the pandemic and a variety of associated policy restrictions have caused consumer prices to increase and producer prices to fall, increasing food insecurity for both urban and rural poor. Many people have also suffered as their employment opportunities in food supply chains have shrunk. As the pandemic brought to light inefficiencies in the food system stemming from pervasive information asymmetries and high transaction costs, it also brought about an opportunity to build the system back better and set it on a more sustainable course. In this respect, digital technologies offer a promising tool.

SCOPE AND STRUCTURE OF THE REPORT

This report examines the pathways through which digital technologies can accelerate the transformation of the agrifood system and how public policy and investment can maximize the positive and minimize the negative impact of digital technologies on this transformation. The report investigates how digital technologies can improve the allocation of physical, natural, and human capital on the farm and reduce transaction costs off the farm, gaining efficiency. It also analyzes the role of digital agriculture in improving equity and environmental sustainability in food systems and highlights the risks that could emerge along the way. We argue that the role of governments is to increase the space for private sector activity, improving the policy and regulatory environment and using public investments to crowd in private sector investment. And in creating incentives to prompt private economic agents to maximize the societal benefits, the public sector must also mitigate the potential (sometimes unknown) risks arising from digital agriculture. This report tells how the World Bank can operationalize its *Build–Boost–Broker value proposition* in the agricultural sector by identifying the building blocks of an enabling environment for digital agriculture and spelling out ways to boost government capacity to adapt to technology-related disruptions and to broker the use of technologies to address the agricultural sector's development challenges (World Bank 2018).

The report is farmer centric and structured as follows. Chapter 2 sets out a framework for analyzing the pathways for digital technologies to enhance the efficiency, equity, and environmental sustainability of the agrifood system. Chapter 3 examines how digital technologies can lower the barriers to sustainable on-farm growth of technical efficiency and can lower information-related transaction costs to improve farmers' access to input and output markets. Chapter 4 explores how mobile money, digital credit scoring, and remote sensing can lower transaction costs to improve farmers' access to credit insurance and savings. Chapter 5 analyzes how digital technologies can redefine the scope of government policies in agriculture and improve their economic efficiency, equity, and environmental sustainability by addressing policy-related transaction costs. Chapter 6 discusses the benefits and challenges of data use in agriculture. Chapter 7 builds on the analysis of the previous chapters to identify public policy entry points for unleashing the power of digital technologies in agriculture. Appendix A introduces an assessment framework to evaluate the state of agricultural and digital development in a country and identify public policy entry points to maximize the efficiency, equity, and environmental sustainability of digital transformation in agriculture. (Greater detail of and methodology for the framework is presented in appendixes B, C, and D.)

REFERENCES

Aksoy, M. A., and A. Isik-Dikmelik. 2008. "Are Low Food Prices Pro-Poor? Net Food Buyers and Sellers in Low-Income Countries." Policy Research Working Paper 4642, World Bank, Washington, DC.

Anríquez, G., and R. López. 2007. "Agricultural Growth and Poverty in an Archetypical Middle-Income Country: Chile 1987–2003." *Agricultural Economics* 36 (2): 191–202.

Barrett, C. B., and P. A. Dorosh. 1996. "Farmers' Welfare and Changing Food Prices: Nonparametric Evidence from Rice in Madagascar." *American Journal of Agricultural Economics* 78 (3): 656–69.

Belleflamme, P. 2016. "The Economics of Digital Goods: A Progress Report." *Review of Economic Research on Copyright Issues* 13 (2): 1–24.

Busch, J., and K. Ferretti-Gallon. 2017. "What Drives Deforestation and What Stops It?" *Review of Environmental Economics and Policy* 11 (1): 3–23. https://doi.org/10.1093/reep /rew013.

Christiaensen, L., L. Demery, and J. Kuhl. 2011. "The (Evolving) Role of Agriculture in Poverty Reduction: An Empirical Perspective." *Journal of Development Economics* 96 (2): 239–54.

Christiaensen, L., L. Demery, and S. Paternostro. 2003. "Macro and Micro Perspectives of Growth and Poverty in Africa." *World Bank Economic Review* 17 (3): 317–47. https://doi .org/10.1093/wber/lhg025.

Cirera, X., and E. Masset. 2010. "Income Distribution Trends and Future Food Demand." *Philosophical Transactions of the Royal Society B* 365: 2821–34. doi:10.1098/rstb .2010.0164.

Das, S., C. Ghate, and P. E. Robertson. 2015. "Remoteness, Urbanization, and India's Unbalanced Growth." *World Development* 66: 572–587.

de Janvry, A., and E. Sadoulet. 2010. "Agricultural Growth and Poverty Reduction: Additional Evidence." *World Bank Research Observer* 25 (1): 1–20.

FAO (Food and Agriculture Organization of the United Nations). 2013. *Food Wastage Footprint: Impacts on Natural Resources.* Rome: FAO.

FAO. 2020. FAOSTAT Statistical Database. Rome. http://www.fao.org/faostat/en/#home.

FAO, IFAD (International Fund for Agricultural Development), UNICEF (United Nations Children's Fund), WFP (World Food Programme), and WHO (World Health Organization). 2020. *The State of Food Security and Nutrition in the*

World 2020: Transforming Food Systems for Affordable Healthy Diets. Rome: FAO. https:// doi.org/10.4060/ca9692en.

FAOSTAT. 2020. "Value of Agricultural Production." FAO. November 3, 2020. http://www .fao.org/faostat/en/#data/QV.

Foley, J. A., R. DeFries, G. P. Asner, C. Barford, G. Bonan, S. R. Carpenter, et al. 2005. "Global Consequences of Land Use." *Science* 309 (5734): 570–74.

FSIN (Food Security Information Network). 2020. *Global Report on Food Crises: Joint Analysis for Better Decisions.* Rome: FSIN. https://docs.wfp.org/api/documents/WFP-0000114546 /download/?_ga=2.71389139.1765439984.1600355938-1204681751.1595275054.

GAFSP (Global Agriculture and Food Security Program). 2014. *Annual Report 2014: Reducing Hunger, Increasing Incomes.* Washington, DC: GAFSP.

Gleick, P. H. 2003. "Water Use." *Annual Review of Environment and Resources* 28: 275–314.

Graeub, B., J. Chappell, H. Wittman, S. Lederman, R. Bezner Kerr, and B. Gemmill-Herren. 2016. "The State of Family Farms in the World." *World Development* 87: 1–15.

Grand View Research. 2019. "Agriculture Equipment Market Size and Share Report, 2019–2025." Database, Grand View Research, San Francisco, January 2019. https://www .grandviewresearch.com/industry-analysis/agriculture-equipment-market.

Grand View Research. 2020. "Animal Health Market Size, Share, Industry Growth Report, 2020–2027." Database, Grand View Research, San Francisco, February 2020. https://www .grandviewresearch.com/industry-analysis/animal-health-market.

Haggblade, S., P. Hazell, and P. Dorosh. 2007. "Sectoral Growth Linkages between Agriculture and the Rural Nonfarm Economy." In *Transforming the Rural Nonfarm Economy: Opportunities and Threats in the Developing World,* edited by S. Haggblade, P. Hazell, and T. Reardon. Baltimore, MD: The Johns Hopkins University Press.

Herrero Acosta, M., P. Thornton, D. Mason-D'Croz, and J. Palmer. 2019. "Transforming Food Systems under a Changing Climate: Future Technologies and Food Systems Innovation for Accelerating Progress towards the SDGs—Key Messages." CCAFS Brief, CGIAR Research Program on Climate Change, Agriculture and Food Security (CCAFS), Wageningen, Netherlands.

IBISWorld. 2019a. "Global Fertilizers and Agricultural Chemicals Manufacturing Industry." Database, IBISWorld, New York, August 2, 2019. https://www.ibisworld.com/industry -trends/global-industry-reports/manufacturing/fertilizers-agricultural-chemicals -manufacturing.html.

IBISWorld. 2019b. "Global Candy and Chocolate Manufacturing Industry." Database, IBISWorld, New York, August 25, 2019. https://www.ibisworld.com/global /market-research-reports/global-candy-chocolate-manufacturing-industry/.

IBISWorld. 2019c. "Global Wine Manufacturing Industry." Database, IBISWorld, New York, November 8, 2019. https://www.ibisworld.com/global/market-research-reports/global -wine-manufacturing-industry/.

IBISWorld. 2019d. "Global Milk and Cream Manufacturing Industry." Database, IBISWorld, New York, November 15, 2019. https://www.ibisworld.com/global /market-research-reports/global-milk-cream-manufacturing-industry/.

IBISWorld. 2020a. "Global Bakery Goods Manufacturing Industry." Database, IBISWorld, New York, January 3, 2020. https://www.ibisworld.com/global/market-research-reports /global-bakery-goods-manufacturing-industry/.

IBISWorld. 2020b. "Global Fruit and Vegetable Processing Industry." Database, IBISWorld, New York, February 23, 2020. https://www.ibisworld.com/global/market-research -reports/global-fruit-vegetable-processing-industry/.

IBISWorld. 2020c. "Agricultural Insurance Industry in the US." Database, IBISWorld, New York, February 29, 2020. https://www.ibisworld.com/united-states/market-research -reports/agricultural-insurance-industry/.

IBISWorld. 2020d. "Animal Health Biotechnology Industry in the US." Database, IBISWorld, New York, February 29, 2020. https://www.ibisworld.com/united-states /market-research-reports/animal-health-biotechnology-industry/.

IBISWorld. 2020e. "Emergency Veterinary Services Industry in the US." Database, IBISWorld, New York, February 29, 2020. https://www.ibisworld.com/united-states /market-research-reports/emergency-veterinary-services-industry/.

IBISWorld. 2020f. "Third-Party Logistics Industry in the US." Database, IBISWorld, New York, February 29, 2020. https://www.ibisworld.com/united-states/market-research -reports/third-party-logistics-industry/.

IBISWorld. 2020g. "Agricultural Banks Industry in the US." Database, IBISWorld, New York, March 17, 2020. https://www.ibisworld.com/united-states/market-research-reports /agricultural-banks-industry/.

IBISWorld. 2020h. "Farm Animal Feed Production Industry in the US." Database, IBISWorld, New York, March 31, 2020. https://www.ibisworld.com/united-states /market-research-reports/farm-animal-feed-production-industry/.

IBISWorld. 2020i. "Meat, Beef and Poultry Processing Industry in the US." Database, IBISWorld, New York, September 29, 2020. https://www.ibisworld.com/united-states /market-research-reports/meat-beef-poultry-processing-industry/.

IBISWorld. 2020j. "Global Cheese Manufacturing Industry." Database, IBISWorld, New York, October 6, 2020. https://www.ibisworld.com/global/market-research-reports/global-che ese-manufacturing-industry/.

IBISWorld. 2020k. "Tractors and Agricultural Machinery Manufacturing Industry in the US." Database, IBISWorld, New York, October 11, 2020. https://www.ibisworld .com/industry-trends/market-research-reports/manufacturing/machinery/tractors -agricultural-machinery-manufacturing.html.

IBISWorld. 2020l. "Global Beer Manufacturing Industry." Database, IBISWorld, New York, November 2, 2020. https://www.ibisworld.com/global/market-research-reports/global -beer-manufacturing-industry/.

IBISWorld. 2020m. "Global Spirits Manufacturing Industry." Database, IBISWorld, New York, December 1, 2020. https://www.ibisworld.com/global/market-research-reports/global -spirits-manufacturing-industry/.

IFIF (International Feed Industry Federation). n.d. "The Global Feed Industry." IFIF, WIEHL, Germany (accessed December 18, 2020). https://ifif.org/global-feed/industry/.

Irz, X., L. Lin, C. Thirtle, and S. Wiggins. 2001. "Agricultural Productivity Growth and Poverty Alleviation." *Development Policy Review* 19 (4): 449–66.

Ivanic, M., and W. Martin. 2008. "Implications of Higher Global Food Prices for Poverty in Low-income Countries." *Agricultural Economics* 39 (supplement): 405–16.

Lal, Rattan. 2004. "Soil Carbon Sequestration Impacts on Global Climate Change and Food Security." *Science* 304 (5677): 1623–27.

Larson, D., A. Dinar, and J. A. Frisbie. 2011. "Agriculture and the Clean Development Mechanism." Policy Research Working Paper 5621, World Bank, Washington, DC.

Larson, D. F., and D. Z. Gurara. 2013. "The Demand for Fertilizer When Markets Are Incomplete: Evidence from Ethiopia," chap. 11 in *An African Green Revolution*, 243–59. Dordrecht, Netherlands: Springer.

Larson, D. F., R. Muraoka, and K. Otsuka. 2016. "Why African Rural Development Strategies Must Depend on Small Farms." *Global Food Security* 10: 39–51.

Lowder, S., J. Skoet, and T. Raney. 2016. "The Number, Size, and Distribution of Farms, Smallholder Farms, and Family Farms Worldwide." *World Development* 87: 16–29.

Marketline. 2018. "Food and Grocery Retail Global Industry Guide 2018–2022." London, Marketline, March 2018. https://store.marketline.com/report/mlig1769-06--food -grocery-retail-global-industry-guide-2018-2022/.

Mehra, Aashish. 2020. "Cold Chain Market Worth $340.3 Billion by 2025." *Markets and Markets*, October 21, 2020. https://www.marketsandmarkets.com/PressReleases/cold-chain.asp.

Meola, A. 2016. "Why IT, Big Data, and Smart Farming Are the Future of Agriculture." *Business Insider*, January 24. http://www.businessinsider.com/internet-of-things-smart -agriculture-2016-10.

Mordor Intelligence. 2019. "Seed Market: Growth, Trends, and Forecast (2020–2025)." Database, Mordor Intelligence, Hyderabad, India, 2019. https://www.mordorintelligence .com/industry-reports/seeds-industry.

Nkonya, E., A. Mirzabaev, and J. von Braun, eds. 2016. *Economics of Land Degradation and Improvement: A Global Assessment for Sustainable Development*. Cham, Switzerland: Springer International.

Pharo, P., J. Oppenheim, C. Ruggeri Laderchi, and S. Benson. 2019. "Growing Better: Ten Critical Transitions to Transform Food and Land Use." The Global Consultation Report of the Food and Land Use Coalition, London. https://www.foodandlandusecoalition.org /wp-content/uploads/2019/09/FOLU GrowingBetter-GlobalReport.pdf.

Pingali, P. L. 2012. "Green Revolution: Impacts, Limits, and the Path Ahead." *Proceedings of the National Academy of Sciences* 109 (31): 12302–08.

Porth, Lysa, and Ken Seng Tang. 2015. "Agricultural Insurance: More Room to Grow?" *Actuary Magazine*, May 2015. https://www.soa.org/globalassets/assets/Library/Newsletters/The -Actuary-Magazine/2015/april/act-2015-vol12-iss2-porth-tan.pdf.

Ravallion, M. 1990. "Rural Welfare Effects of Food Price Changes under Induced Wage Responses: Theory and Evidence for Bangladesh." *Oxford Economics Papers* 42: 574–85.

Statista Research Department. 2015. "Global Agricultural Machinery Market Share by Region 2015." Database, Statista, New York, May 1, 2015. https://www.statista.com /statistics/642496/agricultural-equipment-world-market-region/.

Stevenson, J., N. Villoria, D. Byerlee, T. Kelley, and M. Maredia. 2013. "Green Revolution Research Saved an Estimated 18 to 27 Million Hectares from Being Brought into Agricultural Production." *Proceedings of the National Academy of Science of the United States of America* 110 (21): 8363–68.

Technavio. 2020. "Food Logistics Market by Transportation Mode and Geography: Forecast and Analysis 2020–2024." Database, Technavio, New York, April 2020. https://www .technavio.com/report/food-logistics-market-industry-analysis.

Thompson, F. 1968. "The Second Agricultural Revolution, 1815–1880." *Economic History Review* 21 (1): 62–77. doi:10.2307/2592204.

UNCTAD (United Nations Conference on Trade and Development). 2019. *Digital Economy Report 2019: Value Creation and Capture—Implications for Developing Countries*. Geneva: UNCTAD.

UNIDO (United Nations Industrial Development Organization). 2018. Industrial Statistics Database INDSTAT4. https://stat.unido.org/app/availability/availability.htm?product _key=3&_ga=2.235963969.190343302.1607984761-796643523.1607984761.

Varangis, Pano. 2020. "Agriculture Finance and Agriculture Insurance." World Bank, October 8, 2020. https://www.worldbank.org/en/topic/financialsector/brief/agriculture-finance.

Varian, H. R. 2000. "Buying, Sharing, and Renting Information Goods." *Journal of Industrial Economics* 48 (4): 473–88.

World Bank. 2018. *The Role of Digital Identification in Agriculture: Emerging Applications.* Washington, DC: World Bank.

World Bank. 2020a. *Poverty and Shared Prosperity 2020: Reversals of Fortune.* Washington, DC: World Bank.

World Bank. 2020b. *Harvesting Prosperity: Technology and Productivity Growth in Agriculture.* Washington, DC: World Bank.

Zion Market Research. 2017. "Global Processed Meat Market Will Reach $1,567.00 Billion by 2022." GlobeNewswire, February 8, 2017. http://www.globenewswire.com/news-release/2017/02/08/915112/0/en/Global-Processed-Meat-Market-will-reach-1-567-00-Billion-by-2022-Zion-Market-Research.html.

CHAPTER TWO

Pathways for Digital Technologies to Change the Agrifood System

KEY MESSAGES AND INTRODUCTION

- Digital technologies have enormous potential to boost the efficiency, equity, and environmental sustainability of the agrifood system.
  - o On-farm, digital technologies may help improve the allocation of physical, natural, and human capital.
  - o Off-farm, digital technologies may drastically lower information-related transaction costs associated with farmers' access to upstream and downstream markets, leading to improved allocative efficiency.
  - o Digital technology may narrow economic, spatial, and social divides and boost equity in rural areas.
  - o Digital technology may improve environmental sustainability through resource efficiency, better tracking of externalities, and transformation of the behavior and attitudes of food consumers and producers.
  - o Digital technologies can lower transaction costs associated with agricultural policy design and implementation, enabling governments to deliver more efficient and equitable support to the agricultural sector and to improve environmental outcomes.
- The role of the public sector is to create an enabling environment for digital transformation of the agrifood system with the goal of maximizing efficiency, equity, and environmentally sustainable outcomes.

Digital technologies are likely to have far-reaching impacts on and off the farm as well as throughout the agrifood system. Digital technologies present an opportunity to tackle multiple market failures by greatly reducing the transaction costs of matching buyers and sellers across input, output, and financial markets in the food system—and by better targeting support to poor and vulnerable farmers with digitized services. Digital agriculture can also improve the data-intensive process of farm decision-making for resource allocation and management by processing and analyzing more precise data faster and by providing advice tailored to the individual farm. Digital agriculture may optimize the current agrifood system to increase its value addition and contribution to a healthy economy, healthy people, and a healthy planet. Broadly, the impacts of digital technologies on farms and the agriculture sector are not so different from those on other sectors. But the impacts on the agrifood system are noteworthy because of the complexity of the food production system; agriculture's links to natural resources and contributions to reducing poverty, such as nutrition, human capital, and smallholder development; and development hurdles tied to remoteness.

This chapter sets out a framework for analyzing the pathways for digital technologies to enhance the efficiency, equity, and environmental sustainability of the agrifood system (figure 2.1). For agricultural producers, the impacts of digital technologies can lead to large gains in efficiency, both technical and allocative. On the farm, digital technologies can help producers use their physical, natural, and human capital most efficiently to maximize output by combining detailed data about farmers' fields and animals with information on how to better exploit existing production knowledge (see chapter 3). Off the farm, digital technologies reduce transaction costs arising from farmers' interactions with input and output markets, including rural finance markets and the government, by reducing the time and cost of transmitting enormous amounts of digital information across great distances (see chapters 3 and 4). Cumulatively, these producer gains, coupled with similar efficiency gains along all segments of the agrifood system, can improve the economic efficiency of society. Aggregate efficiency gains at the societal level arise through increases in on-farm efficiency and productivity, rapid diffusion of digital innovations across producers, and reallocation of resources toward the most efficient farms (OECD 2019b).

The potential of digital technologies to enhance the environmental sustainability of the agrifood system is also enormous. They can make on-farm use of production resources more efficient. They can change distribution processes. They can increase the capacity for environmental monitoring. And they can transform the attitudes and behaviors of food consumers and producers about the environmental impact of agrifood production. As digital technologies reduce the costs of exchanging information and accessing markets, they create pathways for commercialization and inclusion in the value chain of producers previously excluded by economic, social, or spatial barriers. Net impacts for agriculture and the overall economy are, however,

FIGURE 2.1 Pathways for Digital Agriculture to Improve Efficiency, Equity, and Environmental Sustainability

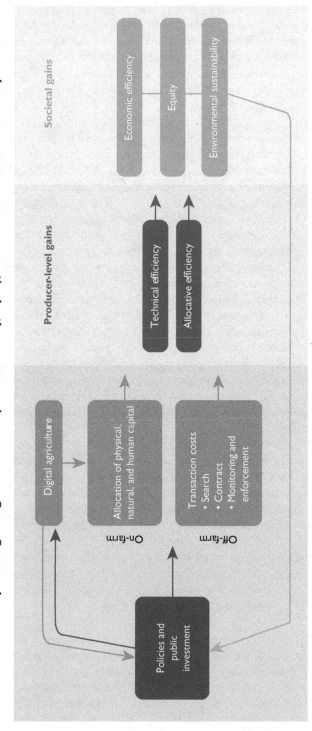

Source: World Bank.

hard to predict, not least because of difficulties in appropriately measuring the digital economy. While digital agriculture holds a tremendous potential to improve agrifood system outcomes, it should not be viewed as a panacea. The virtual economy is embedded in the real, material economy. Complementary investments are required to realize the potential benefits of digital technologies, especially in rural areas, and to address the multiple constraints faced by farmers, as is discussed in this report.

More than affecting the agrifood system directly, digital technologies can enable the design and delivery of more efficient, equitable, and environmentally sustainable policies for the agrifood system. Both the political economy and policy-related transaction costs shape a country's choice of policy instruments, including those influencing the adoption of digital technologies, often leading to the adoption of second-best policy instruments. Policy-related transaction costs are the costs governments incur in gathering information, planning and designing policies, collecting revenue, and implementing and monitoring the policies. Digital technologies hold the promise of lowering many of these costs so that policies can maximize efficiency, equity, and environmental sustainability gains for farmers and consumers (see chapter 5).

The ability to collect, use, and analyze massive amounts of machine-readable data about practically every aspect of the agrifood system is what promises to drastically reduce transaction costs in the agrifood system. Access to data can generate large financial benefits for the private sector and economy, enhance the efficiency of the public sector's support for the agrifood system, spur innovation and entrepreneurship, and lead to enhanced equity and improved environmental sustainability. But to take advantage of the full potential of data in the food system, several data-related technical, social, and legal challenges must be addressed (chapter 6).

How the public sector engages with the agriculture sector will influence the size of the on-farm and off-farm impacts of digital technologies. Governments around the world use policies, public investments, and public goods to shape the development of the agrifood system. Similarly, they can use these tools to create an enabling context for the emergence of digital technologies in that system while ensuring the sustainable distribution of the dividends. Aligning public policy goals for digital agriculture and those for the sector more broadly could maximize the societal gains of efficiency, equity, and environmental sustainability (see chapter 7).

PATHWAYS FOR IMPROVED EFFICIENCY

On the farm, digital technologies promise to increase technical efficiency by (1) reducing informational hurdles to the adoption of existing agricultural technologies and (2) improving information processing and optimization. Technical efficiency is defined as the (managerial) ability of the farmer to produce the maximum attainable output given her resources and available agricultural technology (Fare, Grosskopf, and Lovell 1983; Bravo-Ureta et al. 2007).

Technical efficiency is measured by the gap between the farmer's current output and the level of output she could produce if she were on the production frontier—if she were operating at 100 percent of technical efficiency. Improved decision-making is the main driver of increased technical efficiency, obtained mostly through improved information, education, and experience. Digital technologies improve technical efficiency through two main channels:

1. First, digital technologies close the efficiency gap by reducing the informational hurdles to adopting existing agricultural technologies. The hurdles arise when farmers are unaware of the range of agricultural technologies available to them throughout the agricultural production process (figure 2.2) and how to use them well. Such informational barriers to technology adoption concern available agricultural technologies and best production practices, the relevance of technologies to local growing conditions, the production environment, including the weather, and the environmental effects of farming practices.
2. Second, digital technologies, ranging from weather apps to precision agriculture technologies, support farmers' decision-making through the

FIGURE 2.2 Stages of the Agricultural Production Process and Information Needs

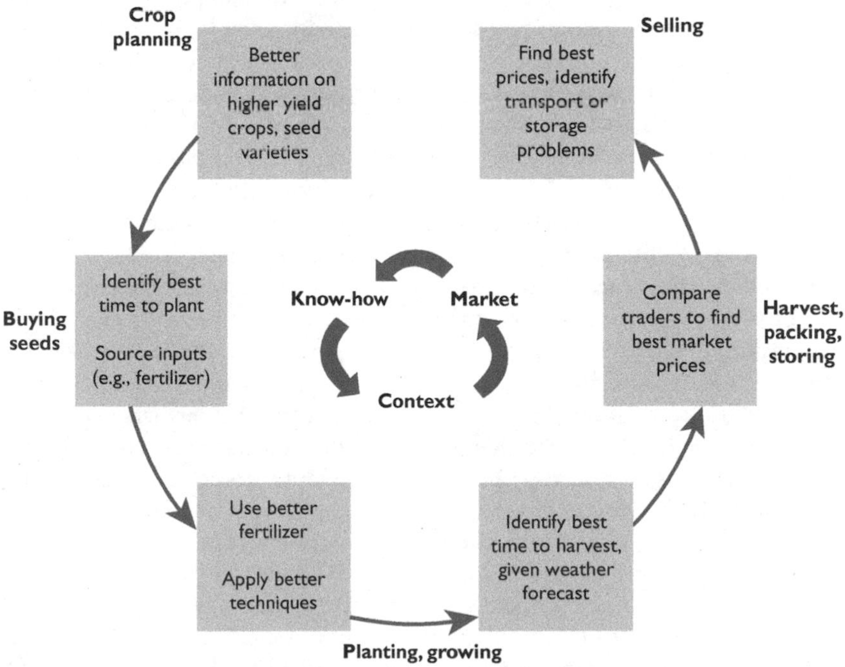

Source: Adapted with permission from Mittal, Gandhi, and Tripathi 2010.

acquisition and leveraging of granular data about fields and animals in combination with accurate, timely, and location-specific weather and agronomic data. For example, if soil quality varies, then precision agriculture tools can help provide correct microdoses of nutrients, improve nutrient use efficiency, and reduce input use (essentially avoiding the waste of fertilizer or water).

Off the farm, digital technologies can sharply reduce the information-related transaction costs of farmer interactions with input and output markets, leading to improved allocative efficiency. Transaction costs—costs associated with the exchange of goods and services between buyer and seller—play a central role in the resource allocation decisions of agricultural producers and, consequently, in resource allocation at the societal level. Specifically, when the cost of a market transaction creates a disutility greater than the utility gain to producers, it results in a market failure (de Janvry, Fafchamps, and Sadoulet 1991). Effectively, transaction costs raise the price to buyers and lower the price received by sellers, creating a price band within which some agents find it unprofitable to either sell or buy. In agriculture, the price band explains why many subsistence farmers lack access to profitable market opportunities and prefer to produce for home consumption (Cuevas 2014).

Transaction costs also explain the emergence of intermediary firms that strive to economize on such costs, resulting in frictions in the economy. A more complex modern agrifood system that requires the supply of products of consistent quantity, quality, and safety creates additional layers of transaction costs, which are often prohibitive for smallholder farmers. The digital agriculture revolution has sharply reduced transaction costs through the increased availability of information, greater transaction trust, and the ability to connect economic agents along the agrifood system. Digital computing power and advances in software have reduced information gaps between farmers and consumers and have decreased the need for traditional intermediaries to secure the transactions. While the biggest impact is on information-related transaction costs, other types of transaction costs, such as delivery costs, are also affected.

Broadly, three types of information-related transaction costs can be distinguished: search costs, bargaining and decision costs, and supervision and enforcement costs (figure 2.3) (Eaton, Meijerink, and Bijman 2008). Search costs are the costs of looking for information on trading partners and on the prices and quality of products. Bargaining costs are the resources put into negotiating the terms of an agreement. Supervision and enforcement costs include the time and other costs of monitoring and enforcing the contract.

While the three types of transaction costs exist in all markets, four inherent features of agriculture result in higher transaction risks and, consequently, in higher transaction costs than in other markets (Eaton, Meijerink, and Bijman 2008). First, the *uncertainty* associated with production variability due to weather conditions, pests, and diseases is a particularly high risk in agriculture. It increases the transaction costs associated with concluding contracts

FIGURE 2.3 Transaction Costs and Risks in Agricultural Value Chains

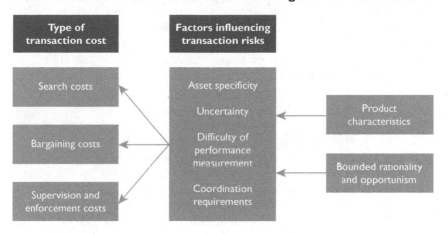

Source: Adapted with permission from Eaton, Meijerink, and Bijman 2008.

because of the potential need to renegotiate in the face of unforeseen events (Williamson 1979).

Second, *asset specificity* is the extent to which investments made by one or both parties to a transaction are specific to that transaction and thus have less value for transactions with other parties (Williamson 1988). For producers, investments in specific assets expose them to the risk of severe bargaining and contractual enforcement problems if a transaction falls through. In farming, these risks are exacerbated by the prevalence of thin markets (meaning few alternative transactions are possible) and the perishability of agricultural commodities (meaning that a product's value is inherently time dependent), both of which arise from farming's context in remote, sparsely populated rural areas (Dorward and Kydd 2003). As a result, asset specificity in rural areas is often highly asymmetric: a powerful intermediary may be the only buyer of farmers' produce, extracting most of the value in the transaction. In such cases, farmers have low incentives to invest in higher quality products, particularly for perishable goods.

Third, the need for *coordination* (connectedness of transactions) is particularly high in agriculture. Transactions rarely take place in isolation but often depend on other transactions in the value chain or sector. For example, producers need to procure inputs (cash, seed, and fertilizer) before they can produce or market a product. All these transaction coordination efforts involve transaction costs.

Fourth, agricultural production makes *performance measurement* difficult, thereby raising the transaction costs associated with performance monitoring. For example, some characteristics of agricultural products may not be easily determined, such as how the product was produced (for example, the use of pesticides in organic produce).

Digital agriculture enables substantial reductions in transaction risks and costs through its influence on the factors that increase them. These reductions are possible because of the ability of digital technologies to generate and transmit massive amounts of data at nearly zero marginal cost and because digital platforms bring together many economic agents at the same time, again at nearly zero marginal cost. In other words, the proliferation of data and digital platforms thickens agrifood markets by increasing the number of potential buyers and sellers that can interact. At the same time, the increased flow of information on every process and customer along the agrifood value chain, underpinned by digital verification that makes it easier to certify the trustworthiness of an economic agent, strengthens trust in transactions.

By lowering transaction costs, digital agriculture affects economic activity in the sector in several ways (Deichmann, Goyal, and Mishra 2016; OECD 2019a; World Bank 2016). Falling transaction costs boost productivity and profitability in the sector. For example, falling transaction costs might lower input costs, increasing per-hectare profits. As transaction costs fall, farms and firms take up economic activities once precluded by high transaction costs. For example, the thickening of agrifood markets through greater transparency and lessened asset specificity creates opportunities for value creation. Production processes can be more readily monitored and evaluated and information more easily transmitted to consumers, who may be willing to pay a price premium for their preferences. As a result, farmers can differentiate their products in a way that opens new markets, domestic and international. And as transaction costs fall close to zero, the structure of value chains can change and new business models emerge that can spark innovation, creating a virtuous cycle leading to further reductions in transaction costs. For example, as information-related transaction costs fall, traders may have a greater incentive to adopt efficient contracting structures than to vertically (or horizontally) integrate.

PATHWAYS FOR IMPROVED EQUITY

Three types of divides—economic, spatial, and social—exist in rural areas and may affect agrifood production. *Economic divides* stem from the unequal allocation of productive resources and differences in cost structures between smallholder farmers and those with larger farms. *Spatial divides* result from disadvantages in accessing markets, infrastructure, and public services in the sparsely populated areas in which farming takes place compared with access in urban or peri-urban communities. *Social divides* may prevent disadvantaged groups in rural areas, such as women and youth, from equitable access to resources or markets because of adverse societal and cultural norms or levels of educational attainment.

Digital agriculture has the potential to alleviate all three types of divides and boost equity. Economic divides can be narrowed through changes to economies of scale; improved access to markets, including financial; and increases in productivity achieved through digital agriculture, all of which can enable smallholder farmers to participate in the value chains and lower poverty in rural areas. Spatial divides can be narrowed though digital technologies that lessen the disadvantages of remoteness by lowering hurdles to information, markets, and services. Finally, social divides can be narrowed through digital technologies that create opportunities to integrate disadvantaged groups into society; the spread of social media and changes in social interaction can also lessen social divides (IIASA 2019).

Digital agriculture can, however, create a new form of inequality: a digital divide. Digital divides can be defined as differences in the capacity to access and use information and communication technologies between individuals, men and women, households, geographic areas, socioeconomic groups, ethnic groups, and so forth. The capacity to access information and communication technologies encompasses both physical access and access to the resources and skills to participate effectively as a "digital citizen." The digital divide relates to a range of inequalities between social groups, genders, age groups, and rural and urban areas, both within and across countries (IIASA 2019). In the agrifood system, such inequalities concern (1) access to and use of digital technologies (including relevant skill sets and the quality and affordability of technologies and services); (2) the concentration of knowledge, power, and revenue in the hands of those who develop and own digital solutions and data; and (3) impacts on the economy through productivity gains and job losses. As a result, while digitalization promises to alleviate divides in the rural areas, it can exacerbate them if not well managed.

Inequality in Access to and Use of Digital Technologies

Digital divides often stem from the same economic, spatial, and social divides that already prevail in rural areas. For example, an analysis of the placement of cell phone towers in Sub-Saharan Africa found that small, isolated communities are less likely to be near a cell phone tower (Buys, Thomas, and Wheeler 2009). Another study found that wealth-related variables, such as income and human capital, largely explain cross-country differences in internet access (Chinn and Fairlie 2007). Wealth also determines the types of devices and services that firms and households can afford. Women and girls face barriers to digital inclusion that reflect gender inequalities in society, in access to education, careers, and opportunities (map 2.1) (IIASA 2019). Skill and education levels also play a role. Larger-scale and better educated farmers are more likely to engage in digital agriculture than smallholder and less educated farmers (World Bank 2019).

The Concentration of Knowledge, Power, and Revenue in the Hands of Those Who Develop and Own Digital Solutions and Data

The cost of infrastructure (telecommunications, security protocols, ledgers, clouds, and so forth) and the advantage of accumulated data tend to favor big actors and first-movers in the development of new digital technologies, while creating barriers for later entrants (World Bank 2016, 2019). As a result, a few

MAP 2.1 Gender Gaps in Mobile Internet Use Are Wide in Low- and Middle-Income Countries, 2019

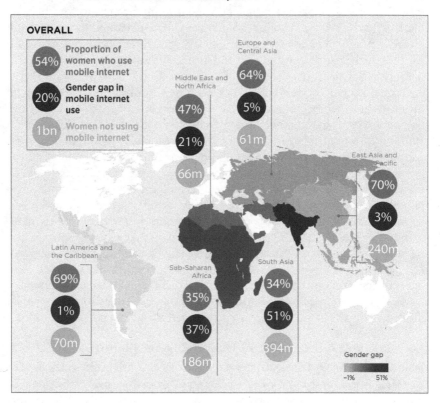

Source: GSMA 2020.

Note: The gender gap refers to how much less likely a woman is to use mobile internet than a man. Mobile internet use is defined as a person having used the internet on a mobile phone at least once in the last three months. Mobile internet users do not have to personally own a mobile phone, so the above figures also include those who used mobile internet on someone else's phone. Based on survey results and modeled data for adults ages 18 years and older. bn = billion; m = million.

powerful companies dominate markets. For example, wealth and power in the digital space are increasingly concentrated in the hands of a small number of so-called global super platforms, including Microsoft, Apple, Amazon, Google, Facebook, Tencent, and Alibaba (UNCTAD 2019). There is also a high geographic concentration in the platform economy, with the United States accounting for 72 percent of the total market capitalization of platforms, followed by Asia, mainly China. Both high market valuations and the speed at which global digital companies have attained high capitalization attests to the value that comes from an ability to quickly collect data and transform it into digital intelligence (UNCTAD 2019). The value of data is also increasingly realized by corporate leaders in traditional sectors, such as agriculture (box 2.1), resulting in a changing market structure.

WHAT'S COOKING: DIGITAL TRANSFORMATION OF THE AGRIFOOD SYSTEM

BOX 2.1 Impacts of Digital Agriculture on Input Industries

The development of digital agriculture influences the input-industry structure in three ways. The first and perhaps most important impact on the industry has been increased investments by new groups of investors and companies from outside what is traditionally considered the agricultural input industry. The first group comprises the big information and communication companies, such as IBM, Google, and Alibaba. Another group comprises start-up companies from universities in computer modeling and big data. Another group of start-ups is made of spinoffs from information technology companies such as ClimateCorp, which spun off from Google, or from machinery companies such as the Chinese drone company XAG, which moved into agriculture in 2013. In the United States, much of the funding for these start-ups comes from venture capital groups that made money investing in computers and software and are now looking at food and agriculture as a new market for their investments. In addition to seeking financial returns, at least some of these investors see themselves as saving the planet through reducing the environmental impact of agriculture by reducing conventional inputs through precision farming.

The second important impact of digital agriculture has been vertical integration of major input firms in the provision of farm management services. There may also be a shift from input-based business models (providing herbicides) toward service-based business models (providing weed-free fields). Seed, biotech, and agricultural chemical companies and machinery companies are buying companies that provide short- and long-term weather predictions, crop and livestock management software, and other components to make digital platforms to provide farm management recommendations to farmers. Part of their motivation is to make money by marketing farm management services through their current dealer networks, but they also want to protect or expand their market shares. Machinery companies buy sensor producers and software companies. Animal health companies are also buying companies that provide sensors and tags for animals (Merck's purchase of Antelliq).

A third change of industry structure involves the relationship between manufacturers and dealers. One important factor is the possibility for machine manufacturers to monitor farmers' current use of their machines by directly accessing data collected by sensors mounted on tractors and machinery and transmitted back to the company. This information allows the manufacturers to do a better job predicting current and future demand for the tractors and machinery and to use this data for refining their products. This information may also reduce the importance of their dealers in providing data for them, which may increase their bargaining power. However, not all farmers use digital solutions. So dealers still remain an important source of information for machine manufacturers. In Germany, it has been observed that machinery manufacturers increasingly request their dealers to use customer management software and share the data provided by this software with them. How the collection and sharing of this information will influence relations among manufacturers, dealers, and farmers remains to be seen. It may foster the already ongoing trend toward more concentrated and more specialized dealer networks.

(Continued)

BOX 2.1 Impacts of Digital Agriculture on Input Industries *(Continued)*

There is less evidence of the role digital agriculture has had on horizontal integration of input firms. Some evidence shows that European Union companies delivering precision agriculture technologies are expanding in size and shrinking in number (European Parliamentary Research Service 2017). However, the key question that remains unanswered and requires further research is the impact of the ongoing changes in the input industry on farmers' access to inputs and the distribution of the value the input companies get from access to farm data.

Concentrations of knowledge and power can lead to information asymmetries in digital markets, increasing transaction costs for participants and affecting the functioning of the markets and ability to innovate. The market dominance of digital platforms is driven by three factors (UNCTAD 2019). The first is a network effect of a large platform—the more users a platform has, the more valuable it becomes to everyone. The second is the ability of digital platforms to aggregate, process, and control data—the more data platform collects the more it can cut its costs, satisfy the consumers, and improve its products relative to competitors. And the third is the dynamics of path dependency—once a platform begins to gain traction, the costs to users of switching to an alternative platform start to increase (Farrell and Klemperer 2007). As a result, large platforms control vast amounts of information about producers and consumers, which can create significant information asymmetries between the platforms and the stakeholders using the platforms. Information asymmetries stemming from the uneven accumulation of data among large and small companies can also reduce the ability of smaller companies to innovate (Nolet 2018). But Engels (2016) makes the case that digital platforms may support competition—product ranges (such as sales of substitute services) provide for competitive conditions, and platform market conditions are regularly disrupted by innovation, so they are perhaps less susceptible to the accumulation of market power than more conventional exchange mechanisms. This has not been proved for the food value chain and justifies further research.

Impacts on the Economy through Productivity Gains and Job Losses

The digital transformation of the agrifood sector creates winners and losers, and the role of the public sector is to ensure that the losers are properly compensated by the winners. The adoption of digital technologies tends to be skill- and knowledge-biased (OECD 2011). As a result, digital technologies tend to increase the demand for skilled labor while decreasing demand for unskilled labor, with implication for wage and income inequality (box 2.2).

BOX 2.2 Impacts of Digital Transformation on Agricultural Jobs

The digital agriculture revolution will likely have far-reaching consequences for the structure of agricultural labor around the world. The precise magnitude and direction of these consequences, however, is not yet clear. Emerging evidence from other industries shows that adopting digital technologies in agriculture may increase demand for higher-paying jobs requiring secondary education and decrease demand for jobs that perform routinized tasks (Autor 2015; Goecker et al. 2015; McKinsey Global Institute 2017). Specifically, the proliferation of digital technologies and automation of various processes displaces employment from jobs with routinized tasks, such as planting and harvesting, to jobs in which humans have a comparative advantage over machines, such as managing data analysis (Acemoglu and Restrepo 2020). A study from the McKinsey Global Institute projects that agriculture has a high potential for automation compared with other sectors (figure B2.2.1). Developed countries such as the United States and Canada, where digital agriculture has become more common than in other countries, provide evidence for the hypothesis. In the United States and Canada, labor demand is increasing for higher-level activities such as farm management and the operation of digital technologies.

As a result, digitalization of agriculture may reinforce social, economic, and spatial inequities in job opportunities and skills development, just as many digital technology divides already reflect existing social divides (Rotz et al. 2019). The effect of the digital transformation of agriculture on employment over time may be strong in countries with a large share of the labor force in agriculture and low productivity, mainly in Sub-Saharan Africa and South Asia. Yet these countries have lower capacity to adopt digital technologies, and any large change in agricultural employment is likely to be gradual (McKinsey Global Institute 2017).

While the displacement of workers is probable, digital agriculture also creates new pathways for employment. Digitalization is revolutionizing how farmers make decisions and how agricultural firms develop products and services. For example, apps such as Climate FieldView enable farmers to collect, store, and visualize critical data to maximize profits and yields (Climate Corporation 2020). The widespread availability of information thanks to digitalization also allows farmers to better understand consumer desires (Freddi 2008). This allows specialized farmers to satisfy evolving consumer tastes for niche products, such as organic foodstuffs and meat alternatives, and services, such as community-supported agriculture cooperatives. The burgeoning ag-tech scene has attracted considerable investor attention and represents a new frontier in farm employment for innovative thinkers. Furthermore, new business models in agriculture are emerging postfarmgate that not only efficiently match supply and demand but also create new marketplaces for services and finance (Paris Innovation Review 2016). Online platforms represent such new employment avenues by reducing barriers to entry into markets and reducing search costs (Evans and Schmalensee 2007), yet the future effect on employment of online platforms across industries is difficult to model (Eichhorst et al. 2016) due to their negligible current role in the labor force (Katz and Krueger 2019). These platforms inevitably pressure the status quo (see Uber and the US taxi industry in Hall and Krueger 2016) and may decrease

(Continued)

FIGURE B2.2.1 Automation Potential across Different Sectors of the Economy

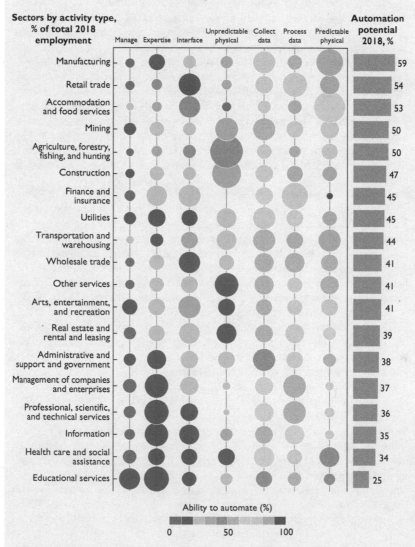

Source: Adapted, with 2018 data, from McKinsey Global Institute 2017.
Note: Size of bubble indicates percentage of time spent in US occupations.

(*Continued*)

employment for just these reasons. To date, the evidence shows that introducing digital platforms does not have a monotonically negative correlation with employment in industries where it has been adopted, as feared. But no significant positive correlation with employment has yet been empirically supported, either, so sweeping conclusions are inevitably misleading (Berger, Chen, and Frey 2018).

The net effect of agricultural labor market transformation is yet to be seen. As change takes place, the key questions become to what extent do job losses occur, to whom, and whether or not the new jobs are shared across social and spatial levels, within economies, and between countries. To mitigate the negative effects brought about by the digital transformation, governments must address digital divides through investments in human capital and job-training programs. To prevent inequitable access to new jobs and educational opportunities, policy should target marginalized groups. Furthermore, policy makers will need to rethink social safety nets and income support for displaced workers, the "losers" in the transformation of the agrifood system (Acemoglu and Restrepo 2020; McKinsey Global Institute 2017). Sound digital agriculture policy can lead to productivity gains, economic growth, and reduced inequality across social and economic levels and places.

To incentivize the positive change toward digital technologies, governments should adopt clear, cross-cutting policies that reduce the cost of adopting new technologies, build trust in the digital transformation of agriculture, and create a positive enabling environment for the private sector to lead the charge in this revolution.

PATHWAYS FOR IMPROVED ENVIRONMENTAL SUSTAINABILITY

Digital agriculture can have direct, enabling, and behavioral effects on the environmental sustainability of the agrifood system. While it is impossible to fully quantify the impacts of digital agriculture on the environmental sustainability of the agrifood system, several pathways of change can be defined conceptually:

- *Direct effects* stem from changes to production and distribution processes that have a direct impact on the use of natural resources or on greenhouse gas emissions. Such effects result from improvements in resource efficiency brought about by digital technologies and enabled through greater production control (such as precision agriculture), dematerialization of products and services on and off the farm, improved coordination of the agrifood system, and greater customization of production due to improved flows of information between producers and consumers.
- *Enabling effects* are attributable to the enhanced scope for environmental monitoring of agricultural production systems. As digital technologies enable the rapid and inexpensive dissemination of large amounts of

environmental monitoring data (Kogan, Powell, and Fedorov 2010; Tsou, Guo, and Stow 2003), they allow for inventorying natural resources at national and global levels, monitoring their use, and ensuring compliance with environmental regulations. In turn, this enables addressing negative environmental externalities.

- *Behavioral effects* result from the transformation of the behavior and attitudes of food consumers and producers that affect the environmental sustainability of the agrifood system. As digital technologies expand the knowledge of the importance of sustainable production practices and allow for enhanced traceability, consumers can more easily act on their preferences to consume food produced in an environmentally responsible way, in turn driving demand for more environmentally sustainable production. At the same time, digital technologies can disseminate information to the producers about the importance of sustainable production practices along with advice on how to implement them. Digital technologies can also strengthen the role of certifications and agreements that aim for environmentally friendly production practices and waste management (Berkhout and Hertin 2004).

The environmental impacts of digital agriculture are expected to be mostly positive, but there are also risks. Digital technologies are essential to measuring, modeling, and communicating the environmental impacts of the agrifood system. The impacts on environmental sustainability are expected to be largely positive. Digital technologies improve resource efficiency through greater process control, while addressing environmental problems at the global level and driving behavioral change among consumers and producers. Still, there are several known risks of digital technologies. For example, digital technologies consume energy (Berkhout and Hertin 2004), generate e-waste, or lead to a so-called rebound effect when efficiency gains, directly or indirectly, stimulate new demand that can offset environmental gains (OECD 2001). Precision agriculture can lead to biodiversity loss (European Parliamentary Research Service 2017). Developing efficient and effective policy responses to improve the environmental sustainability of the agrifood system requires understanding both the pathways through which digital agriculture affects the environment and the potential risks associated with new technologies.

PUBLIC POLICY ENTRY POINTS FOR ACCELERATING DIGITAL TRANSFORMATION OF THE AGRIFOOD SYSTEM

While the creation and use of digital agricultural technologies are fundamentally private sector activities, driven by the private gains of profit-maximizing producers and utility-maximizing consumers, the public sector may need to remedy market failures that distort incentives. Private economic agents may not have the right incentives to make rational decisions because of market or policy failures, lack of public good provision, or inadequate information about their options and the impacts of their decisions. Some of the characteristics of digital goods, such as nonrivalry, nonexcludability, infinite durability, and experience-good nature, may make it challenging for the private sector to supply and use digital technologies in the agrifood system (box 2.3). In such cases, the entry point for public policy is to influence the incentives and decisions of private agents with the goal of maximizing efficiency gains at the societal level and maximizing the equity and environmental sustainability impacts of the adoption of digital agriculture that may not be fully internalized by private economic agents. In creating incentives to prompt behavior among private economic agents that maximizes societal benefits, the public sector must take care also to mitigate the potential (sometimes unknown) risks arising from digital agriculture.

The Maximizing Finance for Development (MFD) framework can help identify public actions needed to facilitate broader development and adoption of digital technologies and harness their impact on food system outcomes (World Bank 2019). MFD looks for ways to crowd in private resources to help

---

BOX 2.3 Properties of Digital Information and Digital Goods Have Implications for Their Supply in Rural Areas

Digital goods are *infinitely durable*, with economic implications for their creators. They are infinitely durable because they work on multiple devices—whether embodied or disembodied—and can be easily transferred from one medium to another (Rayna 2008). While the durability of a device is limited, digital goods can be stored indefinitely if they are transferred to a new device or medium. For example, a video on proper maize planting techniques can be transferred from the device of one farmer to the devices of many others across time and space. For companies trying to get some return on their digital goods, this poses a challenge. Unless producing firms artificially reduce the durability of digital goods (for example, by renting, which limits the product's durability to the duration of the rental period), the expected effect of the infinite durability of digital goods in a competitive setting is a progressive decline in demand and falling prices, limiting profit opportunities.

Digital information and many digital goods typically are *nonrivalrous* and sometimes *nonexcludable* and so can be considered public goods. Because digital datasets and digital goods are, at the margin, nearly free to replicate, they are nonrivalrous from an economic perspective: one person can use a digital dataset or digital good without affecting the quality or quantity available for others to use. While digital information is nonrivalrous, it can also be a component of a physical good—for example, a copyright-protected algorithm programmed into a sensor, which itself is a component of a sowing machine. In this case, the final good is not fully a knowledge good and not strictly digital. So the sowing machine and its knowledge-product components can be marketed as a standard private good. But once nonrivalrous information takes the form of a nonrivalrous, reproducible, and

(Continued)

easily transferred digital good, the nature of the good changes dramatically. Digital goods can also be largely nonexcludable, provided no policy or technical restriction is in place. In such a case, it is hard for anyone to exclude others from consuming them. This implies that reproduction costs are nearly zero. For producers of digital goods, the inability to exclude nonbuyers from using the goods means a loss of potential revenue for their products, undermining their incentive to create. That is why digital goods produced for embodied devices often have technical restrictions created by the manufacturer to prevent nonexcludability. From a public sector perspective, nonexcludability creates a strong incentive to place digital data and some digital goods in the public domain.

In addition to being nonrivalrous, nonexcludable, and durable goods, digital goods are *experience goods*. A good is considered an experience good when full information about its main attributes is unknown without direct experience of the good or when the search for information about the main attributes is more costly or difficult than experiencing the product directly (Klein 1998). The qualities of experience goods, such as compact discs, have implications for consumers and producers. Because it is difficult to make a judgment about a digital good before experiencing it, consumers tend to reward the reputation of established suppliers of digital goods, making it harder for smaller players to enter the markets. Digital good producers need to employ consumer segmentation strategies (such as selling limited versions with fewer features) or offer samples to interested consumers to limit the amount of information consumers must process to decide whether to purchase the good. The experience-good nature of digital agriculture goods has implications for the adoption of digital technologies. In agriculture, a digital good is often judged by the economic outcomes on the farm; for example, if a farmer buys a subscription to an e-advisory service and if following the advice does not result in higher yields or prices at harvest, the farmer will be unlikely to renew the subscription.

The characteristics of digital goods have implications for their supply in rural areas. Because digital goods and services are nonrivalrous, replicable, and easily transferred, the marginal cost of delivering them to network-connected devices is nearly zero, even though the fixed cost of developing the product can be high, particularly for digital goods produced for embodied devices. So, even small gains to a provider of digital goods or services from each nonrivalrous exchange can provide a pathway for the product developer to recover fixed investments and realize profits. Providers of digital goods may employ various pricing approaches, such as bundling and subscription services, consumer segmentation strategies, and bartering for data. Providers can also put technical restrictions or licenses in place that limit the replicability of digital goods and information. Regardless of the strategies employed, the ability of a provider to recover the fixed costs depends on the expected technology adoption by farmers and, hence, the "thicknesses" of the market. So developers of highly sophisticated embodied digital devices and related digital goods must often focus on developing solutions for markets dominated by

(Continued)

achieve development goals, while optimizing the use of scarce public resources. Since digital technologies are primarily generated by the private sector, and since the farmers and agribusinesses adopting these technologies are also private actors, MFD can help identify entry points for public sector actions to facilitate the broader adoption of digital technologies and harness their impact on food system outcomes (see appendix E) (World Bank 2019).

A starting point for the government is to create an enabling environment for the development of the tier 1 enablers for successful digital transformation, led by the private sector (figure 2.4). First, to maximize the efficiency, equity, and environmental sustainability gains from digital agriculture, *good quality, accessible networks* in rural areas are essential. The type of network infrastructure influences the type of digital applications that can be used. For example, second generation networks are more suited for voice and text messaging, while third, fourth, and fifth generation networks enable use of a much broader set of digital devices and applications. The second foundation requires *complementary investments in rural electricity, roads, and logistics* to power digital devices and bridge digital markets. Finally, if the government is to facilitate digital transformation of the agrifood system, it has to develop *governmental capacity to foster digital innovation* and ensure the equitable distribution of the benefits by building data infrastructure and developing human capital. The government needs to be equipped with the physical, digital, and institutional structures that enable and govern the collection, transfer, storage, and analysis of data to produce knowledge and advice for the agrifood system. And it needs to strengthen its own human capital through training or retraining for applying digital technologies and analyzing underlying data, so that it establishes the right goals and instruments to support digital transformation.

To maximize the economic efficiency gains of digital agriculture, as a next step, public and private sectors need to jointly form an innovation ecosystem for digital agriculture to spur the supply of digital agriculture solutions. Building on the tier 1 enablers, the innovation ecosystem needs to include some

FIGURE 2.4 **Enablers of Digital Innovation Ecosystems in the Agrifood System**

Tier 2 enablers
- Access to data
- Digital platforms
- Digital payment systems
- Digital skills
- Digital entrepreneurship

Tier 1 enablers
- Availability and accessibility of digital infrastructure in rural areas
- Availability of nondigital infrastructure
- Basic education and skill levels
- Governmental capacity to foster digital innovation

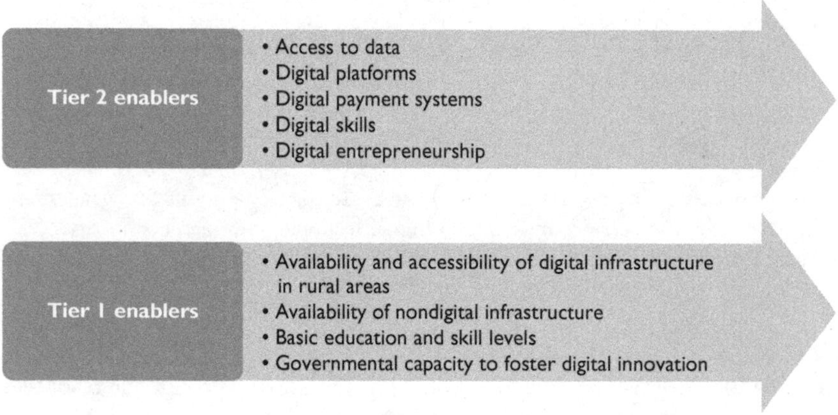

Source: World Bank.

additional elements (tier 2 enablers), such as the availability of open datasets, digital platforms, the digital entrepreneurship environment, digital payment systems, and digital skills to incentivize the development of digital innovation ecosystems. On the government side, supportive public policy interventions should generally provide public goods and create an enabling policy and regulatory environment for the private sector to thrive. Theory and practical experience across many countries indicate that basing spending decisions on this general principle will ensure that public expenditures yield greater bang for the buck and crowd in—rather than crowd out—private sector investments. There may be cases where subsidies for private goods are justified to correct market failures, but these should be exceptions.

To facilitate the adoption of digital agriculture, governments have many tools to increase the uptake of digital solutions in the agrifood system by private economic agents. In addition to skills development, governments can promote the development of relevant, customized digital tools in a suitable format and languages; reduce the cost of adopting digital technologies and facilitate access to finance to enable adoption; and build trust in digital applications, particularly given the fact that digital goods are experience goods. Government interventions should target the whole value chain, not just specific constraints in isolated segments of the value chain. The impact of government interventions will depend on how they affect the prices faced by all actors. Digital technologies that reduce some frictions while leaving others could distort market outcomes, helping some actors and hurting others. For example, if farmers increase production through e-extension services but cannot access markets, they are unlikely to value digital solutions. Digital goods tend to be experience goods, so negative experiences may sharply reduce demand.

To ensure the equitable distribution of digital dividends, governments need to target digital divides as well as economic, spatial, and social divides. While public policy measures targeting economic, spatial, and social divides are not directly within the scope of this report, it is relevant to note that digital technologies offer solutions for tackling these divides. Governments can improve access to and use of digital technologies by marginalized groups; monitor and address concentrations of knowledge, power, and revenue in the digital world; and adopt compensatory measures for potential losers from the digital transformation of the agrifood system.

Governments can increase the environmental sustainability of the agrifood system through digital technologies. The proliferation of digital technologies in agriculture offers enormous potential to enhance the environmental sustainability of the agrifood system. This can be achieved through more efficient use of production resources at the farm level, changes to distribution processes, improved capacity for environmental monitoring, and changes in the behavior of food consumers and producers and in their attitudes toward the environmental impacts of the agrifood system. The role of the public sector is to nudge producers and consumers in the direction of more environmentally sustainable choices. Possible actions include strengthening digital environmental monitoring, incentivizing the use of digital technologies for environmental sustainability, and applying e-education and information dissemination to influence the behavior of producers and consumers.

To identify the most appropriate and effective policies and entry points to spur digital innovation in the agrifood system, governments need clear policy objectives. The goals of increasing efficiency, equity, and environmental sustainability in the agrifood system are largely interdependent. For example, more efficient use of inputs on the farm tends to result in positive environmental outcomes, improved profitability, and greater inclusion even for small producers. Even so, in formulating policies for digital development of the agricultural sector, governments need to prioritize interventions in areas where the gaps are largest, while also anticipating and addressing risks and second-order effects of the interventions along pathways in the efficiency, equity, and environmental sustainability framework. The approach needs to be as holistic as possible. For example, the ability of digital technologies to reduce transaction costs in the agrifood system has the potential to increase market efficiency and competition. At the same time, if digital technologies reduce some frictions but not others, that can distort market outcomes, widening the digital divide. Finally, digital development in the agrifood system should not be considered a goal but rather a means to achieve the societal gains of efficiency, equity, and environmental sustainability. The focus of policy agenda for accelerating digital agriculture transformation in a country would depend on the level of agricultural and digital development in a country. The report's digital agriculture profiling tool introduces an assessment framework to evaluate the state of a country's agricultural and digital development and identify public policy entry points to maximize the efficiency, equity, and environmental sustainability of digital transformations in agriculture (appendix A).

REFERENCES

Acemoglu, D., and P. Restrepo. 2020. "Robots and Jobs: Evidence from US Labor Markets." *Journal of Political Economy* 128 (6): 2188–244. https://doi.org/10.1086/705716.

Autor, D. H. 2015. "Why Are There Still So Many Jobs? The History and Future of Workplace Automation." *Journal of Economic Perspectives* 29 (3): 3–30.

Berger, T., C. Chen, and C. Frey. 2018. "Drivers of Disruption? Estimating the Uber Effect." *European Economic Review* 110: 197–210.

Berkhout, F., and J. Hertin. 2004. "De-materialising and Re-materialising: Digital Technologies and the Environment." *Futures* 36 (8): 903–20.

Bravo-Ureta, B., D. Solís, V. H. Moreira López, J. F. Maripani, A. Thiam, and T. Rivas. 2007. "Technical Efficiency in Farming: A Meta-Regression Analysis." *Journal of Productivity Analysis* 27 (1) (02): 57–72. http://dx.doi.org/10.1007/s11123-006-0025-3.

Buys, P., S. Dasgupta, T. Thomas, and D. Wheeler. 2009. "Determinants of a Digital Divide in Sub-Saharan Africa: A Spatial Econometric Analysis of Cell Phone Coverage." *World Development* 37 (9): 1494–1505

Chinn, M. D., and R. W. Fairlie. 2007. "The Determinants of the Global Digital Divide: A Cross-Country Analysis of Computer and Internet Penetration." *Oxford Economic Papers* 59 (1): 16–44. http://dx.doi.org/10.1093/oep/gpl024.

Climate Corporation. 2020. "Climate FieldView Does the Listening So You Can Get the Most Out of Every Acre." Climate Corporation, San Francisco, CA (accessed August 10, 2020). https://climate.com.

Cuevas, A. C. 2014. "Transaction Costs of Exchange in Agriculture: A Survey." *Asian Journal of Agricultural Development* (2014) 11: 21–38.

Deichmann, U., A. Goyal, and D. Mishra. 2016. "Will Digital Technologies Transform Agriculture in Developing Countries?" *Agricultural Economics* 1 (47): 21–33.

de Janvry, A., M. Fafchamps, and E. Sadoulet. 1991. "Peasant Household Behavior with Missing Markets: Some Paradoxes Explained." *Economic Journal* 101: 1400–17.

Dorward, A., and J. Kydd. 2003. "Implications of Market and Coordination Failures for Rural Development in Least-Developed Countries." Paper presented at the Development Studies Association Annual Conference, Strathclyde University, Glasgow, September 10–12.

Eaton, D., G. Meijerink, and J. Bijman. 2008. "Understanding Institutional Arrangements: Fresh Fruits and Vegetable Value Chains in East Africa." Markets, Chains and Sustainable Development Strategy and Policy Paper, Stichting DLO, Wageningen. http://www.boci.wur.nl/UK/Publications.

Eichhorst, W., H. Hinte, U. Rinne, and V. Tobsch. 2016. "How Big Is the Gig: Assessing the Preliminary Evidence on the Effects of Digitalization on the Labor Market." IZA Policy Paper 17, Institute of Labor Economics, Bonn, Germany.

Engels, B. 2016. "Data Portability among Online Platforms." *Internet Policy Review* 5 (2). https://doi.org/10.14763/2016.2.408.

European Parliamentary Research Service. 2017. "Precision Agriculture in Europe: Legal, Social, and Ethical Considerations." Science and Technology Options Assessment, European Union, Brussels.

Evans, D., and R. Schmalensee. 2007. "The Industrial Organization of Markets with Two-Sided Platforms." *CPI Journal* 3 (1). https://www.competitionpolicyinternational.com/the-industrial-organization-of-markets-with-two-sided-platforms/.

Fare, R., S. Grosskopf, and C. Lovell. 1983. "The Structure of Technical Efficiency." *Scandinavian Journal of Economics* 85: 181–90. https://doi.org/10.2307/3439477.

Farrell, J., and P. Klemperer. 2007. "Coordination and Lock-In: Competition with Switching Costs and Network Effects." In *Handbook of Industrial Organization*, vol. 3, 1967–2072, edited by Mark Armstrong and Robert Porter, 1967–2072. Amsterdam: Elsevier.

Freddi, D. 2008. "Technology Fusion and Organizational Structures in Low- and Medium-tech Companies." In *Innovation in Low-Tech Firms and Industries*, edited by Hartmut Hirsch-Kreinson and David Jacobson. Cheltenham Glos, UK: Edward Elgar.

Goecker, A. D., P. G. Smith, E. Smith, and R. Goetz. 2015. "USDA Employment Opportunities for College Graduates in Food Agriculture, Renewable Natural Resources and the Environment: United States, 2015–2020." US Department of Agriculture, Washington, DC. https://www.purdue.edu/usda/employment.

GSMA. 2020. *The Mobile Gender Gap Report 2020*. London: GSMA.

Hall, J., and A. Krueger. 2016. "An Analysis of the Labor Market for Uber's Driver-Partners in the United States." Working Paper 22843, National Bureau of Economic Research, Cambridge, MA. http://www.nber.org/papers/w22843.

IIASA (International Institute for Applied Systems Analysis). 2019. *The World in 2050: The Digital Revolution and Sustainable Development: Opportunities and Challenges*. Laxenburg, Austria: IIASA.

Katz, L., and A. Krueger. 2019. "Understanding Trends in Alternative Work Arrangements in the United States." Working Paper 25425, National Bureau of Economic Research, Cambridge, MA. http://www.nber.org/papers/w25425.

Klein, L. 1998. "Evaluating the Potential of Interactive Media through a New Lens: Search versus Experience Goods." *Journal of Business Research* 41 (3): 195–203.

Kogan, F., A. Powell, and O. Fedorov. 2010. *Use of Satellite and In-Situ Data to Improve Sustainability*. Dordrecht, Netherlands: Springer.

McKinsey Global Institute. 2017. *A Future That Works: Automation, Employment, and Productivity*. Washington, DC: McKinsey and Company. https://www.mckinsey.com/~/media/McKinsey/Featured%20Insights/Digital%20Disruption/Harnessing%20automation%20for%20a%20future%20that%20works/MGI-A-future-that-works_Full-report.pdf.

Mittal, S., S. Gandhi, and G. Tripathi. 2010. "Socio-Economic Impact of Mobile Phones on Indian Agriculture." Working Paper No. 246, Indian Council for Research on International Economic Relations (ICRIER), New Delhi. http://www.icrier.org/pdf/WorkingPaper246.pdf.

Nolet, S., 2018. "Seeds of Success: Advancing Digital Agriculture from Point Solutions to Platforms. Innovation and Entrepreneurship." US Studies Centre at the University of Sydney. https://www.ussc.edu.au/analysis/advancing-agtech-and-digital-agriculture-in-australia.

OECD (Organisation for Economic Co-operation and Development). 2001. *Impacts of Information and Communication Technologies on Environmental Sustainability: Speculation and Evidence.* Paris: OECD.

OECD. 2011. "Digital Divide: From Computer Access to Online Activities—A Micro Data Analysis." OECD Digital Economy Papers 189, OECD, Paris. http://dx.doi.org/10.1787/5kg0lk60rr30-en.

OECD 2019a. *Digital Opportunities for Better Agricultural Policies.* Paris: OECD.

OECD. 2019b. "Innovation, Productivity, and Sustainability in Food and Agriculture: Main Findings from Country Reviews and Policy Lessons." OECD Working Paper on Agricultural Policies and Markets, Paris. http://www.oecd.org/officialdocuments/publicd isplaydocumentpdf/?cote=TAD/CA/APM/WP(2018)15/FINAL&docLanguage=En.

Paris Innovation Review. 2016. "Agriculture and Food: The Rise of Digital Platforms." February 12. http://parisinnovationreview.com/articles-en/agriculture-and-food-the-rise -of-digital-platforms.

Rayna, T. 2008. "Understanding the Challenges of the Digital Economy: The Nature of Digital Goods." *Communications and Strategies* 71: 13–16.

Rotz, S., E. Gravely, I. Mosby, E. Duncan, E. Finnis, M. Horgan, J. LeBlanc, R. Martin, H. Tait Neufeld, A. Nixon, L. Pant, V. Shalla, and E. Fraser. 2019. "Automated Pastures and the Digital Divide: How Agricultural Technologies Are Shaping Labour and Rural Communities." *Journal of Rural Studies* 68: 112–22. https://doi.org/10.1016/j .jrurstud.2019.01.023.

Tsou, M. H., L. Guo, and D. Stow. 2003. "Web-based Remote Sensing Applications and Java Tools for Environmental Monitoring." *Online Journal of Space Communication* 3. https://www.researchgate.net/publication/237105601_Web-based_Remote_Sensing _Applications_and_Java_Tools_for_Environmental_Monitoring.

UNCTAD (United Nations Conference on Trade and Development). 2019. *Digital Economy Report 2019: Value Creation and Capture: Implications for Developing Countries.* Geneva: UNCTAD.

Williamson, O. 1979. "Transaction–Cost Economics: The Governance of Contractual Relations." *Journal of Law and Economics* 22 (2): 233–61.

Williamson, O. 1988. "Corporate Finance and Corporate Governance." *Journal of Finance* 43 (3): Papers and Proceedings of the Forty-Seventh Annual Meeting of the American Finance Association, Chicago, IL, December 28–30, 1987, 567–91.

World Bank. 2016. *World Development Report 2016: Digital Dividends.* Washington, DC: World Bank.

World Bank. 2019. *Future of Food: Harnessing Digital Technologies to Improve Food System Outcomes.* Washington, DC: World Bank.

PART TWO

The Agrifood System's Digital Transformation

CHAPTER THREE

Transforming Agrifood Value Chains

KEY MESSAGES

- On-the-farm, digital technologies may lower the barriers to agricultural technology adoption through improved access and processing of information.
- Emerging, although limited, evidence shows that improved access to information has positive impacts on farmers' adoption of technology, while studies on precision agriculture show a largely positive impact on farmers' profitability.
- Off-the-farm, digital technologies may lower information-related transaction costs through improved price discovery, buyer-seller matching, digitally enabled collective action, and improved traceability and quality control.
- Emerging evidence shows that better access to upstream and downstream markets with the help of digital technologies has resulted in three types of observable outcomes relevant for farmers: reductions in commodity price dispersion, increased profits and incomes of farmers, and changes in resource allocations and new incentives for quality improvements.
- Evidence on the net effects of digital agriculture on equity remains scarce, while the risks of a digital divide remain significant.
- Digital agriculture offers great promise for improved environmental sustainability in the agricultural value chain, notwithstanding some risks. But empirical evidence on the environmental effects of digital technologies is still scarce.

ON-FARM DIGITAL TRANSFORMATION

Digital technologies lower the barriers to agricultural technology adoption through improved access and processing of information, increasing on-farm technical efficiency.

Barriers to On-Farm Productivity Growth

New agricultural technologies and production practices are key to increasing productivity on the farm, but the adoption of these technologies, particularly by smallholders, has been limited. Most agricultural growth over the past three decades came not from expanding the amount of land, water, and inputs used but from total factor productivity (TFP) growth—from more efficient use of land, labor, capital, and other inputs such as fertilizers through improved technology and production practices (Fuglie et al. 2020; Fuglie 2010, 2015; Gollin 2010). During 2001–15, input growth—area growth, irrigation expansion, and input intensification—accounted for only one-third of the rise in agriculture production globally. TFP growth accounted for two-thirds (Fuglie et al. 2020). Studies show that improved agricultural technologies could increase yields (McDermott et al. 2010; Mueller et al. 2012; Neumann et al. 2010), especially in Sub-Saharan Africa (where yield gaps and poverty are linked) (Mueller et al. 2012; Dzanku, Jirström, and Marstorp 2015). But these improved technologies have faced low uptake by smallholder farmers, particularly in Africa (Dzanku, Jirström, and Marstorp 2015; Larson, Muraoka, and Otsuka 2016; Mueller et al. 2012). In the 2000s, less than 50 percent of the crop area in African countries was planted with modern seed varieties, compared with more than 90 percent in Asia (Fuglie et al. 2020).

Poor access to information about available agricultural technologies, such as seed, fertilizers, and good production practices, is often an impediment to their adoption. To adopt these new technologies, farmers must know that they exist and how to implement them, and they must believe that they will generate higher returns than traditional agricultural technologies (Deichmann, Goyal, and Mishra 2016). They must also assess the risks of adopting the new technology, which are often weather-related shocks—especially in rainfed agriculture—or market-related ones.

Farmers tend to rely on their social networks and local media to learn about new agricultural technologies, but the cost to obtain information can be high. For example, in Sri Lanka, information costs represented 70 percent of transaction costs for farmers (de Silva and Ratnadiwakara 2008). Costs associated with the decision stage—deciding what crop to grow, where, and how much—were the second highest. Smallholder farmers tend to learn from other farmers in their communities, because they lack other information sources (Bandiera and Rasul 2006; Conley and Udry 2010; Foster and Rosenzweig 1995). But that learning is limited by considerable agroclimatic variation between farms, including in land and soil quality, topography, and weather.

In trying to increase farmers' access to information, governments and donors have devoted major resources to extension programs, but their efficacy is unclear (Anderson and Feder 2007; Aker 2011; Davis et al. 2012). Extension services worldwide employed an estimated half-million agents in 2007, 80 percent of them publicly funded (Anderson and Feder 2007). But distance limits extension agents' reach—and remote farmers are less well served (Frisvold, Fernicola, and Langworthy 2001). Farmer field schools emerged in the 1990s, but their high cost limited their scalability (Waddington et al. 2012). In fee-for-service extension, farmers pay service providers for information on agricultural technologies and practices—an approach that overcomes some limitations of the public models, but its efficacy also remains unproved (Rivera, Quamar, and Crowder 2001). In general, traditional extension services suffer from limited scale, mixed impacts, and unsustainability (Rivera, Blum, and Sulaiman 2009).

Poor information about the variability of growing conditions in the field leads to measurement errors in applying inputs and so to lower returns, another barrier to adopting agricultural technology. Knowing soil quality requires determining the amount of fertilizer and other nutrients a crop needs: the poorer the soil quality, the more fertilizer needed. Soil quality varies in the field, so maximizing the returns to technology (such as the yield of hybrid seeds) requires being able to vary input applications spatially at a rate customized to the needs of the plant genetics and the soil conditions at each location. Conventional farm management cannot respond adequately, because it results in the application of fertilizers and pesticides at uniform rates based on average field conditions, so some areas receive too few nutrients, and others too many.

Poor information on local weather conditions also discourages agricultural technology adoption. Weather-related shocks are among the most important sources of risk for smallholder farmers. They are likely to be exacerbated by climate change, making weather information essential (see, for example, Cole et al. 2013). A comprehensive literature review showed that agroclimatic environments were the most important determinant of Green Revolution technology adoption rates (Feder and Umali 1993). Most farmers relied on traditional methods to understand weather predictions. Reliable location-specific weather reports are still a challenge, despite promising developments (Kusunose and Mahmood 2016), and few weather projects have gone beyond the pilot stage (Caine et al. 2015).

Role of Digital Technologies in Lowering Barriers to On-Farm Productivity Growth

Improved access to information

Digital technologies facilitate knowledge transfer and skill acquisition, including low-cost extension advice. Very simple communication technologies can, by themselves, lower information hurdles. Mobile phones speed the spread of information through, for example, social networks—the way farmers frequently learn about new production techniques (Conley and Udry 2010;

Foster and Rosenzweig 1995). Low-cost extension programs, such as those delivered through text messaging (short message service, or SMS) or voicemail, can also help. Using digital technologies to transmit extension advice, such as information on new agricultural technologies, can be faster and cheaper than traditional face-to-face extension. In the Philippines, the Farmers Texting Center uses an SMS-based system to answer farmers' question about rice production (Qiang et al. 2012). Other systems use internet connections through kiosks, smartphones, or computers to provide additional content through videos and searchable databases. Start-up companies such as AccessAgriculture, Farmerline, AgroCenta, and PlantVillage provide digitized extension services. Digital Green has produced and disseminated more than 5,000 locally relevant videos in more than 50 languages in which farmers share knowledge on agricultural production practices (Digital Green 2020). Digital Green videos are primarily screened off-line in communities that have limited electricity and internet connectivity. Digital platforms also support innovative engagement through crowdsourcing. The WeFarm crowdsourcing platform uses machine-learning algorithms to match farmers who have questions with farmers who have answers. Already more than 50,000 WeFarm users in Kenya, Peru, and Uganda have shared more than 8 million pieces of information. Official government extension systems can use digital tools as well.

Promising digital technologies using big data and artificial intelligence are emerging to provide more granular e-extension to farmers. Deep-learning algorithms based on artificial neural networks, convolutional neural networks, and support vector machines have diagnosed plant diseases from photographs with better than 97 percent success (Sladojevic et al. 2016; Ferentinos 2018). Algorithms can use video content to detect lameness in dairy cows (van Nuffel et al. 2016). And researchers are engaged in early efforts to incorporate diagnostic software into smartphone apps, such as Leaf Doctor, created at the University of Hawaii (Pethybridge and Nelson 2015).

Similarly, a thriving ecosystem of mobile apps backed by input providers can help farmers combat pests and manage equipment. Better monitoring allows farmers to respond more quickly to pests and to plant and livestock diseases. For example, the Genuity Rootworm Manager App, developed by Monsanto, determines the risk of corn rootworm at specific field sites, in part by prompting farmers for information about practices and past events (Hopkins 2014). Other apps manage specific equipment. For example, John Deere's SpeedStar Mobile works with the company's planter to collect and report data on seed population rates, seed spacing, and groundspeed row by row.

Digital technologies can also increase the accountability of public extension services, leading to their improved efficacy. They can help farmers hold public service providers accountable—which may be of particular relevance in developing countries, where governance structures are often weak. Digital agriculture solutions can make state-led input distribution more accountable (Daum 2018). In Pakistan, an app-based crowd-sourcing clearinghouse empowers farmers with knowledge of the success rates of veterinarians offering artificial inseminations services. This gave farmers a 37 percent higher insemination rate for their cows compared with a control group (Hasanain, Khan, and Rezaee 2018). And the e-extension approach confronts fewer governance challenges than traditional extension services (Aker 2011; Nakasone and Torero 2016).

Improving information processing and optimization to support on-farm decision-making

Digital technologies improving information processing allow farmers to respond to spatial and temporal variability of production. Conventional farm management methods cannot respond effectively to in-field variability in growing conditions or incorporate real-time information about weather conditions in managing agricultural activities. They apply inputs such as fertilizers and pesticides at uniform rates based on average field and weather conditions and generic crop features, resulting in some areas having insufficient nutrients while others have too much, making crop productivity lower than its potential in some areas and discharging excess nutrients from other areas (Zilberman, Khanna, and Lipper 1997). Brandes et al. (2016) show that even high-yielding fields include areas with low productivity due to poor soil quality and that, in some areas of a field, farmers may lose money by incurring planting and input application costs. The areas that are unprofitable to plant are also likely to be the most environmentally risky ones.

Digital agriculture provides farmers with more data about field conditions and a better way to process the data. For example, the Africa Rice Center developed a decision support tool that helps farmers in Senegal target fertilizer application (Saito et al. 2015). While the app does not capture in-field variations, its field-specific recommendations for fertilizer application allowed rice farmers to raise yields by up to two tons per hectare (from a baseline of five to six tons) and profits by up to $640 per hectare (from a baseline of $1,200–$1,500). Private companies are also active in this area. In Nigeria, the private precision farming company Zenvus promotes the use of soil fertility sensors (Ekekwe 2016). International companies are also exploring smallholder markets. For example, IBM developed a prototype of AgroPad, an artificial intelligence tool for on-the-spot chemical analysis of soil (Steiner 2018). Such apps are often free of charge, but companies use them for product marketing and, if they are widely used, benefit from obtaining big data. The farmers do not necessarily own the technologies themselves. Some apps operating without sensors use a wide range of external data such as weather data and biomass maps to generate recommendations for efficient farm management.

Precision agriculture technologies, combined with other digital technologies, support decision-making by allowing seed planting and fertilizer application to target spatial and temporal variations. Precision agriculture addresses variability in the field by using big data and data analytics to better understand the agronomics of crop production and to improve the accuracy of farmers targeting site-specific conditions. Precision agriculture also addresses temporal variability by combining geocoded technology information with precise meteorological information to inform farmers how much input to apply and when and where to apply it, thereby increasing input use efficiency. Precision agriculture can also improve high-value fruit and vegetable farming through precise irrigation and pest spraying and optimal harvesting based on high-resolution yield, color, and sugar content information (European Parliament 2014).

Digital agriculture can give farmers accurate, timely, and location-specific weather information. Localized satellite weather data are transmitted to farmers through digital technologies such as mobile phones. Such innovations potentially show the best timing for planting and harvesting, increasing productivity. Accurate weather information also increases farmer resilience to weather-related shocks (FAO 2018). Access to better weather data helped Colombian farmers reduce crop losses by up to 7 percent in a randomized controlled trial study (Camacho and Conover 2011). Various parametric weather insurance contracts use high-resolution mapping of weather conditions at the farm level through satellite technologies.

Early warning systems for crop and livestock health can allow proactive and timely management responses. For example, Scouting tool and Plantix, two mobile crop advisory applications, quickly diagnose pests, plant diseases, and nutrient deficiencies based on smartphone photographs (Xarvio 2020). For animal health, VetAfrica, a Scottish start-up, and Cowtribe, a Ghanaian start-up, have developed apps to help farmers diagnose diseases and obtain treatment advice (CTA 2017). Both farmers and extension officers can provide information, as in the Fall Armyworm Monitoring and Early Warning System created by the United Nations Food and Agriculture Organization (Parker 2018). Digital agriculture tools that use remote drone- and satellite-based crop health monitoring can also be used by extension officers, cooperative members, private service providers, and agrochemical dealers who advise farmers (TechnoServe 2018).

Digital technologies help manage livestock diseases and health, breeding, genomics, and fertility management. The potential for smart management of operations is not limited to row-crop agriculture but can also be deployed for improving livestock and dairy farming. Electronic identifiers, motion detectors, rumination monitors, and precision feeding systems can enable better management of animals on an individualized basis by allowing continuous monitoring of nutritional status, feed intake and refusals, and early detection of diseases. For example, iCow, an extension-type mobile app in Kenya founded by a former organic farmer, sends short messages to provide advice based on dairy cattle calendars on cattle feeding, milking, disease control, and fertility management (Gathigi and Waititu 2013). Farmers using iCow increased daily milk yields by two to three liters per cow and reduced calf mortality and veterinary costs (according to iCow estimates, which are not based on independent assessments) (Kahumbu 2012). Tagging cattle with radio frequency identification devices (RFIDs) can provide smallholder farmers valuable data for breeding programs. In India, the Chitale Dairy cooperative in Maharashtra has tagged about 200,000 cows (Bhattacharya 2017). That cooperative also uses Herdman, an app developed by VetWare. Herdman uses quick response (QR) codes to quickly record weight, health, yields, feeding, calving, and disease data that have helped improve feeding, breed more productive animals, and guide veterinary officers by detecting when animals are sick (Bhattacharya 2017). VetWare is currently exploring alternative approaches to identify animals, such as iris recognition (T. Ravichandran, personal information, July 25, 2019). In Africa, the Namibian Livestock Identification and Traceability System uses an RFID-based traceability system to fight bovine diseases (Deichmann, Goyal, and Mishra 2016). The Ugandan mobile service Jaguza also uses data from RFID tags to predict and respond to emerging health issues in livestock herds (Katamba and Mutebi 2017). The University of Hohenheim and the company Fodjan in Germany are piloting a feeding app for dairy cattle for African farmers. After data on animals and available feed and feed costs are entered, the app optimizes diets for feeding costs, rumen health, or milk yield (Doldt 2019).

Emerging evidence on the impacts of digital technologies on farmers' practices and outcomes

E-extension has shown positive impacts on farmers' technology adoption, but evidence of its effect on yields remains mixed. E-extension can shift farmers' input use and crop decisions. A meta-analysis in India and Kenya found that digitally delivered extension increased the likelihood of adopting recommended agrochemical inputs (by an odds ratio of 1:22) (Fabregas, Kremer, and Schilbach 2019). A mobile phone–based educational intervention in Niger improved the diversity of crops planted (Aker and Ksoll 2016). In some instances, more judicious input use and smarter crop choices translate into improved yields; the same meta-analysis in India and Kenya found that digitally delivered extension increased farmers' yields by 4 percent (Fabregas, Kremer, and Schilbach 2019). In Vietnam, internet access was associated with a 7 percent increase in the volume of agricultural output (Kaila and Tarp 2019). In Ethiopia, SMS-based advisory services increased wheat production from one ton per hectare to three tons (ATA 2019). But other studies do not find systematic evidence of yield increases. Avaaj Otalo, a mobile phone–based extension service for Indian farmers, increased the adoption of more effective pesticides and the planting of lucrative but risky crops (Cole and Fernando 2014), but there was no evidence of increased cotton, wheat, or cumin yields, nor evidence of increased profits (Cole and Fernando 2020). Although the first round of a farm cycle–based SMS intervention helped Kenyan sugarcane farmers raise yields by 11.5 percent—especially farmers with limited prior agronomic training—a follow-up trial of the same intervention found no significant effect on yields (Casaburi et al. 2014; Casaburi, Kremer, and

Ramrattan 2019). Differences in season and farmer characteristics between trials suggests that the efficacy of e-extension depends on context (Casaburi, Kremer, and Ramrattan 2019). Timing, context-specific content, and comprehensibility all influence the success of e-extension (Nakasone and Torero 2016). Overall, a comparative analysis of the empirical findings on the impacts of digital technologies on efficiency, equity, and environmental sustainability (EEE) outcomes in the agrifood system remains challenging due to the complexity of the notions of both "digital agriculture" and "EEE outcomes."

Some anecdotal evidence suggests e-extension can improve farmer incomes. For example, e-Dairy, a service linked to a mobile app and to touch-screen kiosks around Sri Lanka, provides dairy farmers with information about animal health, milk prices, feed suppliers, bank loans, and veterinary services. It improved farmer income by $262 per dairy calf, according to one report (Qiang et al. 2011). In one study in India, farmers receiving customized crop cultivation and nutrient management practices via mobile phones and the internet earned 15 percent more income than the control group (Raj et al. 2011). But further empirical work is needed to draw conclusions about e-extension's impact on profits and incomes. Although potential gains in input efficiency, yields, and profits from e-extension may seem small, Fabregas, Kremer, and Schilbach (2019) emphasize the gains are large relative to the cost of information delivery, especially at scale.

Studies find a significant positive relationship between the use of precision agriculture technologies and yield improvements. Tekin (2010) estimated that variable rate nitrogen fertilizer application can increase wheat production between 1 and 10 percent, offering savings in nitrogen fertilization between 4 and 37 percent. According to Biggar et al. (2013), an 8 percent increase in wheat yields (for 10 percent less nitrogen) and 5 percent increase in corn yield (for 21 percent less nitrogen) was shown when GreenSeeker technology was used in Maryland, United States. In Virginia, United States, using again GreenSeeker technology in corn fields, there was nearly 27 kilograms per hectare less nitrogen application than the conventional method with a nearly equivalent yield (Balafoutis et al. 2017).

A review of the studies on precision agriculture's impact on farmers' profitability is largely, but not uniformly, positive, with 68 percent of cases showing increased profits (European Parliament 2014). Another review of 234 articles that discussed economic returns from precision agriculture found that 73 percent of the articles focused on corn reported net benefits, 100 percent of those focused on soybean, 75 percent of those focused on potato, and 52 percent of those focused on wheat (Griffin and Lowenberg-DeBoer 2005). A study of corn farms that adopted at least one of the precision technologies examined found that net returns increased by 1 to 2 percent compared with corn farms that did not (Schimmelpfennig 2016). Studies of variable rate technology for corn production found it profitable only on corn fields with sufficient variability in fertility. These studies, to estimate net benefits, differed in their treatment of time periods, discount rates, capital costs, input costs, and crop yield.

Case specific, they do not provide generalizable conclusions about the conditions under which digital technologies are likely to be profitable. Most examined an earlier generation of precision technologies. Little or no evidence is publicly available on the profitability of big data–enabled precision farming, because the big data being generated at the farm scale are largely in private hands and not readily available to researchers or policy makers.

OFF-FARM DIGITAL TRANSFORMATION

Digital technologies may drastically lower transaction costs associated with the farmers' access to upstream and downstream markets through improved price discovery, buyer-seller matching, digitally enabled collective action, and improved traceability and quality control.

Barriers to Farmers' Access to Upstream and Downstream Markets

Information plays a key role in the connectivity of farmers, particularly smallholders, to the upstream and downstream markets. High costs associated with searching and gathering information, bargaining and negotiating contracts, and monitoring and enforcement weaken the decisions of smallholder farmers to participate in the market, making them less competitive and resulting in the inefficient allocation of goods and resources. The sum of transaction costs faced by a farmer creates a price band that determines the farmer's decision to purchase inputs or sell produce, thus limiting productivity and profitability (de Janvry, Fafchamps, and Sadoulet 1991). Overall, transaction costs tend to be higher for farmers living in remote areas with poor communication and transportation infrastructure, resulting in thin markets (meaning few alternative transactions are possible) and the production of perishable commodities.

High transportation costs due to long distances from rural markets and poor road infrastructure further determine farmers' decisions to participate in these markets. For example, a study in Nigeria found that a 10 percent increase in transportation costs reduces the probability of farmers using mechanized techniques by 2.4 to 3.5 percent. This result is consistent with other studies that found a positive relationship between road quality and participation in input and output markets (de Janvry, Fafchamps, and Sadoulet 1991).

High screening, supervision, and enforcement costs resulting from information asymmetries can make markets fail for agricultural producers, particularly small ones. Market failures due to asymmetric information, as described in a seminal 1970 article, "The Market for 'Lemons,'" occur in all major agricultural markets (Akerlof 1970). The lemon problem arises when sellers know the quality of their goods, but buyers do not. Because buyers cannot distinguish between a high-quality and low-quality product, a low-quality product sells at the same price as a high-quality one. In input markets, large information asymmetries discourage input purchase by farmers, contributing to suboptimal input use, and so to low farm productivity and profitability. In the output markets, buyers of agricultural products from farmers may be uncertain about their quality, so farmers lose transactions or receive lower prices.

Asymmetric information also limits cash-constrained farmers' access to credit, reducing their ability to purchase inputs or make quality-enhancing investments. Smallholder farmers tend to be excluded from credit markets (see chapter 4 for more details). For example, 40 percent of smallholders in Honduras, Nicaragua, and Peru are credit constrained (World Bank 2007). Lack of access to credit decreases farmers' ability to purchase inputs and invest in higher quality products. In one study, Peruvian producers without access to credit used only 50–75 percent as much purchased inputs on average as their counterparts with access to credit, and they earned net returns only 60–90 percent as high (Boucher, Carter, and Guirkinger 2006). Access to credit is especially important for capital-intensive inputs, such as machinery. Farm machinery expenditures average about 20 percent of total farm production expenditures for farms reporting $10,000–$50,000 in gross sales and 11 percent for those reporting $50,000–$100,000. The differences in access to credit create a large gap in agricultural investment between advanced countries and poor ones, where small scale and high cost discourage purchasing such capital-intensive inputs.

Increasing concentration and formalization in the global agrifood system create additional layers of transaction costs for farmers. On the supply side, increasing concentration in processing, trading, marketing, and retailing is being observed in all regions of the world and in all segments of production-distribution chains (Adjemian, Saitone, and Sexton 2016; Sexton and Xia 2018; van Donk, Akkerman, and van der Vaart 2007). Traditional marketing channels with ad hoc sales are being replaced by coordinated links among farmers, processors, retailers, and others. Farmers increasingly face pressures on price and delivery conditions, a reduced number of potential buyers, and more generally, challenges in accessing the downstream food value chain. Pressures of scale and specialization mean that smallholder farmers are more challenged than larger ones, and traditional risk management techniques based on diversification are threatened by specialization.

On the demand side, consumers are becoming more demanding of food quality and safety. Escalating and heavily publicized outbreaks of foodborne diseases have raised the awareness of the need to ensure food quality and safety. According to the World Health Organization (WHO 2020), each year an estimated 600 million people—almost 1 in 10 in the world—fall ill after eating contaminated food and 420,000 die. In addition, $110 billion is lost each year in productivity and medical expenses resulting from unsafe food in low- and middle-income countries. Traceability—from the point of origin to the point of consumption—is increasingly common in public and private systems for monitoring food safety compliance. But increasing demand for safe and traceable food can exclude small-scale producers who lack the resources to comply with strict standards.

Similarly, to participate in international trade, farmers and exporters need to increase the quantity, quality, sophistication, and sustainability of their production and exports. Satisfying the food safety requirements of importing countries has become more complex as the range of items covered by mandatory standards and the stringency of standards increase. Demonstrating compliance with standards has shifted from enforcing product standards at the borders of exporting and importing countries to controls over the way products are grown, harvested, processed, and transported. At the same time, mandatory public standards have increasingly been complemented by collective private standards such as EurepGAP and Safe Quality Food (UNIDO 2006). Complying with these standards puts additional pressure on farmers, particularly smallholders.

Consumers are also increasingly willing to pay premiums for diverse product characteristics, including some not strictly related to food safety (Aertsens et al. 2009; Cicia and Colantouni 2010; Connolly and Klaiber 2014; Dabbene, Gay, and Tortia 2013). That willingness has fostered a proliferation of public and private standards, including those related to organic food, environmental sustainability, animal welfare, and social impact (Grunert, Hieke, and Wills 2014; Guilabert and Wood 2012). Taken together, the standards have led to complex supply chains to deliver food with an array of features that lie at the heart of public health and the business models of supermarkets, food brands, and other agribusinesses. Requirements to comply with the standards and certifications of compliance are often costly and require specific infrastructure, creating an additional layer of transaction costs for farmers, particularly smallholders.

High transaction costs in agrifood value chains explain the emergence of intermediary firms that often create even higher transaction costs for smallholder farmers in upstream and downstream markets. Agricultural markets are often dominated by intermediaries with substantial market power—either suppliers of inputs or buyers of outputs—who are better informed about market conditions, especially the prices further along the supply chain. Opinion is divided as to traders' impact on smallholder market access and market success. Traders can lower transaction costs and offset information asymmetry by providing services such as search, price discovery, and quality definition (Abebe, Bijman, and Royer 2016; Leksmono et al. 2006; Mitra et al. 2018). But intermediaries can also obstruct direct buyer-seller communications, leading to increased transaction costs (Abate et al. 2011). Asset specificity in agriculture can expose farmers to severe bargaining and contract enforcement problems if they face a monopsonistic buying structure for outputs or a monopolistic seller structure for inputs. In such cases, farmers have low incentives to invest in productivity-enhancing measures or higher quality products. Whether middlemen play a positive or a negative role for smallholders' access to markets, their existence stems from the presence of transaction costs in the markets. Hence, there can be large efficiency gains from their removal (Besley and Burgess 2000).

Role of Digital Technologies in Lowering Barriers to Farmers' Access to Upstream and Downstream Markets

Improved price discovery and matching

A broad set of digital technologies can reduce transaction costs associated with searching for market information, compared with traditional methods. Mobile phones, the most available type of digital technology, can expand and complement existing interpersonal networks and speed information flows by reducing the consequences of geographic distance (Aker, Ghosh, and Burrell 2016). The reduced search cost allows farmers to search for information in less time and across a wider geographic area (Aker 2008; Aker and Mtibi 2010). Using a mobile phone is cheaper than physically traveling to the market, because going to the market includes transport cost and the opportunity cost of time.

Digital platforms, by facilitating matching, reduce the need for intermediaries and enable farmers to cater directly to many customers, which helps deconcentrate and thicken the market. Lower search costs let more buyers and sellers use market platforms, allowing previously unprofitable transactions (Deichmann, Goyal, and Mishra 2016). In addition, peer-to-peer digital markets let flexible suppliers enter and exit markets, supplementing the activities of dedicated suppliers (Einav, Farronato, and Levin 2016). And the use of standardized, automatic online processes and secure payments, in turn, reduces contracting and payment costs. One study described India's eChoupal, an integrated digital platform connected to a network of village kiosks created by the India Tobacco Company, which streamlines the procurement of soybeans and other agricultural products from dispersed smallholder producers (Kumar 2004). Another study showed improvements in digital services, such as cloud storage, generating downstream efficiencies in delivering nondigital goods (Rosenthal et al. 2012). Alibaba's Taobao online marketing platform is another case (Li 2019). The county of Shuyang, where 86 of China's 4,310 Taobao villages are located, has undergone a dramatic transformation from one of the poorest counties in Jangsu province to a well-off landmark for agricultural e-commerce. Thanks to a thriving horticulture industry backed by e-commerce, the county's gross domestic product surpassed 80 billion yuan (more than $11 billion) in 2018, and 41,000 people were lifted out of poverty. Various digital platforms have been emerging in the past few years to make agricultural mechanization more accessible, such as TroTro Tractor in Ghana, EM3 and Trringo in India, and Hello Tractor in Ghana, Kenya, and Nigeria. Such platforms match machinery rental services, which buy machines such as underused tractors, with customers who can now rent machines they previously had to buy or else could not access at all, because they could not borrow from banks. Because the marginal cost of matching buyers and sellers through digital platforms is extremely low, saved transaction and search costs reduce the unit costs of renting machinery (box 3.1).

BOX 3.1   Case Studies of Tractor Hire and Drone Hire in India, Nigeria, and China

A variety of digital machinery rental platforms for farmers has been emerging around the world. These platforms promise to increase farmers' access to machinery, but their overall impact so far has been mixed.

EM3 Agri Services in India

In India, EM3 Agri Services aims to "uberize" agriculture (Katz 2016). EM3 allows farmers who own equipment such as tractors, harvesters, and other mechanical implements to rent them out to help pay for their purchase or to generate additional revenue. The renting farmers, typically in remote regions with small holdings and limited capital, get access to quality implements on a pay-as-you-use basis priced by acreage or by the hour. This is especially important, because most farms in India are smaller than three acres, unable to afford even basic mechanization due to the large capital needed. EM3 has established 300 custom hiring centers under an agreement with the state government. The EM3 centers use a franchise model, in which the state provides franchisees with subsidized tractors, and EM3 helps them use digital technology to acquire customers. The franchisees pay 5 percent of every transaction to EM3, and they pay a security deposit that is fully repaid only when they can prove at least 650 machinery hours per year, a level achievable only through providing services. EM3 deploys local representatives in the villages it serves and operates call centers handling requests from machinery owners and prospective renters.

Most farmers contact a franchisee for services directly by walking in or calling by phone, because franchisees were typically private contractors before becoming franchisees and have a trusted working relationship with farmers. The franchisee then uploads the request on an EM3 application, specifying the type of service, date, and farm size. But farmers can also call an EM3 call center, which uses a digital platform to forward the request to the closest franchisee. If local franchisees do not have the requested equipment, the call center contacts franchisees in other areas—this is common for more expensive equipment such as harvesters, rice transplanters, and laser land levelers. Although there is no smartphone app for farmers yet, franchisees can use an app to manage requests, tractors, and operators.

The overall effects seem mixed and are complicated by the state subsidy, although it is too early to arrive at final conclusions. For the farmers who rent services, few differences are recognizable from services through traditional providers, although access to more expensive equipment may be easier. For tractor owners who offered services before EM3, its benefits are equally limited, because most joined only to access the state subsidy (Daum et al. 2020).

Hello Tractor

Hello Tractor, founded in 2014 in Nigeria, aims to connect tractor owners to farmers through a digital app. Key components are a digital booking platform and a device for remote tractor monitoring. The booking platform, by matching

(Continued)

tractors with farmers who request services, increases machinery use and lowers transaction costs. The monitoring device, depending on the version, records global positioning system (GPS) data, maintenance needs, and fuel level, thereby simplifying the supervision of tractors and operators. So far, Hello Tractor has fitted around 600 tractors with the monitoring device. The number of individual Hello Tractor providers is lower than 600, because not all tractor owners offer services. Large contractors and associations owning several hundred tractors dominate the Nigerian tractor market. As of October 2018, 15 contractors and associations were at least partly following the equipment share model (Daum et al. 2020). While the Uber-for-tractors analogy suggests that smallholder farmers use their phones to hire tractors, few Nigerian smallholder farmers yet own smartphones—and even fewer trust them enough to use them for business transactions (Foote 2018). Thus, like the traditional Nigerian tractor markets, Hello Tractor works with booking agents who pool demand from several smallholder farmers for a 10 percent commission. The booking agents often come from locations outside the farming communities, including cities, bringing both advantages and disadvantages. On the upside, the agents, less constrained by rural social norms, are more likely to accept requests from female farmers. On the downside, they are not always trusted—a challenge because the equipment-sharing model requires a commitment fee before service delivery.

The benefits of Hello Tractor for smallholder farmers are largely positive because digitized business models can increase the overall supply of tractor services. Benefits for tractor owners are mixed and depend on their size. For large contractors that own several dozen tractors with services that migrate across agroecological zones, Hello Tractor's technology helps to monitor tractors and to organize customers. For individual tractor owners and small associations offering services within their own community, the benefit is less clear, because they typically have long-standing relationships with customers, and the Hello Tractor app is costly and reduces their control over pricing (Daum et al. 2020).

Farm Friend

Farm Friend, founded in early 2016 in Beijing, is a drone-sharing platform for farmers to submit requests for agricultural drone operators to spray pesticides and fertilizers on crops. Although Farm Friend does not own agricultural drones itself, it currently deploys more than 5,000 drones over 60,000 hectares in 10 Chinese provinces. The app's interfaces for farmers and drone operators are very user friendly. Farmers input their preferred date and time, crop name, fertilizer or pesticide, hectares of farmland, location, and contact information. Farm Friend automatically matches their requests with the closest service providers. Drone operators receive the order information and plan the work. When the work is complete and performance feedback is sent through an app, payments are deposited to operators' accounts.

Lowered transport costs

Digital technologies can decrease transport costs for farmers by redefining distance and remoteness. For example, the Kenya Agricultural Commodity Exchange collaborates with other companies to disseminate market information via voice mail (Munyua, Adera, and Jensen 2009; Qiang et al. 2012). Deichmann, Goyal, and Mishra (2016) describe an information-based initiative by the Zambian National Farmers' Union to enable farmers and traders to get their product to market at the lowest cost. Search costs and information asymmetry are reduced by using a mobile phone to access an information portal where available trucks, available loads, and anticipated routes are advertised. The system includes online directories of paying users, which solves certain excludability problems of information as a public good. Payments and practical issues are then resolved by voice communications between individuals.

Digital technologies also reduce the efficiency and transaction costs of transportation and logistics. Digital technologies can increase agricultural transportation and logistics efficiency by reducing transport costs and markups from input dealers to farmers. Often, delivery service companies invest in data-intensive systems that optimize logistical networks in real time, building on such new transportation technologies as GPS tracking and crowdsourced transit data (Speranza 2018). For example, web-based and SMS systems in South Africa and Zambia let farmers optimize supply chains and coordinate transportation (Deichmann, Goyal, and Mishra 2016).

Digitally enabled collective action

Digital technologies offer new opportunities to producer groups for exploiting network economies. Producer groups have long served as means of addressing smallholder farm performance (Hellin, Lundy, and Meijer 2009) and access to both upstream and downstream markets, with reduced transaction costs as a primary mechanism (Markelova et al. 2009). Digital technologies offer avenues to improve the functionality of producer organizations and better inclusion of the smallholder farmers into the value chains. The pathways for digital technologies to achieve this goal is through improved connection among members, better accounting and administrative processes, the provision of value-added services to the members, and a stronger collective voice (World Bank 2017):

- *Enhanced connections to members.* A major service provided by farmer organizations is to improve members' access to market information and technical know-how. Digital technologies (SMS, apps, and so forth) can serve as tools to share such information. In addition, the topics discussed and decisions made at executive committee meetings can be shared with members not able to attend due to distance or cost.

- *Digital aggregators.* Another service farmer organizations offer their members is aggregating their produce for retail, wholesale, or export markets. Digital technologies reduce the transaction costs associated with connecting farmers. For example, M-Farm in Kenya enables farmers to sell their produce collectively by connecting them directly to markets using mobile devices (Baumüller 2013).
- *Improved accounting and administration.* Digital technologies allow more efficient and transparent record keeping of the activities of farmer organizations, improving members' trust in them.
- *Stronger collective voice.* With the help of digital technologies, farmers are now able to offer their feedback to their executive board, local government, and private sector actors by means not possible before, such as text, voice, and video technologies.

Improved traceability and quality control in input and output markets

Tracing systems are using digital technologies to reduce information asymmetries in input markets by allowing farmers to screen input quality. Several digital technologies are aimed at providing information about the quality of seeds and fertilizers. Specifically, they try to protect brands from counterfeits by tracking products through the supply chain from production to the farmer or consumer. These systems allocate a unique number or code to each unit, which the customer can submit through a cell phone to a platform, where it is checked. Companies that want to protect a brand name have an incentive to join such systems. Examples include QualiTrace, based in Ghana (QualiTrace 2018); mPedigree, operating in India and several countries in Sub-Saharan Africa (mPedigree 2020); SourceTrace, operating internationally (SourceTrace n.d.); and Sproxil, which started in Nigeria (Sproxil n.d.). Many governments and donors have undertaken projects for reducing the distribution of fake seeds and fertilizers through labels farmers can verify using SMS messaging with distributor companies and the government. Digital tracing systems based on bar codes or QR codes are not a new approach to fighting adulteration along the value chains of certified seeds or products. For example, bar codes on bags of certified seeds have been used before, but case study evidence from Ghana shows that such systems cannot necessarily prevent adulteration if inspection capacity is small and political will to enforce regulations is lacking (Poku, Birner, and Gupta 2018). Systems such as QualiTrace aim to empower the farmers themselves to use digital tools for quality control instead of relying on government inspectors. In this way, such systems enable information crowdsourcing or citizen science. This report did not find any studies about their usefulness by third parties or scholars.

Social media information networks are another digital tool that could help farmers address information asymmetries in their access to the input markets. WhatsApp groups are an important example through which farmers could exchange their experience with inputs, including agricultural machinery, and with specific agro-input dealers. On the downside, such social media can also be used to spread fake news about inputs. For example, companies could make unsubstantiated claims about their fertilizers, pesticides, or biologicals in social media. An increasing number of studies examine WhatsApp among farmers, especially in India (for example, Naruka et al. 2017). With smartphones spreading among farmers in developing countries beyond India, such tools may gain increasing importance there, as well.

In the downstream markets, digital technologies can significantly reduce transaction costs associated with food safety and quality requirement compliance. Digital technologies, such as sensors, data management software, and blockchain (box 3.2) are well suited to tracing systems because tracing systems are information-based and digital platforms coordinate information

BOX 3.2 Role of Distributed Ledger Technologies and Smart Contracts for Improved Traceability along the Agrifood Value Chains

Distributed ledger technologies (DLTs) and smart contracts have significant potential to increase efficiency and transparency in agricultural supply chains by improving product traceability and integrity, contract certainty, proof and verification of geographic origin, and compliance with sanitary and phytosanitary requirements. Various traceability functions relate to particular users in the value chain: business-to-business transactions of raw material and its processing performance require different data than do business-to-consumer transactions, which might focus on branding information or food safety. Transactions between elements in the blockchain constitute depersonalized contracts that overcome trust issues. Such transactions enable "smart contracts" (Staples 2017). Some fundamental technical data (production location, agricultural practices used, and so forth) would provide automated verification.

The use of blockchain is nascent, but successful pilots of its use are rapidly spreading. One of the most successful initiatives is the Food Trust consortium, run by IBM, using blockchain technologies for improved food traceability. It brings together large retail and food industry companies from across the world, including Dole, Driscoll's, Golden State Foods, Kroger, McCormick, and several others. As part of this consortium, Carrefour, a supermarket chain in France, uses blockchain to provide consumers with detailed information on purchased chicken, including veterinary treatments, freshness, and other metrics (OECD 2019). Similarly, Barilla, an Italian pasta and pesto sauce manufacturer, is employing blockchain to improve transparency and traceability in its pesto production cycle along the entire supply chain, from farm to fork. There are also many start-ups that aim at shortening agriculture value chains and reducing the role of the middlemen. For example, INS is an e-commerce platform that uses DLTs to directly connect producers and consumers through data integration. Another example is AgriDigital, an Australian

(Continued)

company that uses blockchain-enabled contracts to facilitate interactions among the various players of the grain supply chain. Another Australian example, the BEEFLEDGER blockchain initiative, employs the key tasks of traceability (supply chain knowledge, documentation, and production scheduling) to offer paddock-to-plate assurance in export markets. This is facilitated by sales and distribution of bespoke currency tokens both to businesses and consumers. BEEFLEDGER offers a dedicated platform for information provision, seeking to serve the information needs of diverse stakeholders.

To ensure their scalability and accessibility, DLT solutions require appropriate ecosystems. Although such ecosystems have technology-specific elements, they also entail enabling policy, regulatory, and institutional conditions as well as basic requirements for infrastructure, literacy (including digital), and network coverage (Tripoli and Schmidhuber 2018). In a recent PwC survey, regulatory uncertainty around blockchain-based solutions was identified as a major challenge to scaling up across various sectors (PwC 2018). Other major challenges included interoperability and the potential failure of blocks within the chain to work together.

flows along supply chains from farm to fork. For example, a tracing system might document that a contracted shipment of coffee, originating from a specific farm with an organic certification, arrived at a specific warehouse and that final payments against the contract were issued. Digitally enabled traceability offers advantages such as efficiency through low cost and ease of use, and immutability provides security from tampering. Further, once digital tracing systems are in place, the marginal costs of increasing the number of platform participants or expanding the criteria tracked by the platform are low. For this reason, technologies to address food-safety risks, preserve quality, track inventory, and preserve product identity are often combined (Løkke et al. 2011).

Tracing systems capture digital information to build a complete record of product movements and transformations through time and space. Records are stored in a digital database, which can be accessed when needed. So information about public and private standards are crucial inputs to the design of tracing systems (Badia-Melis, Mishra, and Ruiz-García 2015; Dabbene, Gay, and Tortia 2013). Tracing systems are often integrated into public systems that alert consumers over digital platforms and speed product recall when food hazards are discovered (Potter et al. 2012). Kos and Kloppenburg (2019) argue that digital technologies transform developing countries' access to global value chains by way of "hypertransparency," which enables product traceability based on existing technologies, combined to provide the following functions: automated and continuous data collection, processing for decisions using algorithms, paperless data management through platforms and cloud-based processing, changed responsibilities along the food value chain and onward into services, and changed boundaries of the value chain to include possible new potential product attributes such as information about localities and smallholder practices.

The beef industry in Uruguay offers a good qualitative example of how digital technologies can guard food safety and, by doing so, extend export markets for domestic farmers. Animals are tracked using a double ear-tag system linked to an internet-accessible database on the characteristics of individual animals. The digital database includes information about the sex, breed, place of birth, and owner of the animal, as well as a history of where the animal has been and when and where it was slaughtered. Histories of meat products from the slaughtered animal are built up and linked, so that it is possible to trace exported meat products back to histories of the animal source. The integrated system calms concerns about the quality and safety of Uruguayan beef and helped open high-end markets in the European Union, Japan, and the United States (box 3.3).

Emerging evidence on the impacts of off-farm digital technologies on farmers' outcomes

Better access to upstream and downstream markets are expected to produce three types of observable outcomes relevant for farmers. Increased competition due to falling information costs and the reduced role of middlemen is expected to reduce commodity price dispersion. Lower transaction costs are expected to lift farmgate output prices, increasing profits and incomes. And changes in relative output prices and access to new markets is expected to lead to on-farm shifts in resource allocations and new incentives for quality improvements. The evidence on all three effects is still limited but largely supportive.

Several studies show that price dispersion in local markets declines when mobile service starts, which is indirect evidence that markets are gaining efficiency. Examples include markets for sardines in India (Abraham 2007; Jensen 2007), bananas in Uganda (Muto and Yamano 2009), millet in Niger (Aker 2010), and cowpeas in Niger (Aker and Fafchamps 2015). Parker, Ramdas, and Savva (2016) show that geographic price dispersion increased for agricultural goods in India when bulk text messages were banned unexpectedly for 12 days in 2010. For easily stored commodities, mobile phone use appears to have less impact. For example, Aker and Fafchamps (2015) found no evidence that the price dispersion of millet declined with mobile phone use in Niger, and Riera and Minten (2018) found that cell phone coverage had no impact on an index of cereal prices in Ethiopia. The results are consistent with theory because storage facilitates both spatial and temporal arbitrage (Larson 2007).

Another body of research shows that digital technologies providing market information can raise farmgate prices for certain crops, but the evidence of an impact on farmer incomes is mixed. The positive effect of improved market information on farmers' incomes and prices mostly affects perishable, high-value crops (table 3.1). For example, Courtois and Subervie (2014) found that

The government of Uruguay has a goal of feeding 50 million people by 2050 and has put in place ambitious policies, including sustainable intensification, to help meet this goal. The government's commitment to sustainability is, in part, driven by the desire to support continued growth while maintaining and enhancing the productivity of its natural resources (water, soil, and biodiversity) into the future. The production of high-quality products has allowed Uruguay to access high-value and differentiated markets in North America, East Asia, and Western Europe but implies intensive resource use and risks to soil, water, human health, and biodiversity. Hence the principle of *sustainable intensification* at the core of the government's strategic priorities. Within this context, the challenge becomes how to enhance innovation to reconcile high demand with a low overall agricultural footprint (including greenhouse gas emissions) under principles of circular economy.

To achieve sustainable intensification, the government has developed digital traceability systems for cattle, soil, and agricultural value chains. Ensuring 100 percent traceability of Uruguayan products has several advantages, including increased access to differentiated markets, boosted competitiveness of Uruguayan products, and detailed information about agricultural and livestock impact on the environment. Uruguay has made it a priority to understand the impact of agriculture and livestock on natural resources and has put in place policies and systems to enforce good management practices. Digital agriculture tools help with tracking and enforcing these policies.

Cattle traceability. In response to the foot-and-mouth disease epidemic, the World Bank supported Uruguay in a foot-and-mouth disease program and helped to develop a national system for livestock information. The registration system started with more than 75,000 participants in the agriculture and industrial sectors and paved the way for the individual cattle traceability program. Today, all animals born in September 2006 or later are required to be tagged with one visual ear tag and one radio frequency identification tag, both for traceability purposes (photo B3.3.1). The novel system allowed Uruguay to become the only country in the Americas (and one of only a few in the world) with 100 percent traceability of cattle and allowed consumers, mainly in China, Europe, and North American Free Trade Agreement areas, to know the origin of the beef for reasons of health (fewer diseases with full traceability), social goals (ability to know that the cows were grass fed), and environment (sustainability of natural resources) reasons.

The system, which is free for users and paid for entirely by the government, allows every producer in Uruguay to take part, from farmers with just two cows to those with 30,000 head. The platform is hosted on the National Information System for Livestock website and allows private users to log in and track details about their registered cattle. Information is tracked from birth to slaughter on individual cows, including their travel, feed, medicine, and weight gain, among other indicators. Users not registered in the system can view maps of operators who use it and a map of individual cattle by department.

Soil traceability. One of the pivotal policies for implementing sustainable intensification is Uruguay's soil use and management plans. In 1982, Uruguay passed a law of Soil and Water Conservation (Ley no. 15.239), which established technical rules for the preservation of soils and waters with agricultural use and recovering eroded soils.

(Continued)

PHOTO B3.3.1 Tagged Cow in Uruguay

Credit: Katie Kennedy Freeman. Used with permission; further permission required for reuse.

Following a successful pilot, in 2013 the program was scaled up, and soil-use and soil-management plans became a requirement for any farmer cultivating more than 100 hectares. By 2015, more than 90 percent of the land in Uruguay was covered by soil use and management plans, and in 2017 the policy was expanded beyond agricultural

(Continued)

lands to include range lands. The implementation of these plans is monitored through
remote satellite imagery and through the national agricultural information system
Sistema Nacional de Información Agropecuaria (SNIA).

Agricultural value chain traceability. In 2017, the Ministry of Agriculture started
work on a traceability system for honey. This included mapping quantity and location
of the hives and apiaries in the country. The ministry is working with beekeepers to
develop a supply chain with honey origin linked to an export certificate, allowing
producers to access high-value markets for their honey. These maps are available in
the SNIA system. As a next step for agricultural value chains, the ministry is working
to develop a batch traceability system for rice using blockchain technology.

TABLE 3.1 Summary of the Impact of Digital Technologies on Farmgate Prices

Location, product, medium (source)	Farmer impacts	Comments
India (Madhya Pradesh), soybeans, web-based e-Choupal (Goyal 2010)	+ 1.0–3.0 percent (average: 1.7 percent)	Transfer of margin from traders to farmers, effect seen shortly after e-Choupal established
India (West Bengal), potatoes, SMS (Mitra et al. 2018)	+ 19.0 percent	Showed information to be important both in SMS and on a price ticker board in markets
Sri Lanka, vegetables, SMS (Lokanathan, de Silva, and Fernando 2011)	+ 23.4 percent	Over time, an appreciable price advantage over control, plus benefits such as increased interaction with traders and exploring alternative crop options
India (Kerala), fisheries, mobile phones (Jensen 2007)	+ 8.0 percent	An outlier in the sense that fish catches are highly variable and fishermen have their own boat transportation
Uganda, range of crops, SMS and radio (Ferris, Engoru, and Kaganzi 2008)	Bananas + 36.0 percent Beans + 16.5 percent Maize + 17.0 percent Coffee + 19.0 percent	Awareness of market conditions and prices offers more active farmers opportunities for economic gain
Ghana, maize and groundnuts, mobile-based market information service (Courtois and Subervie 2014)	Maize + 10.0 percent Groundnuts + 7.0 percent	Providing price information to farmers allows them to avoid negotiation failures with traders
Peru, range of crops, SMS (Nakasone, Torero, and Minten 2014)	+ 13.0–14.0 percent (average across crops)	Farmers gained bargaining power against agricultural traders; most of the price increase driven by perishables

Source: Adapted from World Bank 2017.
Note: SMS = short message service (text).

farmers who use a mobile-based market information service received 10 percent higher prices for maize and 7 percent higher prices for groundnuts. But other studies recorded no significant effect of digital technologies on farmgate prices (Aker and Fafchamps 2015; Camacho and Conover 2011; Fafchamps and Minten 2012). The scale of the effect on farmers' prices appears to depend on a number of factors, including the effectiveness of the informal market information networks; the stability of price structure and the way the product is sold (spot market or auction) (World Bank 2017); the degree of market integration (Aker and Ksoll 2016); the level of initial information and communication technology (ICT) penetration; and the commodity's value (Nakasone and Torero 2016). By decreasing the cost and increasing the efficacy of tracing systems, digital technologies are expected to expand the scope of markets for higher valued products and improve farm incomes. For example, among tea growers in Kenya, farmers who used Virtual City, an integrated traceability system that uses smartphones, increased their incomes by an average of 9 percent (Qiang et al. 2012). In India's Dindori Tehsil, a 2013–14 study showed that tomato farmers using an agricultural input management module reduced production costs by about $227 per acre. The module is a digital platform that facilitates the farmer's agricultural input requests, aggregates them, and communicates them to input providers. The platform accumulates a larger group demand for agricultural inputs, thus reducing input costs while helping input suppliers plan production and distribution (Sawant 2016). But most studies cannot draw conclusions about digital information services' impact on farmer incomes, and further research is needed.

Few empirical studies have examined whether digital services providing information on prices or other input characteristics help farmers reduce the prices they pay. A study in India's Kazhi Kadamadai Farmers Federation examined farmers using ICT to get information on input uses and prices. Those farmers spent 9 percent less on seeds and had incomes 15 percent higher than farmers who did not use ICT (Raj et al. 2011). The innovations of iProcure, a start-up founded in 2013 in Kenya, connect farmers and farmer cooperatives to input manufacturers in the last mile of agricultural input distribution (iProcure 2020). In theory, such platforms reduce search and bargaining costs, but there is no evidence about this initiative's impact on such transaction costs.

A related set of studies showed that farmers reacted to the expansion of network coverage by entering new markets or changing their crop mix, both indications of allocative efficiency gains. For example, in the study by Bayes (2001), extending telecommunications to rural areas lowered transaction costs for the poor, turning mobile phones into production goods and increasing the benefits to the rural poor via telephone-based services. Muto and Yamano (2009) found that expansion of mobile phone networks in Uganda reduced marketing costs of rural commodities, increasing banana sales in remote, rural communities and inducing market participation of farmers in these regions. Goyal (2010) found the establishment of internet kiosks in Central India increased information flows and marketing channels for soy farmers, effectively increasing soy prices in regions with kiosks and increasing the functioning of agricultural markets. Nakasone, Torero, and Minten (2014) found that access to mobile phones improved agricultural market performance at the macro level. Overa's (2006) study of vegetables in Ghana showed telecommunications liberalization resulted in increased access to tools allowing improved service and higher profit potential.

CHALLENGES FOR ADOPTION OF DIGITAL TECHNOLOGIES

Adoption of digital technologies depends on their impacts on costs and benefits compared with conventional methods. These vary across space, farm size, land quality, human capital, and other factors (Isik and Khanna 2003; Khanna 2001; Schimmelpfennig and Ebel 2011; Torrez et al. 2016). Existing literature points to a variety of factors in the adoption of digital technologies that range from a farmer's age and education to the perceived usefulness of the technology (table 3.2).

TABLE 3.2 Factors in the Adoption of Digital Technologies

Factor	Explanation	Source
Personality of the farmer	Age, education, gender, willingness to take risks	Daberkow and McBride (2003); Edwards-Jones (2006); Lowenberg-DeBoer and Griffin (2006)
Features of the farm	Farm size, farm type, level of debt, resource endowment	Isgin et al. (2008); Paudel et al. (2011)
Social interactions	Local cultures, social milieu, attitudes	Edwards-Jones (2006); Kutter et al. (2011)
Supporting institutions	Numbers and structures of supporting institutions (dealers, technical support)	Edwards-Jones (2006); Fountas, Pedersen, and Blackmore (2005)
Legal environment	Laws and regulations encouraging adoption of new technologies	Edwards-Jones (2006)
Economic factors	Cost of investment, return on investment, profitability	Whipker and Akridge (2009); Paudel et al. (2011)
Features of technology	Ease of use, perceived usefulness, availability of technical support, complexity of the system, compatibility with other technologies	Fountas, Pedersen, and Blackmore (2005); Edwards-Jones (2006); Paudel et al. (2011); Kutter et al. (2011)
Information about technology availability	Exhibitions, fairs, seminars, demonstration farms	Kutter et al. (2011)
Decision support systems	Ease of data processing, ease and accuracy of decision-making	Fountas, Pedersen, and Blackmore (2005)

Source: Adapted from Say et al. 2018.

From the standpoint of economic theory, the incentives for on-farm adoption of digital technologies are based on their costs and benefits relative to conventional methods of farming. Previous studies have adapted the threshold model introduced by David (1975) to explain incentives for adopting digital technologies based on the costs and benefits of adoption, which incorporates three major components:

1. The first is the objective of the farmer, including maximizing profits or expected utility or minimizing expected losses at a given point in time or over a given period, the dynamics of economic returns, and the costs of adoption relative to the status quo. Risk-averse farmers are likely to be willing to pay a high premium to adopt technologies that reduce risk due, for example, to weather or disease (Zilberman et al. 2014). Farmers who have high discount rates may be less willing to adopt a technology that have high up-front costs or benefits that may be realized over a long horizon.

2. Second is the heterogeneity in the costs and benefits of a technology due to differences in farm size, land quality, human capital, and other factors. For instance, larger farms are more likely to adopt technologies that are either indivisible or have economies of scale. Farm size and diversification are likely to reduce risk aversion and thus encourage the adoption of high-risk, high-return technologies. Larger farm size can also lower the unit costs of inputs, consultants, and physical capital and provide the economies of scale needed to make adoption profitable. For example, Schimmelpfennig (2016) reports that only 12 percent of farms of less than 600 acres adopted each of three main precision technologies (GPS yield mapping, guidance system, and variable rate technologies, or VRT). For farms larger than 1,700 acres, the adoption rates of these technologies were 50 percent, 40 percent, and 23 percent, respectively.

3. Third, not only the decision of whether or not to adopt digital technology, but the timing of adoption and the mix of components to adopt matter. Farmers will often prefer to customize their adoption decisions to meet their individual needs and risk considerations. For example, component technologies that are embodied in indivisible equipment (such as yield monitors) are likely to be adopted by larger farms, while technologies that are divisible, such as grid soil sampling, are likely to be scale neutral. Precision technologies that increase input use efficiency by varying application rates to meet crop needs are likely to be adopted on fields with more spatial variability in soil fertility. Khanna (2001), for example, found that farmers adopted soil testing for fertilizer requirements and VRT sequentially rather than as a package, as many farmers adopted soil testing only to learn if the spatial variability in soil fertility was large enough to make it beneficial to adopt VRT.

The threshold that needs to be crossed for adoption is the profit made with conventional technology for a risk-neutral farmer or the expected utility (accounting for both the profit and the variability in those profits) for a risk-averse farmer (Zilberman et al. 2014).

HAVE DIGITAL TECHNOLOGIES BOOSTED EQUITY AND ENVIRONMENTAL SUSTAINABILITY IN AGRICULTURAL VALUE CHAINS?

Although the net effects of digital technologies on efficiency are likely to be decidedly positive, their net effects on equity are less straightforward, and evidence on the impacts on equity remains scarce. The risks of a digital divide remain significant and require attention of policy makers.

Equity

In theory, digital technologies have a potential to lower spatial and economic divides in agriculture through improved flow of information. Reducing the costs of obtaining information lowers both spatial and economic divides by making information cheaper for smaller and/or poorer farmers, creating an opportunity to reduce productivity gaps between rich farmers and poorer ones. Digital technologies such as mobile phones dramatically reduce the cost of disseminating information—such as extension advice, product prices, or standards—which is traditionally high in sparsely populated rural areas. For example, providing information via SMS in Niger is much cheaper than supporting visits by an extension agent (Aker 2011). Improving extension service efficiency is likely to increase its geographic reach and support more frequent contact by extension agents, increasing smallholders' access to information. E-extension mobile applications also reduce the cost of obtaining information to zero. And the cost of farmers' social learning about new technologies goes to near zero, because farmers do not have to physically visit the members of their social network, which would impose both the cost of transport and the opportunity cost of time.

Digital platforms and digital tracing systems can also lower spatial and economic divides in accessing downstream and upstream markets. With the proliferation of digital platforms, small producers, even in remote areas, can now directly connect to input suppliers, consumers, and even international markets, bypassing traditional middlemen. They also get easier and cheaper access to various services, such as payment services, reducing the cost of negotiating, and undertaking transactions, thus making such transactions possible. In addition, digital tracing systems can extend the reach of tracing networks and lower the hurdles that exclude some farmers, enabling producers to receive price premiums for satisfying the preferences of consumers around the world. For example, a study by Foster et al. (2018) highlight the success of Kenyan smallholder tea producers in accessing global value chains by enhancing their visibility in markets with the help of digital technologies. Similarly, the previously mentioned initiative by the Zambian National Farmers' Union allows for accumulating loads from remotely located farmers, and those selling small product lines, so as to improve equity. Wei, Lin, and Zhang (2019) discuss various models for operation of online trading platforms for food products in China, associated with the Alibaba-derived Taobao Village. Each platform is described by the authors in terms of the connection offered to global production networks, and redressing inequity in rural-urban information asymmetry. Finally, digital technologies can circumvent poor access to expensive advanced farm machinery by enabling mechanization services, such as those emerging in China, or digital platform–based capacity sharing firms, such as Hello Tractor (Yang et al. 2013).

In addition, low-cost digital solutions can narrow the inequality between urban and rural areas, increase youth retention in rural areas, and empower women and smallholders. Many female farmers tend to have less access to extension services and markets than their male counterparts due to social, cultural, economic, and institutional barriers. Digital technologies such as apps, platforms, off-line recordings, and simple SMS messages empower smallholders by providing access to data and knowledge, enabling more informed decision-making. Similarly, mobile-enabled platforms could provide women with access to key market information such as prices and input availability. For example, in Ghana's northern pastoral regions, Cowtribe's Lamisi project uses a cloud-based logistics management system that gives women equal access to veterinary services—including vaccines for cattle—delivered when needed (Domfeh 2019). A study on technology adoption by rural women in Queensland, Australia, showed that rural women use most components of technology three times more often than men do (Hay and Pearce 2014).

Risks of an increased digital divide

Lack of physical and digital infrastructure may lead to digital divides along the value chain. How much digital technologies benefit agricultural sectors and rural communities depends on their access to digital infrastructure. Poor smallholder farmers in remote rural areas face hurdles accessing phone and internet networks. In addition, access to roads, storage, and cold chains still matter for accessing downstream markets, particularly for perishable products. As a result, farmers in areas with better physical infrastructure and network coverage are better positioned to take advantage of opportunities presented by digital technologies.

The low literacy of farmers, particularly smallholders, can also create a digital divide. Farmers need basic skills that enable them to use digital tools such as cell phone messages, apps, and digital platforms. Literacy is also required to critically assess the quality of the information provided. Farmers in developing countries and smallholders in general may lack the skills and knowledge to reap the benefits of digital applications (Baumüller 2018; Lio and Liu 2006). Digital literacy also includes the ability to critically assess the quality of an app or platform. For example, modern sensor technologies appear to drastically simplify measuring basic parameters, such as soil moisture content, needed for precision irrigation. But the measurement accuracy of electromagnetic soil moisture sensors depends on positioning the sensors in the root zone of the crop. And the positioning required for high-level accuracy varies considerably according to soil hydraulic properties, weather conditions, and irrigation system configurations, thus requiring site-specific calibration (Soulis et al. 2015). In this example, using digital technology in agriculture requires specific skills. And because only a larger farm would find investing in those skills worthwhile, the technology also contributes to an economy of scale.

Similarly, a number of researchers have emphasized the critical importance of business structure and planning, supply chain management, and logistics in applying e-commerce (Montealegre, Thompson, and Eales 2007). Smallholder farmers with lower levels of skills and knowledge about these elements could end up excluded from digital markets. Overall, given the low digital literacy on smallholder farms—compared with larger, richer farms—poor-quality digital platforms could widen a digital divide. At the same time, digital technologies offer leapfrogging opportunities for the small-scale farmers to help limit any widening of inequalities due to different skill levels. One example is the use of artificial intelligence to bypass literacy issues.

Numerous studies analyze the link between digital technologies and labor demand and income inequality. However, most of them are not agriculture specific. For example, Mnif (2016) finds that in the Middle East and North Africa region innovations increase the demand for skilled labor while decreasing it for unskilled labor, which has direct implications on wage/income inequality. Furthermore, the study finds that the introduction of ICT resulted in permanent changes in the employment structure in favor of skilled workers. Galbraith (2001) shows that the demand for skilled-labor and capital-intensive investment goods lead to increased inequality, whereas the demand for labor-intensive consumption goods tends to compress the wage distribution. Samoilenko and Osei-Bryson (2011) find that in transition economies ICT investments increase inequality while the impact is conditional on the strength of the economy and the availability of infrastructure. Dell'Anno and Solomon (2014) also report a positive relationship between ICT investment and income inequality, although this relationship is mediated by education and quality of institutions. Using Eurostat data for Portugal, Mendonça, Crespo, and Simões (2015) suggest that ICT can exacerbate and perpetuate existing labor market inequalities. Richmond and Triplett (2018) find that the relationship between ICT and income inequality depends on the type of the ICT infrastructure. While internet usage per se is negatively correlated with inequality, they find a positive association between income inequality and fixed broadband subscription and a negative association between income inequality and mobile cellular subscription. The inequality-increasing effect of fixed broadband subscriptions is larger than the inequality-reducing effect of mobile technology.

Different levels of access to digital technologies can deepen the digital divide between small and large farms. Digital technologies, combined with capital-intensive agricultural equipment, could create a digital divide because of scale. New technologies typically involve large up-front costs, and the ability to finance investment is likely correlated closely with a farmer's wealth and capacity to pledge assets as collateral (Schimmelpfenning 2016; Thompson et al. 2019). For poorer and risk-averse farmers, investments in new digital technologies are likely to be limited, because they can lead to sharply varying incomes, with low or negative income streams in early years when they make the investment, then positive returns in later years (Miao and Khanna 2014). Farmers in poor countries are also less likely to invest in tracing technologies that connect them to the markets (Tey and Brindal 2012; Dawe 2015). Precision agriculture technologies are also more specialized than other capital assets such as land and tractors, so they are more likely to be adopted by large farms that can afford the costs, as has been documented for developed countries (Schimmelpfenning 2016; Thompson et al. 2019). Outsourcing technology services to a custom service provider is another option, but that also imposes costs. When larger farms get more efficient, commodity prices may fall, hurting less efficient small-scale farmers, so digital agriculture may disadvantage smaller farmers in that way.

A digital divide may also emerge between crop producers and livestock growers. While digital technologies in the livestock sector, such as precision livestock farming, have a wide range of applications in industrialized countries, developers of applications for developing country farmers often focus narrowly on crop production. They do so despite the critical role of livestock production for food and nutrition security and despite the multitude of digital agriculture entry points for livestock production, including health, feeding, marketing, breeding, genomics, and fertility management.

Gender disparities in access to digital technologies in rural areas of some countries could result in a digital divide between men and women. For example, in rural Rajasthan, India, village rules prohibit women from using mobile phones or social media. In Bangladesh and Pakistan, men are more likely than women to own a mobile phone (World Bank 2020). Overcoming these barriers is critical for rural women to adopt digital technologies to enhance their productive capacity by accessing more inputs.

ENVIRONMENTAL SUSTAINABILITY

Digital technologies offer a great promise for improved environmental sustainability in agricultural value chains, notwithstanding some risks. However, empirical evidence on the environmental effect of these technologies is still scarce.

Direct effects of digital technologies on environmental sustainability

On-farm, digital technologies can help farmers manage their soil and water more sustainably by reducing input use and waste, directly contributing to environmental sustainability. Precision technologies apply water, fertilizers, herbicides, and pesticides only when and where they are needed, limiting the harm to soil and water resources caused by excessive or inadequate applications (Balafoutis et al. 2017; Berry et al. 2003; Bongiovanni and Lowenbert-Deboer 2004). For example, with better targeted input applications, fertilizer runoff can be reduced and fewer pesticides reach surrounding resources such as water bodies. A pilot large-scale trial found that smallholder farmers could apply cutting-edge internet-of-things technology to increase water use efficiency in rice farming with a 13–20 percent water savings. Similarly, variable-rate irrigation has been found to increase water use efficiency, with implications for reducing water use (see review in Finger et al. 2019). More targeted use of fertilizers and plant protection products can lead to improved soil quality. For example, the company Ecorobotix claims that its high-precision spraying robots reduce herbicide use by 90 percent (Ecorobotix n.d.). Robotic mechanical weeding could even fully replace herbicides (McCool et al. 2018). Digital agriculture can also help reduce the soil compaction caused by machinery in the field by reducing overlaps, automatically adjusting the air pressure in the wheels, or using fleets of small agricultural robots and drones for some activities (Blackmore and Griepentrog 2002). And productivity gains spurred by digital technologies, by reducing the need to bring new land into production, reduce pressures on already vulnerable natural resource systems such as forests and marshlands.

Digital technologies can also reduce greenhouse gas (GHG) emissions. Precision irrigation systems reduce energy use. They also reduce nitrous oxide emissions that stem from overwatering. Precision machinery reduces nitrous oxide soil emissions by reducing nitrogen fertilizer use, which accounts for about 1.2 percent of global GHG emissions (Wood and Cowie 2004). Machine guidance and controlled traffic farming reduces fuel consumption by reducing overlap in farm operations—self-guided machines reduce carbon dioxide emissions by using less fuel (Balafoutis et al. 2017). At the same time, mechanical agricultural solutions typically produce carbon dioxide by burning fuel, an effect that can be reduced by using renewable energy sources. Small robots using the swarm intelligence of decentralized, self-organizing systems may be better suited to using renewable energy, such as electricity from solar power (Anil et al. 2015).

Despite potential benefits for soil fertility and reduced emissions in crop production, empirical evidence on the environmental effect of these technologies is still scarce. A few studies provide causal implications based on observed data. For example, Khanna (2001) estimated the effects of adopting soil testing and VRT for nitrogen application on yield per unit of nitrogen in the Midwestern United States. The study found that the gains in nitrogen productivity were higher on relatively lower quality soils and insignificant on farms with above average soil quality. For farmers that adopted both technologies, it was the adoption of VRT that led to the larger increase in nitrogen productivity (33 percent and 18 percent on below average and above average soil qualities) as compared with the gains due to soil testing (6 percent and 7 percent, respectively) (Khanna 2001). Similarly, Rejesus and Hornbaker (1999) show that VRT application of nitrogen and improved timing of fertilizer application can reduce nitrate pollution from corn-soybean rotations in Illinois, United States. Other case studies show that VRT nitrogen application can decrease nitrogen application and nitrous oxide emission (see the review in Finger et al. 2019). Similarly, site-specific nutrient management in locations in southern India, the Philippines, and southern Vietnam was found to lead to higher yields with increased nitrogen fertilizer use while maintaining low nitrous oxide emissions (Pampolino et al. 2007). Variable rate fertilizer application for potato production and olive production in Greece was also found to lead to large reductions in fertilizer use (van Evert et al. 2017).

Digital technologies used in livestock production can also benefit the environment. More efficient feeding strategies that stem from digital agriculture can reduce feed requirements and so reduce livestock's large indirect land use. Diseases and health issues reduce livestock production efficiency by up to 33 percent (Deloitte 2017). Therefore, by improving animal health, digital technologies increase livestock productivity, which in turn results in decreased global GHG emissions per livestock unit (Havlík et al. 2012). For pastoralist systems, digital technologies may help not only to find grazing grounds and waterholes but also to address problems such as overgrazing. An example is AfriScout in Ethiopia, which is run by the nongovernment organization Project Concern International, the World Food Programme, and the Ministry of Agriculture. AfriScout provides pastoralists with satellite-generated images of water and vegetation every 10 days.

Off-farm, direct effects of digital technologies on environmental sustainability stem from changes to distribution processes. More efficient transport services, better organization of delivery into urban markets, and more effective monitoring of the produce en route from farmers to stores directly improves environmental sustainability across a range of measures, including GHG emissions, food waste, and congestion of urban infrastructure. Digital technologies can be used to enable evaluation of the current situation in transport logistics; they can be used to optimize transportation and logistics processes by monitoring different parameters such as fuel usage, speed, and position, thus making the entire supply chain more efficient (Bilali and Allahyari 2018). Some applications, such as Sourcemap, allow visualizing supply chain information in relation to environmental impact. Digital technologies can also contribute to improved environmental sustainability by transforming food wholesale and retail sales. E-commerce, online ordering, and deliveries can potentially displace traditional retail and allow a better coordination of food distribution (Bilali and Allahyari 2018). Digital technologies let farmers receive information, make requests, and provide feedback instantaneously across long distances. By eliminating the travel otherwise required, they minimize resource waste and benefit the environment.

Enabling effect of digital technologies on environmental sustainability

On-farm, the enabling effect of digital technologies on environmental sustainability could be realized through improved tracking and monitoring of farm production decisions. Digital technologies, computational tools, and data analytics enable detailed record keeping about input application rates, timing, and methods used by a farmer. This information, together with biogeochemical and hydrological models and other environmental models, can link farm management decisions with environmental outcomes, such as soil carbon sequestration, nitrous oxide emissions, nutrient loss, and runoff. By providing site-specific information about production decisions, environmental conditions, crop varieties, and yields, the process can enable analysts to quantify the environmental impacts of agricultural production activities. Information on management practices, crop genetics, weather, and environmental conditions can be combined with process models to predict environmental outcomes. By enabling a data- and science-based links between activities and environmental outcomes, digital technologies can convert nonpoint pollution into point source pollution.

Improved traceability of food from farm to fork can enable food loss reduction in the agrifood system, contributing to environmental gains. According to the World Economic Forum analysis, blockchain-enabled traceability can reduce food loss in food systems by up to 30 million tons annually if blockchain were to monitor information in half of the world's supply chains (WEF 2018). Improved communication along agrifood value chains can also enable producers to meet consumer preferences for more sustainable food production or to supply consumers not sensitive to cosmetic standards, such as ripeness, size, color, or weight. As an example, over 9 million tons of "ugly" produce go to waste in the United States alone every year, rejected by stores. Full Harvest is rescuing that waste by building the first business-to-business marketplace where farmers can connect with food companies to offload surplus or imperfect produce. Buyers of such produce can save up to 40 percent compared with traditional distributors. Finally, digital technologies can also strengthen the role of certifications and agreements that aim for environmentally friendly production practices and waste management.

Behavioral effect of digital technologies on environmental sustainability

Digital technologies can generate data on input harm to the environment and communicate it, promoting systemic changes to the input industry's values and behavior, triggering a behavioral effect. Digital technologies show farmers and input suppliers the input industry's harm to the environment and give them ways to promote environmental sustainability. By generating data on negative environmental impacts, digital tools can have systemic effects. Because interaction between companies, civil society, and regulators is particularly important to reduce negative environmental impacts, such data will help consumers, regulators, and nongovernmental organizations push for greater sustainability.

Digital technologies can disseminate information to producers and consumers about the importance and ways of improving environmental sustainability, particularly reducing food waste, in downstream markets. For example, food waste reduction on the preconsumer side is addressed by Leanpath software that targets overproduction, spoilage, and waste in kitchens. Its analytics platform measures waste, values it, and suggests mechanisms for reducing it (Leanpath 2020). Additionally, the tech giant Siemens has partnered with EIT Food, a pan-European consortium fostered by the European Union, to develop a digital twin management product based on the company's internet-of-things platform. The goal of the project is to improve protected data collection and to create user-friendly apps that facilitate data analysis and distribution. Producers provide data alongside their food products, allowing consumers to make informed choices about the food they buy. The sustainability implications of such a transparency-boosting product are manifold: information regarding a product's environmental contribution that does not fit on packaging could be accessed, such as CO_2 emissions in delivery, fertilizer usage at the farm level, and waste generated along the supply chain (EIT Food 2019). On the consumer side, the UK-based application Too Good to Go has established itself as the world's largest surplus food marketplace. The app links local food distributors to eco-conscious consumers interested in reducing food waste in the supply chain. Partner businesses fill "Magic Bags" of products destined for disposal, and consumers on the app can search daily listings and choose from sellers that suit their tastes and needs. So far, the company estimates that their service has saved over 36,400,000 meals globally and 91,005 tons of CO_2 (Too Good to Go n.d.).

Potential risks of digital technologies for environmental sustainability

Although digital technologies appear to offer win-win benefits to farmers and the environment, they may not always do so. By increasing the efficiency of using such natural resources such as water and land, these technologies could lead to less pollution per unit of input or output. But because they could increase total resource use or increase yield per acre, their total effect on pollution is unclear. And their effect will differ across fields, farms, and locations. Efficiency-enhancing technologies could increase or decrease input use and pollution, depending on how much they increase the effectiveness of input use, change the impact of input use on crop yields, and create a cumulative pollution-reducing effect (Khanna, Isik, and Zilberman 2002). Precision farming can accelerate the depletion of natural resources in the rebound effect well known to energy economists, where efficiency gains lead to increased machinery use, and so to increased energy use and GHG emissions.

In agricultural water management, the rebound effect is increasingly discussed in connection with the risk of rising water withdrawals and uses (Berbel et al. 2015; Chambwera and Heal 2014). More efficient irrigation, complemented by digital technologies such as sensors, could lead to increased water depletion if not contained by stringent environmental policy. Nitrous oxide emissions from irrigated fields can be 50–240 percent higher than those from rainfed fields. So, because water in agriculture is underpriced in many countries, lower-cost precision irrigation systems could prompt investments in new irrigation whose nitrous oxide emissions offset any reductions due to the greater precision.

Precision agriculture can lead to higher marginal abatement costs. Because precision technologies make inputs more productive at the margin, the opportunity cost in forgone profits of not using them is higher as well (Schieffer and Dillon 2014). The impact of digital agriculture on farm biodiversity is also ambiguous. Digital agriculture using robots may also support more diverse farms by allowing for smaller plots and the use of mixed cropping, hedgerows, and agro-silvo-pastoral systems. But digital agriculture could also lead to less diversity and more monoculture because automation might be more efficient in more controlled systems with fewer variables. (The empirical evidence on the environmental effects of digital agricultural technologies is limited.)

REFERENCES

Abate, T., B. Shiferaw, S. Gebeyehu, B. Amsalu, K. Negash, K. Assefa, M. Eshete, S. Aliye, and J. Hagmann. 2011. "A Systems and Partnership Approach to Agricultural Research for Development: Lessons from Ethiopia." Outlook on Agriculture 40 (3): 213–20. http://doi .org/10.5367/oa.2011.0048.

Abebe, G., J. Bijman, and A. Royer. 2016. "Are Middlemen Facilitators or Barriers to Improve Smallholders' Welfare in Rural Economies? Empirical Evidence from Ethiopia." Journal of Rural Studies 43: 203–13. http://doi.org/10.1016/j.jrurstud.2015.12.004.

Abraham, R. 2007. "Mobile Phones and Economic Development: Evidence from the Fishing Industry in India." Information Technologies & International Development 4 (1). http://doi .org/10.1162/itid.2007.4.1.5.

Adjemian, M. K., T. L. Saitone, and R. J. Sexton. 2016. "A Framework to Analyze the Performance of Thinly Traded Agricultural Commodity Markets." American Journal of Agricultural Economics 98 (2). http://doi.org/10.1093/ajae/aav074.

Aertsens, J., W. Verbeke, K. Mondelaers, and G. Van Huylenbroeck. 2009. "Personal Determinants of Organic Food Consumption: A Review." British Food Journal 111(10): 1140–67.

Aker, J. C. 2008. "Does Digital Divide or Provide? The Impact of Cell Phones on Grain Markets in Niger." Working Paper 154, Center for Global Development, Washington, DC. http://dx.doi.org/10.2139/ssrn.1093374.

Aker, J. C. 2010. "Information from Markets Near and Far: Mobile Phones and Agricultural Markets in Niger." American Economic Journal: Applied Economics 2 (3): 46–59.

Aker, J. C. 2011. "Dial 'A' for Agriculture: A Review of Information and Technologies for Agricultural Extension in Developing Countries." Agricultural Economics 42 (6): 631–47.

Aker, J. C., and M. Fafchamps. 2015. "Mobile Phone Coverage and Producer Markets: Evidence from West Africa." *World Bank Economic Review* 29 (2): 262–92. http://doi.org/10.1093/wber/lhu006.

Aker, J. C., I. Ghosh, and J. Burrell. 2016. "The Promise (and Pitfalls) of ICT for Agriculture Initiatives." *Agricultural Economics* 47: 35–48. http://doi.org/10.1111/agec.12301.

Aker, J. C., and C. Ksoll. 2016. "Can Mobile Phones Improve Agricultural Outcomes? Evidence from a Randomized Experiment in Niger." *Food Policy* 60: 44–51.

Aker, J. C., and I. M. Mbiti. 2010. "Mobile Phones and Economic Development in Africa." *Journal of Economic Perspectives* 24 (3): 207–32.

Akerlof, G. A. 1970. "The Market for 'Lemons': Quality Uncertainty and the Market Mechanism." *Quarterly Journal of Economics* 84 (3): 488–500.

Anderson, J. R., and G. Feder. 2007. "Handbook of Agricultural Economics." *Agricultural Extension* 3: 2343–78.

Anil, H., K. S. Nikhil, V. Chaitra, and B. G. Sharan. 2015. "Revolutionizing Farming Using Swarm Robotics." In *2015 6th International Conference on Intelligent Systems, Modelling and Simulation*, 141–47. New York: Institute of Electrical and Electronics Engineers.

ATA (Agricultural Transformation Agency). 2019. *Agricultural Transformation Agency, Annual Report 2017–18*. https://www.ata.gov.et/.

Badia-Melis, R., P. Mishra, and L. Ruiz-García. 2015. "Food Traceability: New Trends and Recent Advances: A Review." *Food Control* 57 (November). http://doi.org/10.1016/j.foodcont.2015.05.005.

Balafoutis, A. T., B. Beck, S. Fountas, Z. Tsiropoulos, J. Vangeyte, T. van der Wal, I. Soto-Embodas, M. Gomez-Barbero, and S. M. Pedersen. 2017. "Smart Farming Technologies: Description, Taxonomy, and Economic Impact." In *Precision Agriculture: Technology and Economic Perspectives*, edited by S. Pedersen and K. Lind. New York: Springer.

Bandiera, O., and I. Rasul. 2006. "Social Networks and Technology Adoption in Northern Mozambique." *Economic Journal* 116 (514): 869–902.

Baumüller, H. 2013. "Enhancing Smallholder Market Participation through Mobile Phone-enabled Services: The Case of M-Farm in Kenya." *Electronic Journal of Information Systems in Developing Countries* 68 (1): 1–16.

Baumüller, H. 2018. "The Little We Know: An Exploratory Literature Review on the Utility of Mobile Phone–Enabled Services for Smallholder Farmers." *Journal of International Development* 30 (1): 154. https://doi.org/10.1002/jid.3314.

Bayes, A. 2001. "Infrastructure and Rural Development: Insights from a Grameen Bank Village Phone Initiative in Bangladesh." *Agricultural Economics* 25: 261–72.

Berbel, J., C. Gutiérrez-Martín, J. A. Rodríguez-Díaz, E. Camacho, and P. Montesinos. 2015. "Literature Review on Rebound Effect of Water Saving Measures and Analysis of a Spanish Case Study." *Water Resources Management* 29 (3): 663–78.

Berry, J. K., J. A. Detgado, R. Khosla, and F. J. Pierce. 2003. "Precision Conservation for Environmental Sustainability." *Journal of Soil and Water Conservation* 58 (6): 332–39.

Besley, T., and R. Burgess. 2000. "Land Reform, Poverty Reduction, and Growth: Evidence from India." *Quarterly Journal of Economics* 115 (2): 389–430.

Bhattacharya, A. 2017. "Milking the Numbers: Thousands of Indian Cows Have Been Fitted with Tiny Sensors to Give Farmers Real-Time Data." *Quartz India*, December 7. https://qz.com/india/1148120/thousands-of-cows-across-india-have-been-fitted-with-sensors-to-provide-dairy-farmers-with-real-time-data.

Biggar, S., D. Man, K. Moffroid, D. Pape, M. Riley-Gilbert, R. Steele, and V. Thompson. 2013. *Greenhouse Gas Mitigation Options and Costs for Agricultural Land and Animal*

Production within the United States. Washington, DC: ICF International, Department of Agriculture Climate Change Program Office.

Bilali, H. E., and M. S. Allahyari. 2018. "Transition towards Sustainability in Agriculture and Food Systems: Role of Information and Communication Technologies." *Information Processing in Agriculture* 5 (4): 456–64.

Blackmore, S., and H. W. Griepentrog. 2002. "A Future View of Precision Farming." In *PreAgro: Proceedings of the PreAgro Precision Agriculture Conference,* edited by D. Berger, A. Bornheimer, A. Jarfe, D. Kottenrodt, R. Richter, K. Stahl, and A. Werner, 131–45. Muncheberg, Germany: Center for Agricultural Landscape and Land Use Research.

Bongiovanni, R., and J. Lowenbert-Deboer. 2004. "Precision Agriculture and Sustainability." *Precision Agriculture* 5 (4): 359–87.

Boucher, S., M. R. Carter, and C. Guirkinger. 2006. "Risk Rationing and Wealth Effects in Credit Markets." Department of Agriculture, University of California, Davis.

Brandes, E., G. S. McNunn, L. A. Schulte, I. J. Bonner, D. J. Muth, B. A. Babcock, B. Sharma, and E.A. Heaton. 2016. "Subfield Profitability Analysis Reveals an Economic Case for Cropland Diversification." *Environmental Research Letters* 11 (1). http://iopscience.iop .org/article/10.1088/1748-9326/11/1/014009.

Caine, A., P. Dorward, G. Clarkson, N. Evans, C. Canales, D. Stern, and R. Stern. 2015. "Mobile Applications for Weather and Climate Information: Their Use and Potential for Smallholder Farmers." Working Paper 150, CGIAR Research Program on Climate Change, Agriculture, and Food Security, Copenhagen, Denmark.

Camacho, A., and E. Conover. 2011. "Manipulation of Social Program Eligibility." *American Economic Journal: Economic Policy* 3 (2): 41–65.

Casaburi, L., M. Kremer, S. Mullainathan, and R. Ramrattan. 2014. "Harnessing ICT to Increase Agricultural Production: Evidence from Kenya." Working Paper, Harvard University, Cambridge, MA.

Casaburi, L., M. Kremer, and R. Ramrattan. 2019. "Crony Capitalism, Collective Action, and ICT: Evidence from Kenyan Contract Farming." Working paper, University of Zurich, Switzerland. http://econ.uzh.ch/dam/jcr:e2ffc4e5-ab32-4405-bfa4-70b0e962aa81/hotline _paper_20191015_MERGED.pdf.

Chambwera, M., and G. Heal. 2014. "Economics of Adaptation." In *Climate Change 2014: Impacts, Adaptation, and Vulnerability Working Group II Contribution to the IPCC 5th Assessment Report.* Geneva: United Nations.

Cicia, G., and F. Colantouni. 2010. "Willingness to Pay for Traceable Meat Attributes: A Meta-analysis." *International Journal on Food System Dynamics* 1 (3): 1–12.

Cole, S., and A. Fernando. 2014. "'Mobile'izing Agricultural Advice: Technology Adoption, Diffusion and Sustainability." Harvard Business School Finance Working Paper 13-047, Harvard University, Cambridge, MA. https://www.hbs.edu/faculty/Publication%20 Files/13-047_155cb6a2-afb5-4744-a62d-929b01fc9e7c.pdf.

Cole, S., and A. Fernando. 2020. "The Value of Advice: Evidence from the Adoption of Agricultural Practices." *Economic Journal* (accepted manuscript). http://doi.org/10.1093 /ej/ueaa084.

Cole, S., X. Giné, J. Tobacman, R. Townsend, P. Topalova, and J. Vickery. 2013. "Barriers to Household Risk Management: Evidence from India." *American Economic Journal: Applied Economics* 5 (1): 104–35.

Conley, T., and C. Udry. 2010. "Learning about a New Technology: Pineapple in Ghana." *American Economic Review* 100 (1): 35–69.

Connolly, C., and H. A. Klaiber. 2014. "Does Organic Command a Premium When the Food Is Already Local?" *American Journal of Agricultural Economics* 96 (4): 1102–16. http://doi.org/10.1093/ajae/aau030.

Courtois, P., and J. Subervie. 2014. "Farmer Bargaining Power and Market Information Services." *American Journal of Agricultural Economics* 97: 953–77. http://doi.org/10.1093/ajae/aau051.

CTA (Technical Centre for Agricultural and Rural Cooperation). 2017. "IT Solutions Are Disruptive: They Change the Way Things Are Working." ICT Update, Issue 85, Technical Centre for Agricultural and Rural Cooperation ACP-EU (CTA), Wageningen, the Netherlands. https://ictupdate.cta.int/en/article/it-solutions-are-disruptive-they-change-the-way-things-are-working-sid0b545abc3-b9ff-410c-9370-12c70a1d6dc6.

Dabbene, F., P. Gay, and C. Tortia. 2013. "Traceability Issues in Food Supply Chain Management: A Review." *Biosystems Engineering* 120: 65–80. http://dx.doi.org/10.1016/j.biosystemseng.2013.09.006.

Daberkow, S. G., and W. D. McBride. 2003. "Farm and Operator Characteristics Affecting the Awareness and Adoption of Precision Agriculture Technologies in the US." *Precision Agriculture* 4: 163–77. http://doi.org/10.1023/A:1024557205871.

Daum, T. 2018. "ICT Applications in Agriculture." *Encyclopedia of Food Security and Sustainability*. Amsterdam: Elsevier.

Daum, T., R. Villalba, O. Anidi, S. M. Mayienga, S. Gupta, and R. Birner. 2020. "Uber for Tractors? Opportunities and Challenges of Digital Tools for Tractor Hire in India and Nigeria." *SSRN* (January 28). http://dx.doi.org/10.2139/ssrn.3526918.

David, P. A. 1975. *Technical Choice, Innovation and Economic Growth*. Cambridge, UK: Cambridge University Press.

Davis, K., E. Nkonya, E. Kato, D.A. Mekonnen, M. Odendo, R. Miiro, and J. Nkuba. 2012. "Impact of Farmer Field Schools on Agricultural Productivity and Poverty in East Africa." *World Development* 40 (2): 402–13.

Dawe, D. 2015. "Agricultural Transformation of Middle-Income Asian Economies: Diversification, Farm Size, and Mechanization." ESA Working Paper 15–04, Food and Agriculture Organization of the United Nations, Rome.

Deichmann, U., A. Goyal, and D. Mishra. 2016. "Will Digital Technologies Transform Agriculture in Developing Countries?" *Agricultural Economics* 1 (47): 21–33.

de Janvry, A., M. Fafchamps, and E. Sadoulet. 1991. "Peasant Household Behavior with Missing Markets: Some Paradoxes Explained." *Economic Journal* 101: 1400–17.

Dell'Anno, R., and H. O. Solomon. 2014. "Informality, Inequality, and ICT in Transition Economies." *Eastern European Economics* 52 (5): 3–31. http://doi.org/10.1080/0012877 55.2014.1004264.

Deloitte (Deloitte Touche Tohmatsu). 2017. "Smart Livestock Farming: Potential of Digitalization for Global Meat Supply." Discussion Paper, Deloitte, London.

de Silva, H., and D. Ratnadiwakara. 2008. "Using ICT to Reduce Transaction Costs in Agriculture through Better Communication: A Case Study from Sri Lanka." *SSRN*. http://ssrn.com/abstract=1565184.

Digital Green. 2020. "Community Videos" (accessed August 10, 2020). http://www.digitalgreen.org/videos/.

Doldt, J., 2019. "Evaluation and Validation of a Feed App for Dairy Farmers in Kenya." Hans-Ruthenberg-Institute of Agricultural Science in the Tropics, University of Hohenheim, Stuttgart, Germany.

Domfeh, K. 2019. "Ghana: Digital Vaccine Delivery Service." *Spore,* February 21. http://spore .cta.int/en/dossiers/article/livestock-vaccines-digital-delivery-service-sid0f8cd8489 -ff6d-4c69-aebd-d779263b5715.

Dzanku, F. M., M. Jirström, and H. Marstorp. 2015. "Yield Gap-based Poverty Gaps in Rural Sub-Saharan Africa." *World Development* 67: 336–62.

Ecorobotix. n.d. "Home" (accessed August 10, 2020). Yverdon-les-Bains, Switzerland. https:// www.ecorobotix.com/en/.

Edwards-Jones, G. 2006. "Modelling Farmer Decision-making: Concepts, Progress and Challenges." *Animal Science* 82: 783–90

Einav, L., C. Farronato, and J. Levin. 2016. "Peer-to-Peer Markets." *Annual Review of Economics* 13 (52): 615–35.

EIT Food. 2019. "Trust the Twin: Digitalisation to Improve Transparency in the Food Value Chain" (accessed August 10, 2020). EIT Food, Leuven, Belgium. https://www.eitfood.eu/news /post/trust-the-twin-digitalisation-to-improve-transparency-in-the-food-value-chain.

Ekekwe, N. 2016. "Zenvus: Intelligent Solutions for Farmers" (accessed August 10, 2020). *Startup.info*. https://startup.info/zenvus/.

European Parliament. 2014. *Precision Agriculture: An Opportunity for EU Farmers— Potential Support with the CAP 2014–2020.* Brussels: European Parliament. http:// www.europarl.europa.eu/RegData/etudes/note/join/2014/529049/IPOL-AGRI _NT%282014%29529049_EN.pdf.

Fabregas, R., M. Kremer, and F. Schilbach. 2019. "Realizing the Potential of Digital Development: The Case of Agricultural Advice." *Science* 366 (6471).

Fafchamps, M., and B. Minten. 2012. "Impact of SMS-based Agricultural Information on Indian Farmers." *World Bank Economic Review* 26 (3): 383–414.

FAO (Food and Agriculture Organization of the United Nations). 2018. *Status of Implementation of e-Agriculture in Central and Eastern Europe and Central Asia: Insights from Selected Countries in Europe and Central Asia.* Budapest: FAO.

Feder, G., and D. L. Umali. 1993. "The Adoption of Agricultural Innovations: A Review." *Technological Forecasting and Social Change* 43 (3–4): 215–39.

Ferentinos, K. 2018. "Deep Learning Models for Plant Disease Detection and Diagnosis." *Computers and Electronics in Agriculture* 145: 311–18.

Ferris, S., P. Engoru, and E. Kaganzi. 2008. "Making Market Information Services Work Better for the Poor in Uganda." CAPRi Working Paper 77, CGIAR Systemwide Program on Collective Action and Property Rights (CAPRi), Washington, DC.

Finger, R., S. M. Swinton, N. El Benni, and A. Walter. 2019. "Precision Farming at the Nexus of Agricultural Production and the Environment." *Annual Review of Resource Economics* 11: 313–35.

Foote, W. 2018. "Meet the Social Entrepreneur behind Africa's 'Uber For The Farm.'" *Forbes.* http://www.forbes.com/sites/willyfoote/2018/08/14/meet-the-social-entrepreneur -behind-africas-uber-for-the-farm/#2a162fc32bc5.

Foster, Christopher, Mark Graham, Laura Mann, Timothy Waema, and Nicolas Friederici. 2018. "Digital Control in Value Chains: Challenges of Connectivity for East African Firms." *Economic Geography* 94 (1): 68–86. https://doi.org/10.1080/00130095.2017.1350104.

Foster, A., and M. Rosenzweig. 1995. "Learning by Doing and Learning from Others: Human Capital and Technical Change in Agriculture." *Journal of Political Economy* 103 (6): 1176–209.

Fountas, S., S. M. Pedersen, and S. Blackmore. 2005. "ICT in Precision Agriculture: Diffusion of Technology." In *ICT in Agriculture: Perspectives of Technological Innovation*, edited by E. Gelb and A. Offer. Haifa, Israel: Samuel Neaman Institute for National Policy Research, Hebrew University, Center for Economic Research in Agriculture, European Federation for Information Technology in Agriculture.

Frisvold, G. B., K. Fernicola, and M. Langworthy. 2001. "Market Returns, Infrastructure and the Supply and Demand for Extension Services." *American Journal of Agricultural Economics* 83 (3): 758–63.

Fuglie, K. 2010. "Total Factor Productivity in the Global Agricultural Economy: Evidence from FAO Data." In *The Shifting Patterns of Agricultural Production and Productivity Worldwide*, chap. 4, 63–95. Ames, IA: Iowa State University, Midwest Agribusiness Trade Research and Information Center.

Fuglie, K., M. Gautam, A. Goyal, and W. F. Maloney. 2020. *Harvesting Prosperity: Technology and Productivity Growth in Agriculture*. Washington, DC: World Bank.

Galbraith, J. K. 2001. "Macroeconomics of Income Distribution." In *Inequality and Industrial Change: A Global View*. edited by J. K. Galbraith and M. Berner, 3–15. New York: Cambridge University Press.

Gathigi, G., and E. Waititu. 2013. *Coding for Development in the Silicon Savannah: The Emerging Role of Digital Technology in Kenya. Re-imagining Development Communication in Africa*. Lanham, MD: Lexington Books.

Gollin, D. 2010. "Agricultural Productivity and Economic Growth." *Handbook of Agricultural Economics* 4 (73): 3825–66.

Goyal, A. 2010. "Information, Direct Access to Farmers, and Rural Market Performance in Central India." *American Economic Journal: Applied Economics* 2 (3): 22–45.

Griffin, T., and J. Lowenberg-DeBoer. 2005. "Worldwide Adoption and Profitability of Precision Agriculture: Implications for Brazil." *Revista de Política Agrícola* 14 (4): 20–37.

Grunert, K. G., S. Hieke, and J. Wills. 2014. "Sustainability Labels on Food Products: Consumer Motivation, Understanding and Use." *Food Policy* 44: 177–89.

Guilabert, M., and J. A. Wood. 2012. "USDA Certification of Food as Organic: An Investigation of Consumer Beliefs about the Health Benefits of Organic Food." *Journal of Food Products Marketing* 18 (5): 353–68. http://doi.org/10.1080/10454446.2012.685028.

Hasanain, A., M. Y. Khan, and A. Rezaee. 2018. "No Bulls: Asymmetric Information in the Market for Artificial Insemination in Pakistan." Agricultural Technology Adoption Initiative (ATAI) Working Paper, ATAI, Cambridge, MA. https://www.atai-research.org/wp-content/uploads/2015/11/livestock_15may2018.pdf.

Havlík, P., H. Valin, A. Mosnier, M. Obersteiner, J. S. Baker, M. Herrero, M. Rufino, and E. Schmid. 2012. "Crop Productivity and the Global Livestock Sector: Implications for Land Use Change and Greenhouse Gas Emissions." *American Journal of Agricultural Economics* 95 (2): 442–48.

Hay, R., and P. Pearce. 2014. "Technology Adoption by Rural Women in Queensland, Australia: Women Driving Technology from the Homestead for the Paddock." *Journal of Rural Studies* 36: 318–27.

Hellin, J., M. Lundy, and M. Meijer. 2009. "Farmer Organisation, Collective Action and Market Access in Meso-America." *Food Policy* 34: 16–22.

Hopkins, M. 2014. "10 Best New Agriculture Apps for 2015." *Croplife* 177 (12): 46.

iProcure. 2020. "Home" (accessed August 10, 2020). https://iprocu.re/.

Isgin, T., A. Bilgic, L. Forster, and M. T. Batte. 2008. "Using Count Data Models to Determine the Factors Affecting Farmers' Quantity Decisions of Precision Farming Technology Adoption." *Computers and Electronics in Agriculture* 6: 231–42.

Isik, M., and M. Khanna. 2003. "Stochastic Technology, Risk Preferences, and Adoption of Site-Specific Technologies." *American Journal of Agricultural Economics* 85 (2): 305–17. http://doi.org/10.1111/1467-8276.00121.

Jensen, R. 2007. "The Digital Provide: Information (Technology), Market Performance, and Welfare in the South Indian Fisheries Sector." *Quarterly Journal of Economics* 122 (3): 879–924.

Kahumbu, S. 2012. "Track Your Cow's Development." In *ICT Innovation*. Wageningen, The Netherlands: CTA.

Kaila, H., and F. Tarp. 2019. "Can the Internet Improve Agricultural Production? Evidence from Viet Nam." *Agricultural Economics* 50: 675–91.

Katamba, R., and B. Mutebi. 2017. "Jaguza Livestock App, the App Transforming Livestock Production and Strengthening Food Security." In *2017 IST-Africa Week Conference (IST-Africa)*, 1–12. Windhoek, Namibia. https://doi.org/10.23919/ISTAFRICA.2017.8102352.

Katz, P. 2016. "What Do You Get When You Cross Uber and Agriculture in India?" *Borgen Magazine*, September 9. https://www.borgenmagazine.com/uber-agriculture-in-india.

Khanna, M. 2001. "Sequential Adoption of Site-Specific Technologies and its Implications for Nitrogen Productivity: A Double Selectivity Model." *American Journal of Agricultural Economics* 83 (1): 35–51. http://doi.org/10.1111/0002-9092.00135.

Khanna, M., M. Isik, and D. Zilberman, 2002. "Cost-Effectiveness of Alternative Green Payment Policies for Conservation Technology Adoption with Heterogeneous Land Quality." *Agricultural Economics* (21) 2: 157–74.

Kos, D., and S. Kloppenburg. 2019. "Digital Technologies, Hyper-Transparency and Smallholder Farmer Inclusion in Global Value Chains." *Current Opinion in Environmental Sustainability* 41: 56–63.

Kumar, R. 2004. "'e-Choupals': A Study on the Financial Sustainability of Village Internet Centers in Rural Madhya Pradesh." *Information Technologies and International Development* 2 (1): 45–73.

Kusunose, Y., and R. Mahmood. 2016. "Imperfect Forecasts and Decision Making in Agriculture." *Agricultural Systems* 146 (2016): 103–10.

Kutter, T., S. Tiemann, R. Siebert, and S. Fountas. 2011. "The Role of Communication and Co-operation in the Adoption of Precision Farming." *Precision Agriculture* 12: 2–17.

Larson, D. F. 2007. "On Inverse Carrying Charges and Spatial Arbitrage." *Journal of Futures Markets* 27 (4): 305–336.

Larson, D. F., R. Muraoka, and K. Otsuka. 2016. "Why African Rural Development Strategies Must Depend on Small Farms." *Global Food Security* 10: 39–51.

Leanpath. 2020. "Home" (accessed August 10, 2020). Portland, OR. https://www.leanpath.com.

Leksmono, C., J. Young, N. Hooton, H. Muriuki, and D. Romney. 2006. "Informal Traders Lock Horns with the Formal Milk Industry: The Role of Research in Pro-Poor Dairy Policy Shift in Kenya." ODI/ILRI Working Paper 266, Overseas Development Institute, London.

Li, D. 2019. "China Offers E-Commerce Lessons for Rural Africa." IFPRI Blog, September 9. https://www.ifpri.org/blog/china-offers-e-commerce-lessons-rural-africa.

Lio, M., and M. C. Liu. 2006. "ICT and Agricultural Productivity: Evidence from Cross-Country Data." *Agricultural Economics* 34 (3): 221–28

Lokanathan, S., H. de Silva, and I. Fernando. 2011. "Price Transparency in Agricultural Produce Markets: Sri Lanka." In *Strengthening Rural Livelihoods: The Impact of Information and Communication Technologies in Asia*, edited by D. J. Grimshaw and S. Kala, 15–32.

Rugby and Ottawa: Practical Action Publishing and International Development Research Centre.

Løkke, M. M., H. F. Seefeldt, G. Edwards, and O. Green. 2011. "Novel Wireless Sensor System for Monitoring Oxygen, Temperature and Respiration Rate of Horticultural Crops Post-Harvest." *Sensors* 11: 8456–68.

Lowenberg-DeBoer, J., and T. W. Griffin. 2006. "Potential for Precision Agriculture Adoption in Brazil." *Site Specific Management Center Newsletter*, June, Purdue University, West Lafayette, IN.

Markelova, H., R. Meinzen-Dick, J. Hellin, and S. Dohrn. 2009. "Collective Action for Smallholder Market Access." *Food Policy* 34 (1): 1–7.

McCool, C., J. Beattie, J. Firn, C. Lehnert, J. Kulk, O. Bawden, R. Russell, and T. Perez. 2018. "Efficacy of Mechanical Weeding Tools: A Study into Alternative Weed Management Strategies Enabled by Robotics." *IEEE Robotics and Automation Letters* 3 (2): 1184–90.

McDermott, J. J., S. J. Staal, H. A. Freeman, M. Herrero, and J. A. Van de Steeg. 2010. "Sustaining Intensification of Smallholder Livestock Systems in the Tropics." *Livestock Science* 130 (1–3): 95–109.

Mendonça, S., N. Crespo, and N. Simões. 2015. "Inequality in the Network Society: An Integrated Approach to ICT Access, Basic Skills, and Complex Capabilities." *Telecommunications Policy* 39 (3): 192–207.

Miao, R., and M. Khanna. 2014. "Are Bioenergy Crops Riskier than Corn? Implications for Biomass Price." *Choices: The Magazine of Food, Farm, and Resource Issues* 29 (1): 1–6.

Mitra, S., D. Mookherjee, M. Torero, and S. Visaria. 2018. "Asymmetric Information and Middlemen Margins: An Experiment with Indian Potato Farmers." *Review of Economics and Statistics* 100 (1): 1–13. http://doi.org/10.1162/REST_a_00699.

Mnif, S. 2016. "Skill-Biased Technological Changes: Case of the MENA Region." *Economic Annals* 61 (210): 101–16.

Montealegre, F., S. Thompson, and J. S. Eales. 2007. "An Empirical Analysis of the Determinants of Success of Food and Agribusiness E-Commerce Firms." *International Food and Agribusiness Management Review* 10 (1): 1–21.

mPedigree. 2020. "Home" (accessed 10 August 10, 2020). http://mpedigree.com.

Mueller, N. D., J. S. Gerber, M. Johnston, D. K. Ray, N. Ramankutty, and J. A. Foley. 2012. "Closing Yield Gaps through Nutrient and Water Management." *Nature* 490 (7419): 254.

Munyua, H., E. Adera, and M. Jensen. 2009. "Emerging ICTs and Their Potential in Revitalizing Small-Scale Agriculture in Africa." *World Conference on Agriculture Information and IT* 2 (1): 3–9.

Muto, M. and T. Yamano. 2009. "The Impact of Mobile Phone Coverage Expansion on Market Participation: Panel Data Evidence from Uganda." *World Development* 37 (12): 1887–96.

Nakasone, E., and M. Torero. 2016. "A Text Message Away: ICTs as a Tool to Improve Food Security." *Agricultural Economics* 47 (S1): 49–59.

Nakasone, Eduardo, Maximo Torero, and Bart Minten. 2014. "The Power of Information: The ICT Revolution in Agricultural Development." *Annual Review of Resource Economics* 6 (1): 533–50. https://doi.org/10.1146/annurev-resource-100913-012714.

Naruka, P., S. Verma, S. Sarangdevot, C. Pachauri, S. Kerketta, and J. Singh. 2017. "A Study on the Role of WhatsApp in Agriculture Value Chains." *Asian Journal of Agricultural Extension, Economics, and Sociology* 20 (1): 1–11.

Neumann, K., P. H. Verburg, E. Stehfest, and C. Müller. 2010. "The Yield Gap of Global Grain Production: A Spatial Analysis." *Agricultural Systems* 103 (5): 316–26.

OECD (Organisation for Economic Co-operation and Development). 2019. *Digital Opportunities for Better Agricultural Policies*. Paris: OECD.

Overa, R. 2006. "Networks, Distance, and Trust: Telecommunications Development and Changing Trading Practices in Ghana." *World Development* 34 (7): 1301–1315.

Pampolino, M. F., L. J. Manguiat, S. Ramanathan, H. C. Gines P. S. Tan, T. T. N. Chi, R. Rejendran, and R. J. Buresh. 2007. "Environmental Impact and Economic Benefits of Site-specific Nutrient Management (SSNM) in Irrigated Rice Systems." *Agricultural Systems* 93: 1–24.

Parker, S. 2018. "Machine-learning App to Fight Invasive Crop Pest in Africa." *Mongabay*. http://news.mongabay.com/2018/10/machine-learning-app-to-fight-invasive-crop-pest-in-africa/.

Parker, C., K. Ramdas, and N. Savva. 2016. "Is IT Enough? Evidence from a Natural Experiment in India's Agriculture Markets." *Management Science* 62 (9): 2481–503.

Paudel, K., M. Pandit, A. Mishra, and E. Segarra. 2011. "Why Don't Farmers Adopt Precision Farming Technologies in Cotton Production?" Paper presented at 2011 AAEA & NAREA Joint Annual Meeting, Pittsburg, PA, July 24–26.

Pethybridge, S., and S. Nelson. 2015. "Leaf Doctor: A New Portable Application for Quantifying Plant Disease Severity." *Plant Disease* 99 (10): 1310–16.

Poku, A.-G., R. Birner, and S. Gupta. 2018. "Why Do Maize Farmers in Ghana Have a Limited Choice of Improved Seed Varieties? An Assessment of the Governance Challenges in Seed Supply." *Food Security* 10: 27–46.

Potter, A., J. Murray, B. Lawson, and S. Graham. 2012. "Trends in Product Recalls within the Agrifood Industry: Empirical Evidence from the USA, UK and the Republic of Ireland." *Trends in Food Science and Technology* 28: 77–86.

PwC (PricewaterhouseCoopers). 2018. "Global Blockchain Survey." PwC, London. http://pwc.com/blockchainsurvey.

Qiang, C. Z., S. C. Kuek, A. Dymond, and S. Esselaar. 2012. *Mobile Applications for Agriculture and Rural Development*. ICT Sector Unit Report 96226-GLB. Washington, DC: World Bank.

Qiang, C. Z., M. Yamamichi, V. Hausman, and D. Altman. 2011. *Mobile Applications for the Health Sector*. Washington, DC: World Bank.

QualiTrace. 2018. "Home" (accessed August 10, 2020). http://qualitracegh.com.

Raj, D. A., A. V. Poo Murugesan, V. P. S. Aditya, S. Olaganathan, and K. Sasikumar. 2011. "A Crop Nutrient Management Decision Support System: India." In *Strengthening Rural Livelihoods. The Impact of Information and Communication Technologies in Asia*, edited by D. J. Grimshaw and S. Kala, 33–52. Rugby, Warwickshire, UK: Practical Action Publishing.

Rejesus, R. M., and R. H. Hornbaker. 1999. "Economic and Environmental Evaluation of Alternative Pollution-reducing Nitrogen Management Practices in Central Illinois." *Agriculture, Ecosystems and Environment* 75: 41–53.

Richmond, K., and R. E. Triplett. 2018. "ICT and Income Inequality: A Cross-national Perspective." *International Review of Applied Economics* 32 (2): 195–214. http://doi.org/10.1080/02692171.2017.1338677.

Riera, O. and B. Minten. 2018. "Mobile Phones and Agricultural Market Performance in Ethiopia." Paper presented at International Association of Agricultural Economists 2018 Conference, Vancouver, British Columbia, July 28–August 2, 2018.

Rivera, W. M., M. Blum, and R. Sulaiman. 2009. "Extension: Object of Reform, Engine for Innovation." *Outlook on Agriculture* 38 (3): 267–73.

Rivera, W. M., M. K. Quamar, and L. V. Crowder. 2001. "Agricultural and Rural Extension Worldwide: Options for Institutional Reform in the Developing Countries." Food and Agriculture Organization of the United Nations, Sustainable Development Department, Rome.

Rosenthal, D. S. H., D. C. Rosenthal, E. L. Miller, I. F. Adams, M. W. Storer, and E. Zadok. 2012. "The Economics of Long-Term Digital Storage." In *The Memory of the World in the Digital Age: Digitalization and Preservation.* https://www.filesystems.org/docs/unesco12 /UNESCO2012-storage-econ.pdf.

Saito, K., S. Diack, I. Dieng, and M. K. N'Diaye. 2015. "On-farm Testing of a Nutrient Management Decision-support Tool for Rice in the Senegal River Valley." *Computers and Electronics in Agriculture* 116: 36–44.

Samoilenko, S., and K. Osei-Bryson. 2011. "The Spillover Effects of Investments in Telecoms: Insights from Transition Economies." *Information Technology for Development* 17 (3): 213–31.

Sawant, M. 2016. "Organized Data and Information for Efficacious Agriculture Using PRIDE™ Model." *International Food and Agribusiness Management Review* 19 (A): 115–30.

Say, S. M., M. Keskin, M. Sehri, and Y. E. Sekerli. 2018. "Adoption of Precision Agriculture Technologies in Developed and Developing Countries." *Online Journal of Science and Technology* 8 (1): 7–15.

Schieffer, J., and C. Dillon. 2014. "The Economic and Environmental Impacts of Precision Agriculture and Interactions with Agro-environmental Policy." *Precision Agriculture* 16: 46–61. http://doi.org/10.1007/s11119-014-9382-5.

Schimmelpfennig, D. 2016. *Farm Profits and Adoption of Precision Agriculture.* Economic Research Report ERR-217. Washington, DC: United States Department of Agriculture.

Schimmelpfennig, D., and R. Ebel. 2011. "On the Doorstep of the Information Age: Recent Adoption of Precision Agriculture." Economic Research Service Paper EIB-80, United States Department of Agriculture, Washington, DC.

Sexton, R. J., and T. Xia. 2018. "Increasing Concentration in the Agricultural Supply Chain: Implications for Market Power and Sector Performance." *Annual Review of Resource Economics* 10: 229–51. http://doi.org/10.1146/annurev-resource-100517-023312.

Sladojevic, S., M. Arsenovic, A. Anderla, D. Culibrk, and D. Stefanovic. 2016. "Deep Neural Networks Based Recognition of Plant Diseases by Leaf Image Classification." *Computational Intelligence and Neuroscience* (2016): 3289801.

Soulis, Konstantinos X., Stamatios Elmaloglou, and Nicholas Dercas. 2015. "Investigating the Effects of Soil Moisture Sensors Positioning and Accuracy on Soil Moisture–Based Drip Irrigation Scheduling Systems." *Agricultural Water Management* 148 (January): 258–68. https://doi.org/10.1016/j.agwat.2014.10.015.

SourceTrace. n.d. "Home" (accessed August 10, 2020). http://www.sourcetrace.com.

Speranza, M. G. 2018. "Trends in Transportation and Logistics." *European Journal of Operational Research* 264 (3): 830–36.

Sproxil. n.d. "Home" (accessed August 10, 2020). https://sproxil.com.

Staples, M. 2017. "Software Engineering Research for Blockchain-Based Systems." PowerPoint. Canberra, Australia: Commonwealth Scientific and Industrial Research Organisation. http://www.ict.griffith.edu.au/network/Mark%20Staples_SDLT2017.pdf.

Steiner, M. 2018. "AI-powered Technology Will Help Farmers Health-Check Soil and Water" (accessed August 10, 2020). IBM Research Blog. https://www.ibm.com/blogs /research/2018/09/agropad/.

TechnoServe. 2018. *Eyes in the Sky for African Agriculture, Water Resources, and Urban Planning*. Sydney, Australia: University of New South Wales.

Tekin, A. B. 2010. "Variable Rate Fertiliser Application in Turkish Wheat Agriculture: Economic Assessment." *African Journal of Agricultural Research* 5: 647–52.

Tey, Y. S., and M. Brindal. 2012. "Factors Influencing the Adoption of Precision Agricultural Technologies: A Review for Policy Implications." *Precision Agriculture* 13: 713–30.

Thompson, N. M., C. Bir, D. A. Widmar, and J. R. Mintert. 2019. "Farmer Perceptions of Precision Agriculture Technology Benefits." *Journal of Agricultural and Applied Economics* 51 (1): 142–63.

Too Good to Go. n.d. "Home" (accessed August 10, 2020). http://toogoodtogo.com/en-us.

Torrez, C., N. Miller, S. Ramsey, and T. Griffin. 2016. "Factors Influencing the Adoption of Precision Agricultural Technologies by Kansas Farmers." Kansas State University Department of Agricultural Economics Extension. https://www.agmanager.info/sites /default/files/pdf/Precision%20Ag%20Technology%20Adoption.pdf.

Tripoli, M., and J. Schmidhuber. 2018. *Emerging Opportunities for the Application of Blockchain in the Agrifood Industry*. Rome and Geneva: FAO and ICTSD. http:// www.fao.org/e-agriculture/news/new-publication-emerging-opportunities -application-blockchain-agrifood-industry.

UNIDO (United Nations Industrial Development Organization). 2006. *Global Value Chains in the Agrifood Sector*. Working paper, UNIDO, Vienna. https://www.unido.org/sites /default/files/2009-05/Global_value_chains_in_the_agrifood_sector_0.pdf.

van Donk, D. P., R. Akkerman, and J. T. van der Vaart. 2007. "Opportunities and Realities of Supply Chain Integration: The Case of Food Manufacturers." *British Food Journal* 110 (2): 218–35.

van Evert, F. K., D. Gaitán-Cremaschi, S. Fountas, and C. Kempenaar. 2017. "Can Precision Agriculture Increase the Profitability and Sustainability of the Production of Potatoes and Olives?" *Sustainability* 9: 1863. http://doi.org/10.3390/su9101863.

van Nuffel, A., T. van De Gucht, W. Saeys, B. Sonck, G. Opsomer, J. Vangeyte, K. C. Mertens, B. De Ketelaere, and S. Van Weyenberg. 2016. "Environmental and Cow-related Factors Affect Cow Locomotion and Can Cause Misclassification in Lameness Detection Systems." *Animal* 10 (9): 1533–41.

Waddington, H., B. Snilstveit, J. G. Hombrados, M. Vojtkova, J. Anderson, and H. White. 2012. "Farmer Field Schools for Improving Farming Practices and Farmer Outcomes in Low- and Middle-Income Countries: A Systematic Review." *Campbell Systematic Reviews* 10 (6). https://doi.org/10.4073/CSR.2014.6.

WEF (World Economic Forum). 2018. *Innovation with a Purpose: The Role of Technology Innovation in Accelerating Food Systems Transformation*. Cologny, Switzerland: WEF. https:// www.weforum.org/reports/innovation-with-a-purpose-the-role-of-technology-innovation -in-accelerating-food-systems-transformation.

Wei, Y., J. Lin, and L. Zhang. 2019. "E-Commerce, Taobao Villages and Regional Development in China." *Geographical Review* 110 (3): 380–405.

Whipker, L. D., and J. T. Akridge. 2009. "2009 Precision Agriculture Services Dealership Survey Results." Purdue University West Lafayette, IN.

WHO (World Health Organization). 2020. "Food Safety Fact Sheet." WHO, Geneva. https:// www.who.int/news-room/fact-sheets/detail/food-safety.

Wood, S., and A. Cowie. 2004. "A Review of Greenhouse Gas Emission Factors for Fertiliser Production." IEA Bioenergy Task 38, Orange, Research and Development Division, State Forests of New South Wales, Australia.

World Bank. 2007. *World Development Report 2007: Development and the Next Generation.* Washington, DC: World Bank.

World Bank. 2017. *ICT in Agriculture: Connecting Smallholders to Knowledge, Networks, and Institutions.* Washington, DC: World Bank.

World Bank. 2020. "World Development Indicators." World Bank, Washington, DC.

Xarvio. 2020. "Scouting" (accessed August 10, 2020). Xarvio, Munster, Germany. www.xarvio.com/global/en/SCOUTING.html.

Yang, J., Z. Huang, X. Zhang, and T. Reardon. 2013. "The Rapid Rise of Cross-Regional Agricultural Mechanization Services in China." *American Journal of Agricultural Economics* 95 (5): 1245–51.

Zilberman, D., M. Khanna, S. Kaplan, and E. Kim. 2014. "Technology Adoption and Land Use." In *The Oxford Handbook of Land Economics,* edited by J. Duke and J. Wu, chap. 2. Oxford: Oxford University Press.

Zilberman, D., M. Khanna, and L. Lipper. 1997. "Economics of New Technologies for Sustainable Agriculture." *Australian Journal of Agricultural and Resource Economics* 41 (1): 63–80.

CHAPTER FOUR

Transforming Rural Finance Markets

KEY MESSAGES

- High transaction costs due to isolation, small scale, and risk hinder access to credit, savings, and insurance in rural areas, particularly for smallholder farmers. Digital technologies, such as mobile money, digital credit scoring, and remote sensing for insurance design, promise to reduce these transaction costs:
  - o Mobile money reduces the transaction cost of depositing and withdrawing savings in formal institutions.
  - o Digital credit scoring reduces the transaction costs associated with loan application processing by predicting a customer's creditworthiness.
  - o Remote-sensing data can reduce the transaction costs associated with monitoring traditional insurance contracts.
- Public policy could ease constraints on developing and adopting digital technologies for agricultural finance and should focus on creating an enabling regulatory environment, supporting the innovation ecosystem to design innovative financial solutions, and ensuring interoperability between mobile operators and financial institutions.

BARRIERS TO FINANCIAL INCLUSION

Financial Flows

All financial transactions require three flows between clients and financial service providers:

1. *Money transfers.* These may be deposits and withdrawals for savings, loans, loan repayments, or premium and indemnity payments for insurance.
2. *Information transmissions.* These may communicate loan and insurance demands, client characteristics, or business outcomes.
3. *Information verifications.* These may verify fixed client characteristics in advance, such as agroecological risk profile or moral characteristics, or outcomes afterward, such as investment, client behavior, or they may verify actual weather. Clients, in turn, may verify the trustworthiness of those providing savings and insurance services.

Three key rural features—isolation, small scale, and risk—taken together or separately hinder financial and information flows. Rural communities are isolated due to sparse populations and low-quality transportation and communication infrastructure. The scale of transactions is often small in rural areas, although the fixed costs of collecting information remain large per dollar loaned or insured. Finally, agriculture, the dominant economic activity in rural areas, is highly vulnerable to risks. Throughout the growing season, a smallholder farmer faces random exogenous market and weather changes. Covariate risks, which are calamities such as droughts that affect all farmers and borrowers at the same time, discourage banks from lending to agriculture.

Savings

Isolation limits smallholder farmers' access to formal savings because it increases the cost of moving money. Barriers to savings consist primarily of the cost of moving money, not the flow of information. The cost of individuals moving paper money to bricks-and-mortar bank accounts is often high, since many developing regions have fewer than 2–10 commercial banks per 100,000 people (map 4.1). With banks concentrated in urban areas and poor infrastructure linking rural and urban areas, trips to deposit money safely are long. For individuals in such an environment, both the direct cost of moving money and the cost of forgoing other opportunities to do so render most physical banking systems impractical. First, the saver must trust that an external institution will appropriately guard savings (Coupé 2011; Karlan, Ratan, and Zinman 2014). Then the saver confronts a major barrier to formal savings in the transaction costs of making and retrieving deposits, while the financial institution bears the burden of record keeping.

MAP 4.1 Commercial Bank Branches per 100,000 People Worldwide

Source: World Bank 2020.

Credit

Together, isolation, small scale, and risk also result in high transaction costs and market failures that make access to credit unattractive or impossible for smallholder farmers. The three barriers limit the terms, the cost, and the availability of standard formal credit. For example, for a credit-issuing institution, these conditions complicate discerning who could repay a loan, even without considering an individual's willingness to repay a given lender. Credit bureaus, which verify creditworthiness based on official repayment records, are often limited, if they exist at all, in rural areas. Furthermore, mechanisms to ensure repayment or claim collateral in case of default also tend to be lacking.

In general, loan contracts face two sources of asymmetric information. Although potential borrowers know their own characteristics (such as the risks they face and their willingness to default) and behavior (whether they work diligently and whether they are likely to divert credit from its intended use), potential lenders do not. This asymmetry induces two adverse effects in every transaction between a lender and a borrower:

1. *Adverse selection.* As the interest rate increases, the lower-risk borrowers exit the market first. As lenders increase interest rates to account for high-risk borrowers, the opportunity cost simultaneously increases for lower-risk borrowers who are not willing to pay high interest rates, eventually driving them to exit the market. So the lender, if unable to distinguish low-risk from high-risk borrowers, may find expected profits decreasing even though the interest rate is increasing. (Note that solving this information problem about fixed borrower risk would require a single transmission of verified information.)

2. *Adverse incentives (or moral hazard).* As the interest increases and collateral decreases, incentives increase for diverting labor and credit from the activity supported by the loan, making low business income for the borrower more likely. This information problem is complex, since the morally hazardous diversion of resources emerges from a sequence of decisions that play out over time.

Isolation, small scale, and risk make it prohibitively costly for lenders to overcome the asymmetric information problem. The cost of acquiring information on borrowers can be prohibitively high for lenders. When remote borrowers seek small loans, the fixed cost of acquiring information per dollar loaned becomes excessive. Making matters worse, the presence of exogenous risk prevents lenders from inferring borrower behavior from outcomes: Did a crop fail due to bad weather or to the borrower's morally hazardous credit diversion?

Asymmetric information and high transaction costs truncate the menu of loan contracts available to smallholder farmers. A competitive lender that did not face information and enforcement costs would be able to offer potential borrowers a full menu of loan contracts. The contracts could range from low collateral–high interest rate contracts to high collateral–low interest rate contracts. In that world, borrowers could pick the contract that best meet their needs given their available collateral and risk tolerance. But when rural isolation, small scale, and risk make it prohibitively costly for lenders to overcome asymmetric information, interest rates and collateral no longer automatically substitute for each other, because lenders cannot profitably offer low collateral–high interest rate contracts (Boucher, Carter, and Guirkinger 2008; Carter 1988; Stiglitz and Weiss 1981).

The reduced menu of loan contracts creates an inequitable and inefficient credit market biased against less wealthy borrowers lacking required collateral or the ability to risk losing collateral. First, eliminating low collateral contracts will cull potential borrowers who lack the necessary collateral assets, an effect known as quantity rationing (figure 4.1a). Even individuals who have adequate collateral to borrow, despite the truncated menu of available contracts, may choose not to because high collateral contracts pass large shares of risk to borrowers. In this case, the individual borrower is "risk rationed." Credit rationing can introduce substantial inefficiencies. One study reported evidence from four countries that quantity rationed and risk rationed agricultural entrepreneurs use about 40 percent fewer inputs and enjoy incomes about 50 percent lower than their neighbors who are not credit rationed (Boucher, Carter, and Guirkinger 2008). In Peru, credit rationing lowers small farm agricultural production by as much as 25 percent (Guirkinger and Boucher 2011).

Joint liability microlending programs, which make neighbors jointly liable for each other's debt, are a well-known device to relieve credit rationing harm to low-wealth borrowers. But the success of joint liability programs is unclear. Joint liability lending aligns borrower incentives with lender incentives so that both the borrower and the lender want to minimize default. Physically nearby coborrowers know each other and, presumably, each other's exogenous risk. Most joint liability programs, by allowing borrowers to form their own group, assume that borrowers avoid high-risk coborrowers to avoid adverse selection and that they can, at near-zero cost, monitor coborrower diversions of effort and capital that create endogenous risk of default (figure 4.1b). They can then use nonstandard social collateral to punish wayward coborrowers. But the success of microfinance in controlling endogenous risk is unclear. Recent experiments suggest that a modicum of conventional individual collateral in joint liability loan groups would help reduce morally hazardous behavior (Flatnes and Carter 2019).

Digital technologies provide additional information that enables microfinance institutions to predict risk among low-asset populations (figure 4.1c). Such lending still misses some safe credit risks but expands the financial services frontier (shown by the backward-sloped curve in panel c) among less risky individuals besides those typically eligible for asset-based or social capital–based approaches.

Insurance Markets

Decades of research have highlighted the efficiency cost of uninsured risk, but isolation and small scale make traditional crop insurance unfeasible in the rural areas of developing countries. Traditional crop insurance, which addresses production risks, is available in many developed and developing countries (Mahul and Stutley 2010; Smith and Glauber 2012). But such insurance products are expensive because of high processing and monitoring costs caused by isolation and small scale. Hazell (1992) offers several striking examples of conventional loss-adjusted contracts for which the insurance provider cannot cost-effectively verify losses. Traditional insurance also suffers from information asymmetries (adverse selection and moral hazard). So these contracts are rarely offered without large government subsidies (Hazell 1992; Glauber 2013). For example, a survey of crop insurance programs in 48 developed and developing countries found that all receive major public support, amounting to 50–150 percent of the premium paid by farmers (Mahul and Stutley 2010).

Index insurance, an alternative to traditional crop insurance in developing countries, has the potential to overcome asymmetric information. The insurance payout trigger in index insurance is objective (for example, the rainfall at a weather station), so field visits to verify losses are unnecessary, substantially reducing costs. Although the index is designed to be highly correlated with the losses of the insured, the actions of the insured do not affect payout triggers, mitigating moral hazard problems. Index-based insurance allows extending protection to more farmers across the globe at much lower cost.

FIGURE 4.1 **Rural Credit**

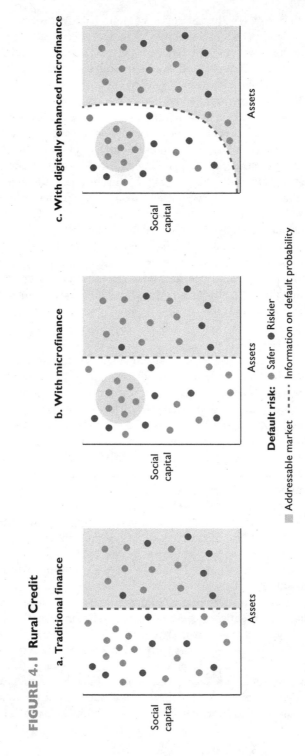

a. Traditional finance

b. With microfinance

c. With digitally enhanced microfinance

Social capital

Assets

Default risk: ● Safer ● Riskier - - - - Information on default probability

▧ Addressable market

Source: World Bank.

Experience with index insurance is growing, with 30 agricultural index insurance pilot programs in 19 developing countries in 2010 (Hazell et al. 2010). Still, few pilots have been scaled up. Most index insurance pays out against abnormal weather events (such as drought, excessive rain, or frost) or when area crop yields are low (Miranda and Farrin 2012).

Although index insurance has the potential to cost-effectively offer coverage to small-scale farmers, first generation contracts have largely not fulfilled their potential, crippled by low predictive power. Despite enthusiasm, the first generation of index insurance contracts from recent decades—largely based on estimated rainfall—suffered from an inability to comprehensively predict losses that farmers (or lenders) might want to insure. This problem creates *basis risk*, or what this chapter alternatively calls *uncompensated losses*. In a nutshell, the same uncompensated loss can arise from two main issues, alone or in combination: unusual variance and flawed design.

PATHWAYS FOR IMPROVED EFFICIENCY, EQUITY, AND ENVIRONMENTAL SUSTAINABILITY

Digital technologies promise to boost financial inclusion in rural areas while at the same time boosting equity, efficiency, and environmental sustainability. These technologies would increase equity by serving smallholder farmers, who are disproportionately excluded from financial services. They would support economic efficiency by reducing transaction costs for isolated populations and thus expanding access to financial services. Finally, digital technologies enable "green finance" by providing a platform to offset carbon emissions and reward environmentally friendly behavior in real time—but the overall environmental impact of these technologies remains inconclusive.

Three digital technologies are examined in this chapter: mobile money or mobile payment systems, digital credit scoring, and remote sensing for insurance design. They were chosen because they are the most suitable technologies for the smallholder context whose impact has been studied empirically. They are used to address isolation, small scale, and risk in financial markets. The chapter also discusses how these technologies affect environmental sustainability.

Mobile Payments Enhance Access to Savings and Informal Insurance

Mobile payments refer here to transactions using mobile devices. These transactions can be conducted on feature phones with basic cell-phone messaging capabilities as well as smartphones with advanced touch-screen and internet applications. Sometimes mobile payments or repayments require using a mobile payment agent network—in this case, the *mobile* qualification rests in avoiding the need for individuals living in remote areas to visit scarce bricks-and-mortar institutions concentrated in urban environments—and in agents using mobile devices for more rapid data collection and transmission. A classic example is M-PESA in Kenya. Mobile payments have generally focused on individuals, although they are increasingly used in individual-to-business transactions and government-to-individual payments.

Mobile money services are increasingly available for rural customers. By the end of 2015, 272 mobile money services had been deployed in 90 countries from Argentina to Zambia, with many more under development. Although mobile money has its largest presence in urban environments, the GSM Association—which represents over 750 mobile operators worldwide—found that more than half the mobile money operators responding to its 2018 survey had a product targeted to rural customers or intended to launch one in the year ahead (GSMA 2018).

Mobile money may have a major impact on savings by reducing the transaction cost of depositing and withdrawing savings in formal institutions. As explained earlier, the barrier to savings rests primarily in the cost of moving money, not in the flow of information. Systems that transmit money digitally create a sort of space-time compression, replacing the need to visit distant bricks-and-mortar financial institutions with the ability to use nearby nodes of a dispersed network of mobile money agents.

Transitioning from cash to mobile money payments can also result in business growth. One study found a strong positive correlation between the use of mobile money payments in Kenya and access to different kinds of finance for businesses, such as trade credit (Beck et al. 2015). Using a general equilibrium model, they found that the availability of mobile money technologies increases gross domestic product by 0.33–0.47 percent. Another study showed that mobile money can also increase microentrepreneurs' profits (Frederick 2014). And a third found that mobile money also reduces salary administration costs (Blumenstock et al. 2015).

Mobile money, by allowing isolated smallholder farmers in need to access friends' and family's savings, enables informal insurance. A small but provocative literature shows that mobile money systems can help mitigate harm from adverse shocks. Jack and Suri (2014), for example, found that negative income shocks between 2008 and 2010 did not affect the consumption patterns of Kenyan households using the M-PESA mobile money system, while the average consumption of non–mobile money users in their study dropped 7–10 percent. Enhanced remittances served as the channel for this consumption cushion: mobile money users were about 13 percent more likely to receive remittances than non–mobile money users, and the amounts they received were larger and came from more diverse individuals throughout their social network. Similarly, Blumenstock, Eagle, and Fafchamps (2016) found further evidence of mobile systems enabling responsiveness to shocks: after a significant earthquake in 2008, individuals living close to the epicenter received significant transfers of phone credit (air time) from people farther away. The country lacked a working mobile money system at the time, so money transfers were not possible. But the phone credit transfers suggest that increasing individuals' access to resources may have helped them gather information, including alternative strategies for coping with the earthquake's aftermath.

Mobile money can also reduce transaction costs for formal insurance due to rural isolation. The Index-based Livestock Insurance program (IBLI) in the arid rangelands of Northern Kenya originally delivered indemnity payments by traversing rural areas in rugged vehicles—a process that often cost more than the value of the indemnity payments, especially in serving livestock herding communities on the move to find the best forage areas (Chantarat et al. 2013). When this chapter was written, IBLI insurance companies had still not paid indemnities to all insured clients based on the 2011 drought, because the companies had been unable to find the clients. Since that drought, IBLI insurance providers have shifted to mobile payment technologies, reducing the delivery cost to a mere fraction of the former cost of in-person payments. That improvement contributes to the long-term financial sustainability of the insurance program (Mude 2017).

Straddling these informal and formal insurance systems are peer-to-peer digital insurance and credit platforms. Digital insurance platforms rely on mobile money and other digital technologies to link anonymous individuals in a mutual insurance system. Although there has been little investigation of such systems, Feng, Abdikerimova, and Liu (2019) report that e-commerce giant Ali Baba and other platforms already link 260 million individuals in China in a complex web of mutual but largely unregulated insurance. Pending further research, this peer-to-peer insurance seems best described as a generalized informal insurance, allowing individuals to access others' savings in times of need. Similarly, the evidence on the impacts of digital credit platforms is scarce. A study on the US-based credit platform Lending Club showed that it increased financial inclusion and reduced the cost of credit to underbanked populations (Jagtiani and Lemieux 2017).

Mobile money, by reducing transaction costs for isolated populations, expands access to financial services. It seems able to support economic efficiency, facilitating trade and enhancing welfare for its users without harming others. The possibilities of increasing efficiency through continuing innovation in applying mobile money transfers—including transfers and payments between people and from governments to people; bill, bulk, and merchant payments; and international remittances—seem likely to expand further.

Digital Credit Scoring Promises to Allow Farmers to Prove their Trustworthiness to Lenders

Digital credit scoring refers to using nontraditional data—information besides the formal credit history traditionally captured by credit bureaus—to predict individual default risk and determine credit terms. Much of the data for constructing digital credit scores comes either from the growing digitized information about individuals and their behavior or from more accessible information about their agricultural systems and income profiles. Data include cell phone usage, device records, social information, agricultural production information, and value chain information (box 4.1).

Besides reducing the transaction costs of moving people and money, mobile data collection systems help to more quickly collect and digest surveys and loan applications, reducing the turnaround time for acting on the information they contain. Although computer-aided or digitally assisted surveys are not novel—their use dates back to the 1980s—processing speeds, storage sizes, device portability, and device cost-effectiveness have improved, enhancing the applicability of collecting mobile data in remote, rural environments (Caviglia-Harris et al. 2012). Such systems may not be appropriate in all environments—especially where trust in technology is low, security concerns are prevalent, or reliable data uploading infrastructure is rare. But the evaluation literature generally finds digital systems ahead of their paper counterparts across many domains, if developers can dedicate sufficient time to testing and debugging the survey

BOX 4.1 Data Used to Generate Digital Credit Scores

Agricultural cash flow and capacity data. The Frankfurt School of Finance and Management has developed the Agricultural Loan Evaluation System (ALES) to help overcome barriers to specialized knowledge required to evaluate agricultural loans. ALES combines archetypical production information for over 1,300 agricultural products and associated risks with local agricultural data (such as average yields, selling prices, working capital needs, production processes, and related costs). This information is used to predict risk and suggest loan amounts and terms for commercial banks with otherwise limited agricultural knowledge to use in evaluating applicants. To date, the ALES system has been deployed in Azerbaijan, Senegal, Tajikistan, and Turkey. Although specific evaluations of the ALES system are not readily available to the public, the principle of quickly and efficiently identifying agricultural costs and production potential that underpins the ALES approach is broadly recommended as a best practice among rural digital finance practitioners (Mercy Corps 2017). Mercy Corps' AgriFin Accelerate approach (Mercy Corps 2017) and the AusAid-funded Strengthening Agricultural Finance in Rural Areas (Safira) program in Indonesia suggest partnering with mobile network operators and supply chain actors to ingest additional information about previous input purchases and sales. This partnership can further help in developing appropriate loans, in effect substituting information based on a farmer's experience growing and selling a particular crop for formal credit scores.

Transactional data. These can include calling, texting, airtime, emergency top-up purchase patterns and habits, and mobile money transactions (Aron 2018). The Brazilian telecom company Oi, in partnership with the organization Cignifi, reported using calling records to generate a "significant" discriminator of credit risk in its application, although it did not provide quantitative specifics on what features had predictive power (Caire et al. 2017).

(Continued)

BOX 4.1 Data Used to Generate Digital Credit Scores *(Continued)*

Device data. These can include "media content, call logs, contacts, personal communications, location information, or online social media profiles" (see, for example, Wei et al. 2015). Many reports suggest social information can be fruitfully used in discriminating default risk—and several companies operate on this model. But few programs publicly describe how well social information performs in assessing credit risk compared with other information sources, and many report that social information can be manipulated by consumers who try to change behavior they know is being monitored (Eichelberger 2013). Such systems may rely on assumptions about how individuals relate to their network—perhaps that individuals flock to others with similar risk scores, so that risk scores can be ascribed to individuals from the scores of others in their network or be derived from their degree of connectedness. Some researchers have warned about possible "digital redlining" in such approaches (Caeyers, Chalmers, and De Weerdt 2010; Tomkys and Lombardini 2015). But others promote them as a way for individuals to gain access to resources that might otherwise be out of reach.

---

tools at the outset of the project, protect participant confidentiality, and avoid environments where digital technologies might otherwise unduly influence results (Caeyrs, Chalmers, and De Weerdt 2010; Tomkys and Lombardini 2015).

The value of information embedded in digital footprint data often matches or exceeds that of credit scoring information alone, showing promise for extending credit where official scores are lacking. Berg et al. (2020) studied 250,000 transactions from a German e-commerce company with a "ship first, pay later" approach that effectively functioned as a short-term loan. The researchers then merged transaction information with customer digital footprint information and customer credit scores from a private credit bureau that were required for purchases for more than 100 euros. They found that digital footprint variables such as device characteristics (a proxy for income), reputation (were emails in the purchaser's own name?), and impulse control (did the purchaser come to the company's website from a price comparison website, in contrast to an advertisement?) all predicted credit scores and forecast credit score changes. Digital footprints provided a benefit beyond that of credit scores alone, as default rates decreased 45 percent once the platform included both credit scores and digital footprint information in its customer evaluation procedures (Berg et al. 2020).

Digital credit scoring and similar approaches reduce the marginal cost of providing credit, making more customers eligible for loans. Numerous companies have begun to evaluate how nontraditional data sources and big data analytics, by predicting a customer's creditworthiness, reliability, and purchasing power, can support loan contracts (Costa, Deb, and Kubzansky 2015). In a striking example, digital data analytics can reduce the marginal cost of providing a $200 loan in Tanzania by more than 40 percent, according to a recent estimate. Those cost savings, if passed to consumers, could routinely reduce entry barriers for a larger swath of the population (Costa, Deb, and Kubzansky 2015). As cellular usage and individual digital footprints spread globally, the number of consumers who could benefit—those who have some digital footprint but live in areas where formal financial services are not widespread—will reach an estimated 625 million to 1.2 billion.

To date, there is little evidence on the ability of digital credit scoring methods to predict default risk. Risks are both exogenous and endogenous. Although it is fairly easy to imagine that digital data could distinguish individuals that have low exogenous risk from those with high exogenous risk, it is less apparent that digital data can reduce endogenous risk by monitoring individuals' behavior or deterring resource diversion. It is not apparent how well even joint liability lending works in reducing endogenous risk without collateral of some kind. One of the few studies currently available on digital credit evaluated the impacts of M-Shwari, the dominant player in the Kenyan market (Suri and Gubbins 2018). It found that the digital option boosts loan uptake by 11 percentage points. Although the result may be attributable to education efforts by M-Shwari, this finding holds out some promise that digital credit can alter the credit rationing landscape. The study also found that such loans do not affect assets, perhaps because small, short-term loans are not well suited to investment (particularly in agriculture).

Under some assumptions, digital credit might allow a low-cost way to discern borrower type. The economic model of credit rationing discussed earlier assumes (in standard economics style) that all individuals will divert resources if it is in their narrow interest to do so. But perhaps willingness to divert is a fixed characteristic, and some types of people will not engage in morally hazardous diversion even when material incentives point them in that direction. If so, then endogenous risk is to some extent a fixed characteristic. The question would then become whether, say, an individual's sterling cell phone repayment record signals a low moral hazard person or simply signals the efficacy of incentives in the cell phone contractual environment. If willingness to engage in morally hazardous behavior is in fact a fixed characteristic, then digital technologies open the door to low-cost ways of discerning type.

Cheaper methods of discerning borrower type could open the door to progressive nanoloans for smallholder farmers. Following a progressive lending model, microfinance organizations have for years made only small loans to individuals at first, gradually making larger loans once the borrowers prove their creditworthiness. Digital technologies open the door to progressive nanoloans (nanoloans are loans of less than $20). In environments where historical or transactional information is limited, some organizations offer progressively larger nanoloans following successful repayment of a previous loan, as in an M-Shwari Savings and Loan product launched in 2012 with Safaricom and Commercial Bank of Africa. In a digital environment, the loan amounts can be smaller than in the traditional microlending model, given the lower cost and faster pace of requesting and delivering funds. Progressive nanoloans are a valuable source of short-term capital that is needed by farmers.

Remote Sensing is Expanding the Reach of Formal Insurance Markets to Smallholder Farmers

Advances in remote sensing have opened new avenues for studying change on the earth's surface and atmosphere—including applications for evaluating crop growth and health over time (box 4.2). Earth observation technologies have been featured in economic analyses since at least the 1930s, when the US Agricultural Adjustment Agency employed aerial photography of farm areas to aid conservation and land-use decisions (Monmonier 2002). Aerial photography gave rise to multiple satellite earth observation missions during the space race of the 1950s and 1960s. Especially in recent decades, the detail that can be efficiently resolved from frequent satellite earth observation technologies ("spaceborne photography") has increased markedly, enhancing enthusiasm for using satellite earth observation in ever wider applications.

Remote-sensing data can reduce the monitoring costs of traditional insurance contracts. As shown earlier, traditional insurance fails in rural areas because of high monitoring costs and asymmetric information. Remote-sensing technologies have the potential to reduce monitoring costs by augmenting and eventually displacing field visits. For example, these technologies can enhance the ability to assess crop, hail, and insect damage (Gallo et al. 2012; Puig et al. 2015; Silleos, Perakis, and Petsanis 2002; Zhou et al. 2016).

BOX 4.2 Publicly Available Remote-Sensing Data

Satellite imagery data has evolved impressively. The Landsat and the Moderate Resolution Imaging Spectroradiometer (MODIS) program satellites have been classic workhorses for many general earth observation tasks. Researchers and practitioners have applied their data to estimate land cover change and biomass, detect fires and volcanic eruptions, explore water quality, evaluate land surface temperature, and more. These satellites regularly orbit the planet. The most recent Landsat satellites orbit every 16 days at 30 meter optical resolution across 7–12 spectral bands, and MODIS satellites orbit four times a day using two different instruments at 250 meter to 1 kilometer resolution with 36 spectral bands. They passively collect and transmit information across the globe. In the past several years, European Space Agency Sentinel spacecraft have started to capture data at a higher spatial resolution (about 10–60 meters, depending on the wavelength) with a fairly high revisit frequency (about every five days) to help pinpoint changes in crop phenology. In addition, the Sentinel-1 satellite launched in 2014 includes active radar imaging, which allows the satellite to acquire data even through cloud cover. Besides publicly available systems, private satellites with submeter spatial resolution and frequent revisits have also become available. Some 594 earth observation satellites were launched between 2003 and 2017, compared with 26 in the previous decade. This corresponds with a shift to lighter (lower mass) remote-sensing instruments (Radiant Earth 2018).

The greater availability and detail of remote-sensing data and advanced computing capacity have improved yield estimates, conceivably reducing the design risk that plagued first-generation index insurance contracts (box 4.3). The use of satellite remote-sensing information to improve crop yield estimation dates to at least the 1970s, when researchers at Kansas State University employed Landsat 1 and 2 data to estimate winter wheat yields at scale on contract with the US National Aeronautics and Space Administration (Kanemasu 1977). So although the idea is not new, the capabilities of the newer, higher resolution sensors coupled with enhanced data-processing platforms offer the promise of evaluating agricultural systems in diverse, smallholder environments—places that face the trio of isolation, small scale, and risk exposure that plague the traditional applications of rural microfinance.

Remote-sensing methods could also lower the cost of index insurance contracts. Although covering idiosyncratic risk fundamentally falls outside the scope of index insurance programs (Jensen, Mude, and Barrett 2018),

BOX 4.3 Remote Sensing to Predict Yield

A recent example of using remote sensing in a smallholder context is Burke and Lobell's (2017) green canopy vegetative index, derived from satellite data at differing resolutions to predict smallholder maize production in western Kenya in 2014–15. Yield predictions based on earth observation data performed similarly to yield predictions based on more costly self-reported farmer field surveys. Both accounted for approximately 40 percent of overall variation in maize yields. Data from higher resolution sensors (roughly 1 meter and 5 meters) led to better predictions and tighter confidence intervals than data from coarser resolution sensors. A subsequent study in Uganda by the same researchers with World Bank collaborators compared predictions based on remotely sensed yields with predictions based on three forms of ground data: farmer self-reports (surveys), subplot crop cuts (actual measurement of the area and production of a subplot), and full plot crop cuts (measurement of the area and production of a full plot) (Lobell et al. 2018). The satellite data themselves supported three estimates—one calibrated to subplot crop cuts, one to full plot crop cuts, and one based on crop model simulations rather than crop cut data. Two especially relevant results appeared. First, self-reported data explained little of the variation (less than 1 percent) in either crop cut–based dataset. Second, all versions of the remotely sensed yields captured over half the variation in the full crop cut data for pure stand (that is, not intercropped) plots larger than 0.10 hectare. Although further work is needed to understand the conditions under which satellite-based measurements best reflect estimated realized crop production, these results point to the possibility of fruitfully using inexpensive, publicly available earth observation data to characterize yield distributions, not just across a wider geographical expanse than surveys, but potentially with higher correspondence to actual farmer yields. Field surveys should not be discontinued, however—they can still contribute useful information on household experiences, outcomes, and numerous other features unobserved from the skies.

remote-sensing data that correspond to yield variability patterns offer the opportunity to increase the homogeneity in insured zones. As an example, earth observation data could help identify in advance systematic breaks in agricultural conditions or outcomes that might otherwise increase the likelihood of basis events due to individual plots deviating from a poorly demarcated regional average, such as what can be termed *avoidable idiosyncratic variation*. Increasing the homogeneity of an insurance zone would enhance the value of index insurance contracts to a farmer. Information about zone homogeneity can also contribute to lowering insurance provider costs. For example, a recent project by the Consultative Group to Assist the Poor and the Pula insurance agency in north-central Nigeria and Kenya employed data-driven approaches to defining the boundaries of insurable areas. By determining in advance which areas were similar, they could avoid oversampling in areas with similar yields, thereby reducing the overall cost of the crop cuts used to trigger area-yield insurance contracts (Hernandez, Goslinga, and Wang 2018).

Has Digital Finance Boosted Equity and Environmental Sustainability?

Although the net effects of mobile money systems on financial efficiency are likely to be decidedly positive, their net effects on equity are less straightforward. As a tool that can facilitate private transactions, mobile money has the potential to alter bargaining dynamics within a household and influence intra- and interhousehold resource allocations (Aker et al. 2016; Duflo and Udry 2004; Jakiela and Ozier 2016). Mobile money opportunities could target less powerful individuals. If so, the ability to conduct private transactions could empower those—especially women—who otherwise have less privacy and less access to property (Aker et al. 2016; Aron and Muellbauer 2019). So far, mobile money for remittances tends to concentrate among wealthier populations who may have other options for mitigating risk. In general, remittances through mobile money are fairly small (Bharadwaj, Jack, and Suri 2019; Blumenstock, Eagle, Fafchamps 2016; Costa, Deb, and Kubzansky 2015). Although small amounts will not transform the day-to-day environment, mobile money sent to alleviate acute adverse conditions is fruitful when it averts disaster.

Mobile money provides a platform to offset carbon emissions and reward environmentally friendly behavior in real time, but the overall environmental impact of this technology remains inconclusive. Creative social enterprises are leveraging detailed consumer data and the ease of mobile payments to reward users for making "green" decisions. For example, the Alibaba company in China began using its Alipay app to track how users had decreased carbon emissions in 2016. Once users reached a certain threshold, partner organizations would plant a tree in Inner Mongolia (UNEP 2019). In the United States, the mobile app PIPs Rewards (Positive Impact Points) provides incentives for consumers to make environmentally friendly decisions. Users are rewarded with points for socially responsible actions, such as taking public transit or recycling, that can be redeemed as real currency at other eco-friendly businesses. Despite the hope that a transition away from cash transactions would improve environmental outcomes, the relative contribution of the information and communication technologies sector to the global footprint is expected to grow from 3.5 percent in 2020 to 14 percent by 2040 (Belkhir and Elmeligi 2018). Carbon emissions stem mostly from the production of smartphones, due to the mining of precious metals, and from data storage and processing (Rochemont 2018). Positive environmental impacts will stem from a shift to renewable energy generation and changing consumer behavior (that is, reducing the turnover of mobile phones).

In theory, digital credit scoring could have positive impacts on equity. Figure 4.1c illustrated how digital credit scoring might work. In principle, if digital credit scoring can distinguish low- from high-risk borrowers, then it would predictably open credit access to a broader swath of potential borrowers who have few tangible assets and poor social connections. This could be especially important for women farmers.

The evidence is thin but growing on how well digital credit scoring works across different data contexts, but its ability to accurately predict the creditworthiness of marginalized populations is questionable. There is some criticism that the ability of digital credit scoring to predict creditworthiness is weak, leaving both risk and interest rates high. And in practice, digital lending still skews to educated, urban, wealthy men despite its potential to broaden access to lower income populations (Gubbins and Totolo 2018). This is partially attributable to the fact that digital credit does not inherently address power imbalances or marginalized groups. Without complementary interventions to expand access to different groups, digital credit helps expand access to groups that already have higher social capital. To shift the dynamics to include more marginalized groups among borrowers (influence the composition of borrowers)—rather than amplify underlying biases favoring other population segments—customized policies should highlight groups that otherwise have not accessed those systems.

Digital lending practices that merely ingest and process existing data will generate models skewed toward individuals who associate with people about whom there is information. This way of characterizing people relies for accuracy on individuals being nested within comparable groups (Gubbins and Totolo 2018). But for an individual who exhibits many features not common to the groups the model was trained on, the likelihood of mistakenly being excluded from credit is high.

Finally, predatory lending, limited competition, and monopoly pricing are concerns with digital credit, because they disproportionately affect the poorest population segments. Unscrupulous actors can use predictions to target individuals likely to produce revenue through late fees or penalties, instead of highly creditworthy individuals. Although this concern is not unique to digital credit, the accelerated pace of transactions and the segmentation of the population in digital lending could amplify the consequences. Literacy constraints can leave people vulnerable to predatory practices (Aker and Blumenstock 2015). Furthermore, especially with privacy and data ownership regimes unclear, farmer incomes could be gouged. For example, a supplier that can better predict a farmer's income can set input prices that the farmer is just able to meet, or a buyer can set output prices that the farmer is just willing to accept. In either case, rent extraction wrests away margins that the farmer could otherwise use to build savings.

In short, some enthusiasm for digital credit may reflect an oversimplified lending model that fails to distinguish between adverse selection and moral hazard incentives. There is much to learn. It is thus far from obvious that digital technologies can eliminate the need for tangible collateral. If even digital credit requires some element of collateralization, then the problem of risk rationing reappears, with some low-risk agents refusing loan contracts that push exogenous risk onto them. And exogenous variability, coupled with the ease of receiving financial services, can lead to future exclusion from further credit for individuals who take on seemingly easy loans but become unable to repay them or are not fully aware of the terms. The risk affects a large portion of the population. More than half the individuals who took out mobile loans had a missed payment, according to a recent Consultative Group to Assist the Poor report. And in Tanzania, for example, nonrepayment results in being blacklisted from future credit. Some 20 percent of individuals reported reducing food spending in order to repay mobile loans, in another consequence of inability to repay as anticipated or of borrowing with poor information (Kaffenberger, Totolo, and Soursourian 2018). Especially in these circumstances, complementary financial instruments—including microinsurance—can prove especially useful.

This chapter has offered reasons for optimism about the potential for emerging digital technologies to fundamentally remake the rural microfinance landscape. But the evidence remains scant about the real potential of mobile money, digital credit scoring, and remote sensing to fundamentally alter rural financial markets. Although these technologies will likely improve the security and rates of return on savings, reduce credit rationing, and make higher quality insurance products available, ongoing medium-term inefficiencies will ration credit to those who can meet collateral prerequisites and lead to insurance offered only sporadically and at high cost.

While further digital innovations to improve this situation are sought, blended financial products incorporating savings, credit, and insurance could be considered. Own savings is likely to remain the cheapest form of finance, although the one with the highest prerequisites, in which managing risk and investment requires substantial wealth. At the other extreme, insurance to manage risk has the fewest prerequisites but continues to be very expensive. Across index insurance projects, $1.00 in expected insurance payout frequently costs $1.50. And insurance demands a healthy trust in the reliability of financial institutions. Credit is somewhere between savings and insurance, requiring lower wealth than savings, but with the cost per dollar somewhere between cost of a saved dollar and the cost of a dollar obtained through an insurance contract.

These observations suggest an approach that allows households to flexibly move among savings, credit, and insurance instruments as their wealth changes and their understanding and trust in financial institutions evolve. Interestingly, the kind of indexes that underlie index insurance contracts can also be used to trigger the release of funds from commitment savings accounts and the opening of contingent lines of credit. We thus might imagine that early in its life cycle, a low-wealth household with few assets and little trust in financial institutions might begin with index-linked savings accounts. With trust and understanding established, the household might switch to insurance to manage its major risks until it has built up enough collateral and reputation assets to open a contingent line of credit. Finally, as the household grows further in resources, it might return to self-finance and self-insurance.

REFERENCES

Aker, J. C., and J. E. Blumenstock. 2015. "The Economics of New Technologies in Africa." In *The Oxford Handbook of Africa and Economics*, vol. 2, edited by C. Monga and J. Y. Lin, 353–71. Oxford, UK: Oxford University Press.

Aker, J. C., R. Boumnijel, A. McClelland, and N. Tierney. 2016. "Payment Mechanisms and Antipoverty Programs: Evidence from a Mobile Money Cash Transfer Experiment in Niger." *Economic Development and Cultural Change* 65 (1): 1–37.

Aron, J. 2018. "Mobile Money and the Economy: A Review of the Evidence." *World Bank Observer.* http://academic.oup.com/wbro/article/33/2/135/5127166.

Aron, J., and J. Muellbauer. 2019. "The Economics of Mobile Money: Harnessing the Transformative Power of Technology to Benefit the Global Poor." Working paper, Oxford Martin School, UK. https://www.oxfordmartin.ox.ac.uk/downloads/May-19-OMS -Policy-Paper-Mobile-Money-Aron-Muellbauer.pdf.

Beck, Thorsten, Haki Pamuk, Burak R. Uras, and Ravindra Ramrattan. 2015. "Mobile Money, Trade Credit and Economic Development: Theory and Evidence." 2015–23. Discussion Paper, Tilburg University, Center for Economic Research. https://ideas.repec.org/p/tiu /tiucen/3d35ab30-05ef-4a31-8710-f845325b8ce4.html.

Belkhir, L., and A. Elmeligi. 2018. "Assessing ICT Global Emissions Footprint: Trends to 2040 and Recommendations." *Journal of Cleaner Production* 177: 448–63.

Berg, T., V. Burg, A. Gombovic, and M. Puri. 2020. "On the Rise of FinTechs: Credit Scoring Using Digital Footprints." *Review of Financial Studies* 33 (7): 2845–97.

Bharadwaj, P., W. Jack, and T. Suri. 2019. "Fintech and Household Resilience to Shocks: Evidence from Digital Loans in Kenya." Working Paper 25604, National Bureau of Economic Research, Cambridge, MA.

Blumenstock, J. E., M. Callen, T. Ghani, and L. Koepke. 2015. "Promises and Pitfalls of Mobile Money in Afghanistan: Evidence from a Randomized Control Trial." In *Proceedings of the Seventh International Conference on Information and Communication Technologies and Development*, p. 15. New York: Association for Computing Machinery.

Blumenstock, J. E., N. Eagle, and M. Fafchamps. 2016. "Airtime Transfers and Mobile Communications: Evidence in the Aftermath of Natural Disasters." *Journal of Development Economics* 120 (C): 157–81.

Boucher, S. R., M. R. Carter, and C. Guirkinger. 2008. "Risk Rationing and Wealth Effects in Credit Markets: Theory and Implications for Agricultural Development." *American Journal of Agricultural Economics* 90 (2): 409–23.

Burke, M., and D. B. Lobell. 2017. "Satellite-Based Assessment of Yield Variation and Its Determinants in Smallholder African Systems." *Proceedings of the National Academy of Sciences* 114 (9): 2189–94.

Caeyers, B., N. Chalmers, and J. De Weerdt. 2010. "A Comparison of CAPI and PAPI through a Randomized Field Experiment." *SSRN.* https://ssrn.com/abstract=1756224.

Caire, D., L. Camiciotti, S. Heitmann, S. Lonie, C. Racca, M. Ramji, and Q. Xu. 2017. *Handbook: Data Analytics and Digital Financial Services.* Washington, DC: World Bank. https://www.ifc.org/wps/wcm/connect/region__ext_content/ifc_external_corporate_site/sub-saharan+africa/resources/dfs-data-analytics.

Carter, M. 1988. "Equilibrium Credit Rationing of Small Farm Agriculture." *Journal of Development Economics* 28 (1): 83–103.

Caviglia-Harris, J., S. Hall, K. Mulllan, C. Macintyre, S. C. Bauch, D. Harris, E. Sills, D. Roberts, M. Toomey, and H. Cha. 2012. "Improving Household Surveys through Computer-assisted Data Collection: Use of Touch-screen Laptops in Challenging Environments." *Field Methods* 24 (1): 74–94.

Chantarat, S., A. Mude, C. B. Barrett, and M. R. Carter. 2013. "Designing Index-Based Livestock Insurance for Managing Asset Risk in Northern Kenya." *Journal of Risk and Insurance* 80 (1): 206–37.

Costa, A., A. Deb, and M. Kubzansky. 2015. "Big Data, Small Credit: The Digital Revolution and Its Impact on Emerging Market Consumers." *Innovations: Technology, Governance, Globalization* 10 (3–4): 49–80.

Coupé, T. 2011. "Mattresses versus Banks: The Effect of Trust on Portfolio Composition." Discussion paper 40, Kyiv School of Economics and Kyiv Economics Institute, Ukraine.

Duflo, E., and C. Udry. 2004. "Intrahousehold Resource Allocation in Côte d'Ivoire: Social Norms, Separate Accounts and Consumption Choices." Working Paper 10498, National Bureau of Economic Research, Cambridge, MA.

Eichelberger, E. 2013. "Your Deadbeat Facebook Friends Could Cost You a Loan." *Mother Jones,* September 18. https://www.motherjones.com/politics/2013/09/lenders-vet-borrowers-social-media-facebook/.

Feng, R., S. Abdikerimova, and C. Liu. 2019. "The Rise of Peer-to-Peer Insurance and Its Mathematical Modeling." Working paper, University of Illinois, Urbana-Champaign.

Flatnes, J. E., and M. R. Carter. 2019. "A Little Skin in the Microfinance Game: Reducing Moral Hazard in Joint Liability Group Lending through a Mandatory Collateral Requirement." *Journal of Economic Behavior and Organization* 164: 199–214.

Frederick, L. I. 2014. "Impact of Mobile Money Usage on Microenterprise Evidence from Zambia in Urban Opportunities: Perspectives on Climate Change, Resilience, Inclusion and the Informal Economy." Wilson Center, Washington, DC. https://www.wilsoncenter.org/sites/default/files/media/documents/event/Urban%20Opportunities.pdf.

Gallo, K., T. Smith, K. Jungbluth, and P. Schumacher. 2012. "Hail Swaths Observed from Satellite Data and Their Relation to Radar and Surface-based Observations: A Case Study from Iowa in 2009." *Weather Forecasting* 27: 796–802. https://doi.org/10.1175/WAF-D-11-00118.1.

Glauber, J. W. 2013. "The Growth of the Federal Crop Insurance Program, 1990–2011." *American Journal of Agricultural Economics* 95 (2): 482–88.

GSMA. 2018. *State of the Industry Report on Mobile Money: 2018.* London: GSMA.

Gubbins, P., and E. Totolo. 2018. "Digital Credit in Kenya: Evidence from Demand-Side Surveys." FSD Kenya, Nairobi. https://fsdkenya.org/research-and-publications/datasets/digital-credit-in-kenya-evidence-from-demand-side-surveys.

Guirkinger, C., and S. R. Boucher. 2011. "Credit Constraints and Productivity in Peruvian Agriculture." *Agricultural Economics* 39 (3): 295–308.

Hazell, P. B. 1992. "The Appropriate Role of Agricultural Insurance in Developing Countries." *Journal of International Development* 4 (6): 567–81.

Hazell, P., J. Anderson, N. Balzer, A. H. Clemmensen, U. Hess, and F. Rispoli. 2010. "The Potential for Scale and Sustainability in Weather Index Insurance for Agriculture and Rural Livelihoods." World Food Programme, Rome.

Hernandez, E., R. Goslinga, and V. Wang. 2018. *Using Satellite Data to Scale Smallholder Agricultural Insurance.* Washington, DC: Consultative Group to Assist the Poor. https://www.cgap.org/research/publication/using-satellite-data-scale-smallholder-agricultural-insurance.

Jack, W., and T. Suri. 2014. "Risk Sharing and Transactions Costs: Evidence from Kenya's Mobile Money Revolution." *American Economic Review* 104 (1): 183–223.

Jagtiani, J., and C. Lemieux. 2017. "Fintech Lending: Financial Inclusion, Risk Pricing, and Alternative Information." Working Paper 17-17, Research Department, Federal Reserve Bank of Philadelphia.

Jakiela, P., and O. Ozier. 2016. "Does Africa Need a Rotten Kin Theorem? Experimental Evidence from Village Economies." Working paper, University of Maryland and World Bank, College Park, MD, and Washington, DC. http://pamjakiela.com/JakielaOzier-VillageEconomies-2015-06-04.pdf.

Jensen, N., A. Mude, and C. Barrett. 2018. "How Basis Risk and Spatiotemporal Adverse Selection Influence Demand for Index Insurance: Evidence from Northern Kenya." *Food Policy* 74: 172–98.

Kaffenberger, M., E. Totolo, and M. Soursourian. 2018. "A Digital Credit Revolution: Insights from Borrowers in Kenya and Tanzania." Consultative Group to Assist the Poor, Washington, DC. https://www.cgap.org/research/publication/digital-credit-revolution-insights-borrowers-kenya-and-tanzania.

Kanemasu, E. T. 1977. "Estimated Winter Wheat Yield from Crop Growth Predicted by Landsat." Report prepared by the Kansas Evapotranspiration Laboratory, Kansas State University, for the National Aeronautics and Space Administration.

Karlan, D., A. L. Ratan, and J. Zinman. 2014. "Savings by and for the Poor: A Research Review and Agenda." *Review of Income and Wealth* 60 (1): 36–78.

Lobell, D. B., G. Azzari, M. Burke, S. Gourlay, Z. Jin, T. Kilic, and S. Murray. 2018. *Eyes in the Sky, Boots on the Ground: Assessing Satellite- and Ground-Based Approaches to Crop Yield Measurement and Analysis in Uganda.* Washington, DC: World Bank.

Mahul, O., and C. Stutley. 2010. *Government Support to Agricultural Insurance: Challenges and Options for Developing Countries.* Washington, DC: World Bank.

Mercy Corps. 2017. "Digital Financial Services for Smallholder Farmers: What Data Can Financial Institutions Bank On?" Mercy Corps, November 10, 2017. http://mercycorpsagrifin.org/wpcontent/uploads/2018/01/Digital-Agro-Data-Edited_Final.pdf/.

Miranda, M., and K. Farrin. 2012. "Index Insurance for Developing Countries." *Applied Economic Perspectives and Policy* 34 (3): 391–427.

Monmonier, M. 2002. "Aerial Photography at the Agricultural Adjustment Administration: Acreage Controls, Conservation Benefits, and Overhead Surveillance in the 1930s." *Photogrammetric Engineering and Remote Sensing* 68 (12): 1257–62.

Mude, A. 2017. "The Role of Mobile Technologies in Promoting Sustainable Delivery of Livestock Insurance in the East African Drylands: Towards Sustainable Index-Based Livestock Insurance (IBLI) for Pastoralists." Paper presented at the Crawford Fund annual conference, "Transforming Lives and Livelihoods: The Digital Revolution in Agriculture," August 7–8, 2017, Canberra, Australia.

Puig Garcia, E., F. Gonzalez, G. Hamilton, and P. Grundy. 2015. "Assessment of Crop Insect Damage Using Unmanned Aerial Systems: A Machine Learning Approach." In *Proceedings of MOD- SIM2015, 21st International Congress on Modelling and Simulation,* edited by T. Weber, M. J. McPhee, and R. S. Anderssen, 1420–26. Canberra, Australia: Modelling and Simulation Society of Australia and New Zealand.

Radiant Earth 2018. "The View from Above." Radiant Earth Foundation, Washington, DC. https://www.radiant.earth/infographic/the-view-from-above/.

Rochemont, S. 2018. *A Cashless Society: Risks and Issues.* London: Institute and Faculty of Actuaries. https://www.actuaries.org.uk/system/files/field/document/Issue%2021-%20Environmental%20Sustainability%20of%20a%20Cashless%20Society%20-%20disc.pdf.

Silleos, N., K. Perakis, and G. Petsanis. 2002. "Assessment of Crop Damage Using Space Remote Sensing and GIS." *International Journal of Remote Sensing* 23 (3): 417–27. https://doi.org/10.1080/01431160110040026.

Smith, V. H., and J. W. Glauber. 2012. "Agricultural Insurance in Developed Countries: Where Have We Been and Where Are We Going?" *Applied Economic Perspectives and Policy* 34 (3): 363–90.

Stiglitz, J., and A. Weiss. 1981. "Credit Rationing in Markets with Incomplete Information." *American Economic Review* 71 (3): 393–410.

Suri, T., and P. Gubbins. 2018. "How Is Digital Credit Changing the Lives of Kenyans? Evidence from an Evaluation of the Impact of M-Shwari." Financial Sector Deepening (FSD) Kenya, Nairobi.

Tomkys, E., and S. Lombardini. 2015. *Going Digital: Using Digital Technology to Conduct Oxfam's Effectiveness Reviews.* Oxford, UK: Oxfam.

UNEP (United Nations Environment Programme). 2019. "Chinese Initiative Ant Forest Wins UN Champions of the Earth Award." Press Release, September 19. https://www.unenvironment.org/news-and-stories/press-release/chinese-initiative-ant-forest-wins-un-champions-earth-award.

Wei, Y., P. Yildirim, C. Van den Bulte, and C. Dellarocas. 2015. "Credit Scoring with Social Network Data Marketing." *Science* 35 (2): 234–58. http://dx.doi.org/10.1287/mksc.2015.0949.

World Bank. 2020. "World Development Indicators." World Bank, Washington, DC.

Zhou, J., M. J. Pavek, S. C. Shelton, Z. J. Holden, and S. Sankaran. 2016. "Aerial Multispectral Imaging for Crop Hail Damage Assessment in Potato." *Computers and Electronics in Agriculture* 127: 406–12.

CHAPTER FIVE

Transforming Agricultural Policies

KEY MESSAGES

- Agriculture policy can help maximize the potential of the agrifood system to achieve sustainable development objectives.
- Policy-related transaction costs can lead to the adoption of agricultural policies that result in inefficient and inequitable public resource allocations, which can also sometimes result in unsustainable environmental outcomes.
- Digital technologies can help agricultural policies improve the use of public funds and identify the most efficient options for achieving a given policy or service objective.
- Realizing the potential of digital technologies for agricultural policy design, delivery, and monitoring requires public investments in modern data infrastructure and human development, as well as an enabling regulatory framework for the use of digital technologies.

ROLE OF TRANSACTION COSTS IN AGRICULTURAL POLICIES

Governments provide support to their agricultural sectors for a range of reasons. Support can be aimed at, for example, ensuring an adequate level of farmer income or ensuring sufficient and affordable food supplies for the population. But governments may also target other objectives for the sector, including supporting the development of more competitive and innovative industries and, increasingly, ensuring environmentally sustainable production systems that are resilient to climate change and other risks.

Support to the agricultural sector globally is high. The 53 countries covered by the Organisation for Economic Co-operation and Development's (OECD's) *Agricultural Policy Monitoring and Evaluation 2019*—all OECD and European Union (EU) countries and 12 emerging economies—provided $705 billion in support to the sector in 2017–18, of which $528 billion a year was direct support to farmers (OECD 2019a). Yet at the same time, several emerging economies implicitly taxed their farmers through policies that artificially depressed prices, reducing farm revenues by $83 billion a year. Moreover, most of these transfers to and from producers, around 70 percent (although there are significant differences across countries), originated in measures that are particularly production- and trade-distorting, including by artificially keeping domestic farm prices above or below levels in global markets or using payments based on output quantities or on the unconstrained use of variable inputs. In contrast, only around $105 billion was spent on public goods and services for the sector, such as research and development, extension and training, biosecurity inspection services, and infrastructure, all of which are needed to equip the agricultural sector for future challenges.

While there has been some reform, many countries still provide the majority of support to agriculture through measures that distort production and trade and harm poorer households. Over the past 20 years, the level of support provided to farmers in many countries has fallen. Support provided to farmers is also more decoupled from production—meaning that many farmers no longer receive payments or higher prices for producing a specific commodity. Nevertheless, coupled policies such as market price support, output payments, and input subsidies remain widely used. Yet, as noted, these measures distort price signals faced by farmers and are poorly targeted and inefficient. For example, higher market prices disproportionally hurt poorer consumers by raising the price of food. This includes smallholder farmers, who may be net buyers of agricultural products. These highly distorting forms of support are also inefficient for raising farm incomes, compared with payments largely or fully decoupled from individual production decisions (Henderson and Lankoski 2019). Studies have also shown that output-based payments benefit commercial-sized farms more than smallholder farms, since payments are roughly proportional to a farm's expected revenue (Glauber, Sumner, and Wilde 2017). Some studies have also shown that policies that target specific commodities can have consequences for consumer choice and health. For example, a policy bias toward sugar, refined grains, and processed oils has had a negative impact on the health of low-income consumers and children (Wiggins and Keats 2014).

Domestic price supports, output payments, and subsidies for the unconstrained use of variable inputs can also have negative impacts on the sustainability of the sector. In OECD countries, coupled support policies not only distort trade flows and production decisions, they also have great potential to harm the environment (Henderson and Lankoski 2019). This is because the measures are contingent on production, and so they provide additional incentives to increase production; market price support and payments based on outputs can lead to more intensive use of inputs such as fertilizer and pesticides, while support for variable inputs without constraints increases the risk of their over- or misuse. And because measures often target specific commodities, they can reduce resilience and adaptation to climate change by encouraging farmers to plant specific crops, even if they are not well suited to changing local climate conditions (Jouanjean et al. 2020). In contrast, fully decoupled support measures are associated with the least environmental damage (Henderson and Lankoski 2019).

While the choice of policy instruments can be driven by political economy considerations, policy-related transaction costs may also lead governments to use second-best policy instruments. High policy-related transaction costs (PRTCs) may make it difficult for governments to use more efficient and effective policies to target farm households in need or stimulate improved agri-environmental outcomes. PRTCs are the costs governments incur in gathering information, planning, and designing policies, collecting revenue, and implementing, monitoring, and checking policy outcomes (figure 5.1). They occur in the interactions between and within government agencies, private organizations, and program participants. Costs incurred by farmers when transacting with the government—to obtain information on polices and claim benefits—are also PRTCs (OECD 2007). PRTCs can differ significantly across policies and affect the choice of policy instruments. The total size of PRTCs is positively correlated with high numbers of transactions, high numbers of interactions, and complex monitoring mechanisms. Yet more targeted policies—for example, aimed at specific policy objectives or beneficiaries—may not be preferred if implementation costs for governments and stakeholders (including farmers) are higher than those for untargeted ones.

PRTCs affect government policies in several ways. First, and perhaps most important, they can constrain the set of feasible policy alternatives, potentially limiting the scope of available policies or policy mechanisms, thus potentially precluding first-best options. Second, within the set of feasible alternatives, PRTCs can diminish the effectiveness or efficiency of policy implementation. This partially explains the difficulty some governments have in implementing new types of more targeted policies. For example, the use of results-based policies may not be possible where necessary monitoring information is prohibitively costly or technically impossible to collect. Third, a lack of information can cause moral hazard, as when governments are unable to know whether certain practices have actually been adopted by farmers before extending payments. Fourth, other activities that are not monitored might offset the expected results. Last, the government may be unable to obtain complete information about the impact of a policy on efficiency, equity, or environmental sustainability goals.

WHAT'S COOKING: DIGITAL TRANSFORMATION OF THE AGRIFOOD SYSTEM

FIGURE 5.1 Policy-related Transaction Costs for the Provision of Budgetary Payments

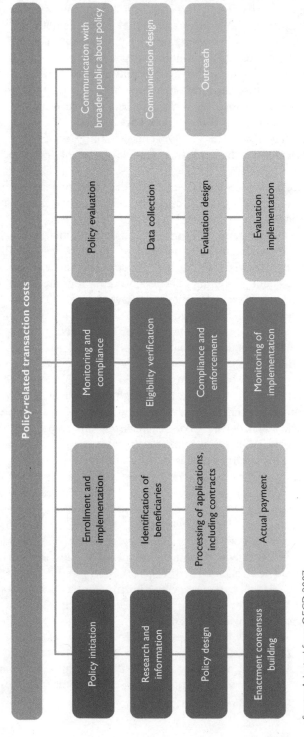

Policy-related transaction costs

Policy initiation	Enrollment and implementation	Monitoring and compliance	Policy evaluation	Communication with broader public about policy
Research and information	Identification of beneficiaries	Eligibility verification	Data collection	Communication design
Policy design	Processing of applications, including contracts	Compliance and enforcement	Evaluation design	Outreach
Enactment consensus building	Actual payment	Monitoring of implementation	Evaluation implementation	

Source: Adapted from OECD 2007.

Note: Differently colored cells contain policy-related transaction costs that are expected to differ across policies.

DIGITAL OPPORTUNITIES FOR REDUCING TRANSACTION COSTS IN AGRICULTURAL POLICIES

Digital technologies can lower these PRTCs, enabling governments to deliver more efficient and equitable support to the agricultural sector and to improve environmental outcomes. While some first-best policy options may not have been feasible in the past, this could change with technological and institutional innovation. The volume and speed of generating and transmitting data about various aspects of the agrifood system can change the calculation of which policy options are the most effective and efficient. These opportunities exist in all phases of the policy-making cycle where missing information and information asymmetries shape the options available to policy makers. (Figure 5.2 offers a representation of the phases of designing, implementing, and evaluating agricultural policy.). Digital technologies can help improve implementation of existing policies and enable new policy approaches with more targeted policy design. In both cases, they can support the more efficient and effective use of public funds.

Governments can also develop more effective policies informed by data—either by making better use of their existing data or by drawing on new sources of data. Government use of digital technologies is not new: for example, governments have been using Landsat data to monitor agricultural production since the 1970s (Leslie, Serbina, and Miller 2017). However, advances in digital technologies have increased the spatial and temporal resolution of agricultural data and the capacity to merge and process large datasets. Policy makers and administrators can make use of this new capacity: for example, higher quality data from remote sensors can be used to monitor important changes in production conditions, while in-situ sensors can enable automated measurement of many aspects of agricultural production. Access to this more granular information can, in turn, inform and enhance policy making across the policy cycle.

Policy Design and Enrollment

The greater availability of data may reduce the transaction costs associated with policy design. Agricultural policy design requires an understanding of complex relationships in the agrifood system, among stakeholders as well as between producers and ecosystems. Choosing the best mechanism to achieve any given policy objectives also requires assessing the likely costs (for both the public sector and farmers) and impacts of different policy options. For example, a voluntary scheme that imposes a large administrative burden on farmers is unlikely to see wide adoption. Access to better data can allow policy makers to use more holistic models to set realistic, measurable goals that better account for the spatial heterogeneity of agricultural production and the complex interactions among various stakeholders. Data analysis and models can also be used to integrate goals of efficiency, equity, and environmental sustainability.

Digital technologies can support the transition from pay-for-practice to results-based policies. Many agrienvironmental policies pay farmers to

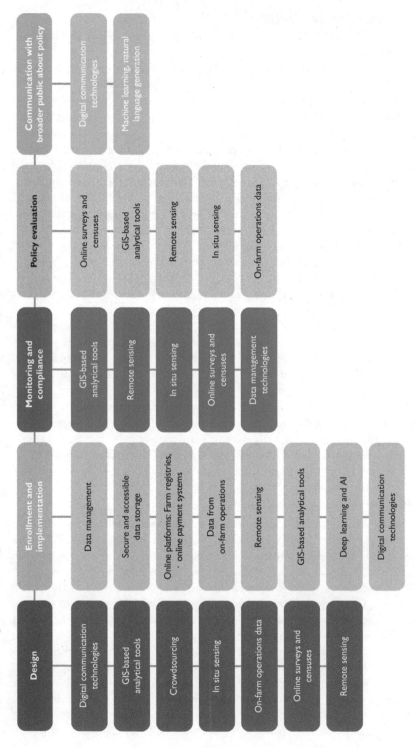

FIGURE 5.2 Digital Technologies Can Reduce Transaction Costs along the Policy Cycle

Design	Enrollment and implementation	Monitoring and compliance	Policy evaluation	Communication with broader public about policy
Digital communication technologies	Data management	GIS-based analytical tools	Online surveys and censuses	Digital communication technologies
GIS-based analytical tools	Secure and accessible data storage	Remote sensing	GIS-based analytical tools	Machine learning, natural language generation
Crowdsourcing	Online platforms: Farm registries, online payment systems	In situ sensing	Remote sensing	
In situ sensing	Data from on-farm operations	Online surveys and censuses	In situ sensing	
On-farm operations data	Remote sensing	Data management technologies	On-farm operations data	
Online surveys and censuses	GIS-based analytical tools			
Remote sensing	Deep learning and AI			
	Digital communication technologies			

Source: Adapted from OECD 2019b.

Note: The phases in the policy cycle are set out linearly, acknowledging that the phases and their ordering for a particular policy will depend on context. The emphasis here is on the usefulness of digital technologies in each phase. AI = artificial intelligence; GIS = geographic information system.

implement practices linked to producing environmental services. Such pay-for-practice policies are considered less efficient and targeted than results-based policies, which reward producers directly for specific environmental outcomes and leave producers free to choose the best means to achieve them given their circumstances (Burton and Schwarz 2013; Savage and Ribaudo 2016; Shortle et al. 2012). For example, results-based policies governing water access and use linked to river, aquifer, or storage levels can be enabled by sensors and advanced models. That said, many policies that pay based on some kind of outcome or performance measure are still, in most cases, based on modeled results rather than direct measurement of results achieved. While sensors offer one measurement option, investing in better models leveraging the increased availability of data and the capacity to combine data from different sources can also be important.

Policy design and initial outreach and enrollment can be enriched and facilitated by improved communication with stakeholders, enabled by digital technologies. Those technologies can facilitate both the outreach and enrollment phases of policy implementation—helping to organize stakeholders who may be in different physical locations and who have limited time to contribute and communicate about policies and programs (Picazo-Vela, Gutiérrez-Martínez, and Luna-Reyes 2012). Digital technologies can lower information search costs and increase program participation, allowing for multidirectional communications among stakeholders and improving public awareness about proposed programs (OECD 2019b).

Policy Implementation

Digital technologies may also help streamline and automate administrative processes and enhance regulatory transparency. Policy implementation can involve a range of different activities and processes, depending on the specific policy mechanism, a number of which can be facilitated by digital technologies, including, for example, executing contracts, administering tradable permits, and administering digital payments to eligible farmers (box 5.1).

Government digital platforms, such as farmer registries, can support farmer identification and verification, streamline the administration of state support payments, facilitate farmer access to services, and reduce the cost and effort of data collection (CTA 2019). Digital registries, developed around a unique digital ID, can help farmers formally register their land and livestock and track the creation or registration of property rights and subsequent changes in ownership and location as trades take place and, as a result, create opportunities for them to access mobile, financial, and other services (World Bank 2018). For example, using detailed farmer registries, including global positioning system coordinates of fields, can provide assurances to financial service providers that they are basing their credit decisions on an accurate understanding of the situation of the smallholder farmers with whom they are working (CTA 2019). Information collected from farmer registries can also provide governments with the necessary data to tailor extension services to farmers' needs,

Digitizing policy-related payments in agriculture yields three main types of benefits: reductions in leakages, in fraudulent payments, and in the costs of payment processing within government. Many countries have digitized social transfers, but digitizing payments related to agricultural policy is in a fairly early stage. Digitizing such payments is producing substantial benefits in some countries.

Colombia. In 2007, the Colombian Coffee Growers Federation, responsible for delivery of government payments to coffee growers, started the transition to digital payments. A tender to offer digital payment services was won by Banco de Bogotá, which introduced the Cédula Cafetera Inteligente (or the Coffee Smart ID Card, referred to here as the Cédula). By June 2013, 82 percent of coffee growers had a Smart ID card, enabling them to withdraw benefits from automated teller machines (ATMs) and special point of sale (POS) devices at coffee purchase points and rural merchants. In 2014, the Cédula was relaunched as a full savings account with access to all ATM and POS devices through a personalized prepaid card with a magnetic stripe and chip.

Between 2007 and 2013, the Cédula program served more than 15 subsidy programs, disbursing $740 million in 5.3 million transactions. The growers' federation reduced costs by up to 79 percent relative to cash delivery, saving $15.5 million. (The cost of Cédula between 2007 and 2013 was $4.1 million. Cash disbursements would have cost $19.6 million, and check disbursements $13.6 million.) The cards and the supplementary database of farmers and their farms allowed the disbursement of subsidies to be better targeted, increasing efficiency, transparency, speed, and security. The system also reduced leakage from fraudulent subsidy claims and was also used for other government programs, in part because it guaranteed traceability and transparency for the disbursement of government funds. The Cédula ensured that more money reached farmers both by eliminating leakages and by replacing the checks that some farmers were cashing at a discount of up to 5 percent of the value.

Estonia. In 1994, the government implemented an innovative e-governance policy. Today 99 percent of public services are available online 24/7, allowing residents with an electronic identification (e-ID) to access public and private services and transactions. Online identity verification and authentication is provided through X-Road. Together e-ID and X-Road are the backbone of e-Estonia. Estonian farmers can access their agricultural state support payments using their e-ID and the X-Road infrastructure. Farmers apply for these subsidies online using data they have already provided to the government. Based on the data and digital infrastructure, mobile applications have been developed for farm management, such as VitalFields, eAgronom, and Terake.eu. Use of these apps has substantially reduced the amount of time farmers spend on paperwork and automates compliance reporting to the payment agency. Filling in paper forms at the Estonian Agricultural Registries and Information Board previously took 300 minutes; this has now declined to 45 minutes for an online application. Developing an accountable and accessible e-service

(Continued)

environment benefited from clear and established legal parameters for personal information privacy, an independent enforcement mechanism for these parameters, and one of the highest internet penetration rates in the world.

Nigeria. In November 2011, the Federal Ministry of Agriculture and Rural Development enacted the Growth Enhancement Support (GES) scheme to launch a pilot to transition the provision of vouchers for fertilizer subsidies to electronic wallets using mobile phones (USAID 2016, 57). The government's role changed from direct procurement and distribution of fertilizer to facilitating the procurement, regulation of quality, and promotion of private-sector fertilizer value chains (Grossman and Tarazi 2014, 6).

Under the scheme, state and local government officials registered eligible smallholders. After farmers manually completed a machine-readable form, their data were added to a national database and farmers were issued a GES ID number. The scheme assigned farmers a subsidy credit associated with their GES ID number; no funds are transferred to the farmer. Instead, farmers visited their local agrodealer redemption center to purchase their inputs.

In 2014, under the second phase of the GES, the ministry partnered with the National Identity Management Commission to capture the biometrics of all farmers and issue them national identification numbers and cards (USAID 2016, 57). Their IDs were tied to a basic account with the Bank of Agriculture, enabling them to save and to access credit, insurance, and other agricultural financial services (Senyo 2015).

The scheme registered more than 12 million farmers in its first three years, increasing the proportion of farmers benefiting from 11 percent to 92 percent. In 2014, 7.2 million farmers received a total subsidy transfer of $420 million on their mobile phones. The government reported saving $192 million in 2012 through GES disbursements (GSMA Intelligence 2016, 37). The mobile phone e-vouchers saw the subsidy cost per farmer drop by more than 80 percent from 2011 to 2012 (Grossman and Tarazi 2014, 7–8).

Still, some challenges remain, related to poor mobile network connectivity in rural areas and lack of airtime to process redemptions. Registration has not been fully automated, which has caused delays between registration and validation of eligibility.

help promote the development of customized farm inputs, and strengthen value chains through increased traceability and transparency. In addition, well-designed farmer registries can provide a better understanding of agricultural policy impacts on women, youth, and other marginalized groups. As a result, by increasing transparency about policy administration and encouraging multidirectional communication, registries can increase trust between parties. But for the farm registries to achieve these goals, several principles need to be taken into account during their design (box 5.2).

The European Union (EU) provides a comprehensive policy framework and significant financial resources to its agriculture and rural development sectors. Upon joining the EU, the member states must adhere to Common Agricultural Policy (CAP), subordinating their national agricultural policies under the common goals and strategies. That said, while the CAP provides a common framework, it also provides the EU member states with freedom to choose among a wide range of CAP policy instruments.

To ensure transparency in administration, control, and execution of agriculture and rural development support schemes, EU member states are tasked with establishing an integrated administration and control system (IACS). In physical terms, IACS consists of a number of computerized and interconnected databases. The interconnected databases include information on farmers and farms, the land registry, payment entitlements, and an animal registry. The three main databases are (1) the Farm Registry, (2) the Land Parcel Identification System (LPIS), and (3) the Animal Registry. These databases enable effective and efficient processing of agriculture support applications, carry out administrative controls, facilitate the selection of physical on-the-spot controls, and calculate subsidies, which are then accounted and executed by the paying agency. In practice, based on the experience of recent accessions to the EU, new member states required three to five years to develop a fully operational IACS with its integral components. Within the three databases, the LPIS is the most demanding, but experience shows that starting with the Farm Registry brings the greatest benefit. Overall, the challenge lies in defining the software programs that administer and control the payments, and thereby ensuring efficient and proper use of EU—and possibly also national—funds.

Experiences from EU member states reveal that a well-integrated Farm Registry is needed to effectively leverage, mobilize, and absorb EU funds. Overall, the key determinants of an effective Farm Register are the following:

Timeliness in information technology development, in particular making sure that the concerned administration prioritizes the development of the Farm Registry over other IACS databases, has positive implications, and limits the burden on the national budget.

Simplicity by limiting the amount of data in the Farm Registry to core data on farm and business units and their managers has a positive impact on active participation by farmers while also reducing the transaction costs during the preparation, submission, and processing of data for the administration.

(Continued)

BOX 5.2 Good Practices for the Establishment of Farm Registries
for Administration of Agriculture Support: Experiences
from EU Member States *(Continued)*

Selectivity and coherence in early definition of the farm size population increases the effectiveness of the Farm Registry, while at the same time providing sufficient space for a broadened farm population and data that has proved to be effective.

Accessibility to the Farm Registry has positive spillovers, as the exchange of data with other public institutions enables verification, limits additional bureaucracy for farmers, and increases the overall effectiveness of public administration.

The data in the Farm Registry should facilitate communication between public entities and farm holdings, build the interface to other databases, and also provide more transparency. Minimum contents of a Farm Registry should include the following:

- *Name of beneficiary:* the farmer (natural person), full names in case of married couple, or name of legal entity
- *Type of beneficiary:* the legal status of the beneficiary, which could be a natural person, married couple, or legal entity (various forms)
- *Unique digital ID:* the unique number assigned to the beneficiary (farm/business unit), which follows different logics depending on the member state (see subsequent chapter)
- *Address of farm:* the physical address where the farm/business unit is located
- *Bank account details:* included in the Farm Registry, as all agriculture support payments have to be traceable and, thus, no cash payments are permitted
- *Contact information:* information on means of communicating with the beneficiary (such as email address, phone number)
- *Information on other farms:* other farms (separate ID number, address) that are managed by the same beneficiary, as IACS foresees that only one application can be submitted by the beneficiary for the total number of farms (holding)

The development of a Farm Registry has several benefits. The data included in the Farm Registry should enable governments to communicate with farmers, especially in order to (1) facilitate statistical surveys (census), (2) manage and carry out payments of agricultural support measures, (3) react and respond quickly in case of animal- and foodborne diseases, and (4) monitor the impact of policies and strategies. In the case of Austria, the IACS Farm Registry was established upon accession to the EU in 1995, while the Statistical Agency had already had a Farm Registry since 1970. The many interfaces that the Farm Registry may have can enable cross-checks with other data sources (figure B5.2.1).

(Continued)

FIGURE B5.2.1 Umbrella Farm Register in Austria

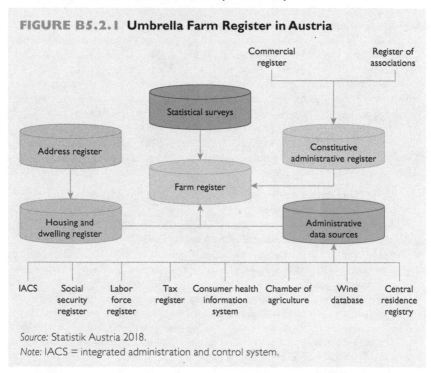

Source: Statistik Austria 2018.
Note: IACS = integrated administration and control system.

Better access to data allows policy administrators to implement more targeted and flexible policies. Improved data are helping policy makers to better understand farmer incomes and activities and the environmental impacts of agriculture. They are also helping policy makers to target specific beneficiaries and objectives, enabling more equitable and environmentally sustainable outcomes. For example, by making use of more granular datasets, the objectives of policy programs can be refined to better account for spatial heterogeneity in the environmental and productivity performance of agriculture, enabling closer tailoring of policies to different conditions across a country. Digital technologies are also enabling policies to operate at a landscape scale through, for example, collective governance mechanisms, wherein policy administrators deal with groups of farmers and other stakeholders, rather than individuals.

Policy Monitoring and Compliance

Policy makers can use digital technologies to improve policy monitoring and compliance systems. One objective of agriculture policies is to realign farmers' incentives so that public goods are taken into account in production decisions.

Some agricultural policies actively seek to alter farmer behavior, usually through regulatory or market-based mechanisms, introducing conditional penalties or rewards that are intended to be dependent on farmers' own actions. In particular, governments can use digital technologies to rethink monitoring and compliance systems and reduce associated costs, enabling more efficient implementation. Monitoring many policies relies on on-the-spot controls, usually based on random checks of a certain percentage of stakeholders. Now, digital automation of compliance, controls, and payments can reduce the burden for producers and the public costs of administering, monitoring, and ensuring compliance with policy. Data from remote sensing, digital data from precision agriculture, and automation algorithms are some of the most promising technologies for improving the efficiency of monitoring and compliance in agriculture (Nikkilä et al. 2012).

Remote sensing could enable 100 percent checks, while reducing costs. For example, under the EU CAP for 2014–20, national payment agencies are required to perform yearly on-the-spot checks for at least 5 percent of beneficiaries. Under the new CAP, administrators will move toward new "data intensive" compliance approaches based on high rates of remote monitoring (near 100 percent) (Devos et al. 2017). In addition to increasing coverage, remote sensing–based spot checks can also drastically reduce the administrative costs associated with policy monitoring. One study showed that use of satellite data to monitor land conversion under the US water quality trading program reduced an administrator's time commitment from 10 hours for on-site visits to 15 minutes (DeBoe and Stephenson 2016).

Digital technologies could shift from penalty-based systems to positive support mechanisms. The possibility offered by technology for high-rate monitoring (near 100 percent) can also change the approach to compliance more fundamentally. Today, governments incentivize farmers to comply with many policies through a system of penalties on those found to be noncompliant, which requires the consequences of noncompliance to be high enough to deter actors from cheating even when they might not be checked regularly. Digital technologies open new approaches that can allow farmers to be rewarded for going beyond compliance rather than relying on heavy penalties. They can also support the targeting of other government services, such as extension services for farmers struggling to comply with policies.

Policy Evaluation

Digital technology can assist in creating and maintaining the knowledge base for policy evaluation. Policies implemented and monitored through digital technologies can also be periodically evaluated and recalibrated more easily and at lower cost. For example, combining administrative data with farm performance data can better evaluate current policies and assist in future policy planning. In addition, digital technologies can foster collaboration among relevant actors to ensure that evaluation takes into account both qualitative and quantitative feedback on policies (OECD 2019b).

Policy Communication

Policy communication with a broader audience can help improve trust between the general public and policy makers, increase participation by different stakeholders in policy discussions, and foster positive stewardship narratives for agriculture. By increasing transparency about policy administration and encouraging multidirectional communication, digital communication technologies can also help overcome issues arising from a lack of trust among parties, often resulting from information asymmetries. Use of web-based technologies may also allow for increased participation in policy making by different stakeholders simply by fostering awareness of policies and opportunities to become involved (OECD 2019b). Finally, communications technologies and high-resolution agricultural data can also improve farmers' awareness of environmental issues and their contribution to them. Overall, by increasing transparency on compliance and on policy impacts, digital communication tools can support better engagement by farmers. Digitally enabled results-based policies could thus be an opportunity to improve program participation and foster a community approach to improving agriculture's environmental performance.

KEY BARRIERS, RISKS, AND IMPLEMENTATION CONSIDERATIONS

While use of digital technologies and data to improve agricultural policies is increasing, further opportunities exist. In 2018, the OECD developed a questionnaire to take stock of the actual and planned use of digital technologies for agrienvironmental policies by public agencies in its member countries (figure 5.3) (OECD 2019b). The results show that government agencies are already using some digital technologies, but their use is often ad hoc, and the decision to adopt digital solutions is taken at the level of individual policies or programs. In general, the prevalence of digital technologies is still rather low. Policy administrators use the same data sources and digital technologies as civil society: general purpose digital communications technologies, including social media and web-based video conferencing. The use of remote sensing data, digital data visualization technologies, and GIS-based analytical tools is still sporadic, but increasing.

While governments see great potential in digital technologies, use remains limited to certain policy areas. Almost all entities responding to the OECD questionnaire considered that digital technologies could improve communications with other government bodies and with producers, facilitate new programs and services, and reduce organizational costs. The most common policy areas using digital technologies were water quality and biodiversity, with the most common mechanisms being extension services, information provision, and agrienvironmental payments or subsidies. The intensity of technology seemed to vary with specific applications. For example, environmental taxes are more technology intensive than trading schemes (environmental markets).

FIGURE 5.3 Digital Technologies Currently Used in the Policy Cycle

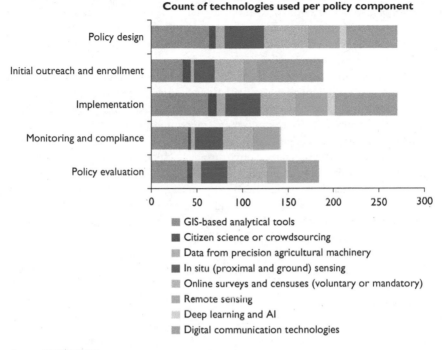

Count of technologies used per policy component

Legend:
- GIS-based analytical tools
- Citizen science or crowdsourcing
- Data from precision agricultural machinery
- In situ (proximal and ground) sensing
- Online surveys and censuses (voluntary or mandatory)
- Remote sensing
- Deep learning and AI
- Digital communication technologies

Source: OECD 2019b.
Note: AI = artificial intelligence; GIS = geographic information system.

GIS-based analytical tools, digital communication tools, and online surveys or censuses are used more intensively for administering economic instruments (environmental property rights, environmental taxes, agrienvironmental payments, or environmental markets) than for regulatory instruments (activity prohibitions or environmental standards).

Policy makers and program administrators face a range of challenges that can affect the successful uptake of digital technologies. Institutional rigidities can constrain government bodies from adopting new policy methods and approaches using digital technologies. More broadly, governments' digital transformation—and indeed, the digital transformation of the agricultural sector—must unfold consistently with objectives of security, privacy, confidentiality, and intellectual property protection. Resource constraints for up-front investments are also a significant issue, notably in the context of lower connectivity in rural areas.

Barriers

Migration to digital technologies requires up-front and maintenance costs for infrastructure and personnel. The cost of the transition—including setting up and maintaining new digital infrastructure, both hardware and software, as well as investments in hiring and retraining staff—can affect the incentive and ability of government bodies to adopt digital technologies. Workflows can also be disrupted in going digital, requiring time and effort to steer adjustments to new systems. The benefits of such potential investments may also not be obvious at first or easy to quantify.

Migration to digital technologies can also be constrained by institutional and technical path dependencies. Path dependency is likely to be an obstacle for the agricultural community to move toward a more data-intensive policy. Both procedural and substantial requirements of regulations may reflect preexisting levels of technological feasibility. The adoption of new technologies might require adapting the regulatory environment, which can take time. Moreover, policy makers may find it difficult to build consensus around new concepts, processes, standards, and parameters relevant for agricultural policy. Enabling digital innovation in, and through, policy design also depends on the interoperability of digital systems and data standards, to be able to combine data generated on-farm or by other entities with data from multiple sources. Achieving such technical interoperability can also entail significant organizational challenges and investments and require overcoming technical path dependencies.

Risks

Digital technologies in the policy space can risk exclusion for those who cannot access them. In assessing whether digital technologies can lead to more efficient policies, governments need to be mindful of creating new divides between those who can use digital tools and those who cannot. This is first a question of hard infrastructure for digital connectivity. Different broadband coverage creates disparities among regions and their capacity to participate in digitally enabled agricultural schemes. Investment in infrastructure is essential, as is creating tools and applications that can be used off-line. But the risk of a divide arises also where new digitally enabled policy designs rely on the monitoring and tracking of activities on-farm that require farmers (and other stakeholders) to adopt certain technologies in order to be able to demonstrate compliance. While this could have positive spillover effects by stimulating uptake of digital tools in the sector, if participation in certain regulatory schemes is mandatory, it could also create an additional burden for regulated actors, forcing investments, not only in new equipment, but also in training for acquiring the skills to use these technologies. Governments should recognize the risks of a digital divide when adopting and designing digitally enabled policies, ensuring that technology adoption does not become a force for exclusion. One important way to mitigate the risks is for governments to involve stakeholders early in the policy process.

Implementation Considerations

Digital technologies need to be applied transparently. From an organizational perspective, policies and policy designs that integrate digital technologies should continue to be transparent and accountable, especially where decisions rely on algorithms (as for agricultural payments related to damages from a natural disaster). All stakeholders should understand the results of algorithms that affect them. Regulators should oversee the development and implementation of such algorithms, guaranteeing that they suit their purpose and putting safeguards in place to avoid unintended outcomes (as with the right to appeal and the access to remedies).

Agriculture policy makers and administrators should be aware of how other policy and regulatory domains may affect the use of digital technologies in agriculture. This means looking into policy domains beyond agriculture ministries and agencies. For example, the use of drones might not be possible if the flying zones are too restrictive. Using technologies to gather and assess monitoring data might require a registration and testing phase, delaying their operation—a particular issue given the fast pace of innovation in the digital era.

Increased use of digital technologies for agricultural policies and service provision will require a sound data governance framework to ensure trust in the system. Guarantees against misuse of data are key to the "social license" for collecting the data needed for new approaches to agricultural policy. If the government is too intrusive or confidentiality is not maintained, the trust and buy-in of producers and other stakeholders may be jeopardized. Data breaches are also increasingly a concern for farmers and other agrifood actors who fear their data may be accessed without their permission. As governments move toward the digital collection and storage of information, it will be important to invest in data security measures and maintain high security standards that reflect evolving technological capabilities.

Regulators need to strike the right balance between protecting the privacy and confidentiality of data and making it possible to leverage the potential of data for the sector's growth and innovation. Resistance to data sharing in some agricultural communities, as well as existing regulatory setups, may hamper the use of digital technologies and data by policy administrators. The extent to which governments can make use of digital technologies and data for agricultural policy will depend on data policies, which shape the ability of all stakeholders to access, share, and reuse data. Governments also need to invest in appropriate data security measures and support inclusive communication and processes around regulations to stimulate trust in the system. For example, agricultural censuses and surveys conducted by or on behalf of government agencies often contain strict confidentially requirements that limit the ability of agencies to combine them with data from other sources or share with policy researchers. Amending existing confidentiality obligations or devising new ways for different government agencies and researchers to share data can improve access to agricultural data and unleash their potential for policy design and use. Technological advances in data encryption and decentralized management systems might also represent potential solutions to some of these issues.

To realize the potential of digital technologies for agricultural policies, governments must also consider the wider enabling environment for digitalization.

The broader data infrastructure—including hard infrastructure and the digital and institutional structures enabling and governing the collection, transfer, storage, and processing of agricultural data to produce knowledge and advice—influence how digital technologies can be used throughout the policy cycle and by agricultural stakeholders more widely. Addressing these issues will require a whole-of-government approach, and policy makers must ensure that agricultural stakeholders have a voice in these broader digital policy discussions, given the importance of digital technologies for the sector.

REFERENCES

Burton, R., and G. Schwarz. 2013. "Result-oriented Agri-environment Schemes in Europe and Their Potential for Promoting Behavioural Change." *Land Use Policy* 30 (1): 628–41.

CTA (Technical Center for Agriculture and Rural Cooperation). 2019. *The Digitalization of African Agriculture Report.* Wageningen, the Netherlands: CTA. https://doi.org/10.1093/oxfordjournals.afraf.a094187.

DeBoe, G., and K. Stephenson. 2016. "Transactions Costs of Expanding Nutrient Trading to Agricultural Working Lands: A Virginia Case Study." *Ecological Economics* 130 (C): 176–85.

Devos, W., D. Fasbender, G. Lemoine, P. Loudjani, P. Milenov, and C. Wirnhardt. 2017. "Discussion Document on the Introduction of Monitoring to Substitute OTSC." JRC Technical Reports, European Commission, Brussels.

Glauber, J., D. Sumner, and P. Wilde. 2017. "Poverty, Hunger, and US Agricultural Policy: Do Farm Programs Affect the Nutrition of Poor Americans?" American Enterprise Institute, Washington, DC.

Grossman, J., and M. Tarazi. 2014. "Serving Smallholder Farmers: Recent Developments in Digital Finance." Focus Note 94, Consultative Group to Assist the Poorest, Washington, DC.

GSMA Intelligence. 2016. *Market Size and Opportunity in Digitizing Payments in Agricultural Value Chains.* London: GSMA.

Henderson, B., and J. Lankoski. 2019. "Evaluating the Environmental Impact of Agricultural Policies." OECD Food, Agriculture, and Fisheries Papers 130, Organisation for Economic Co-operation and Development, Paris.

Jouanjean, M.-A., F. Casaline, L. Wiseman, and E Gray. 2020. "Issues around Data Governance in the Digital Transformation of Agriculture: The Farmers' Perspective." OECD Food, Agriculture and Fisheries Papers 146, Organisation for Economic Co-operation and Development, Paris. https://doi.org/10.1787/53ecf2ab-en.

Leslie, C., L. Serbina, and H. Miller. 2017. "Landsat and Agriculture: Case Studies on the Uses and Benefits of Landsat Imagery in Agricultural Monitoring and Production." US Geological Survey, Reston, VA.

Nikkilä, R., J. Wiebensoh, E. Nash, I. Seilonen, and K. Koskinen. 2012. "A Service Infrastructure for the Representation, Discovery, Distribution and Evaluation of Agricultural Production Standards for Automated Compliance Control." *Computers and Electronics in Agriculture* 80: 80–88. https://doi.org/10.1016/j.compag.2011.10.011.

OECD (Organisation for Economic Co-operation and Development). 2007. *The Implementation Costs of Agricultural Policies.* Paris: OECD.

OECD. 2019a. *Agricultural Policy Monitoring and Evaluation 2019.* Paris: OECD.

OECD. 2019b. *Digital Opportunities for Better Agricultural Policies*. Paris: OECD.

Picazo-Vela, S., I. Gutiérrez-Martínez, and L. F. Luna-Reyes. 2012. "Understanding Risks, Benefits, and Strategic Alternatives of Social Media Applications in the Public Sector." *Government Information Quarterly* 29 (4): 504–11.

Savage, J., and M. Ribaudo. 2016. "Improving the Efficiency of Voluntary Water Quality Conservation Programs." *Land Economics* 92 (1): 148–66.

Senyo, I. 2015. "Kogi Govt Accredits over 145,000 Rural Farmers for NAPI Loans." *World Stage*. June 21, 2015. http://www.worldstagegroup.com/worldstagenew/index.php?active =news&newscid=22955&catid=36Shortle et al. 2012.

Shortle, James S., Marc Ribaudo, Richard D. Horan, and David Blandford. 2012. "Reforming Agricultural Nonpoint Pollution Policy in an Increasingly Budget-Constrained Environment." *Environmental Science and Technology* 46 (3): 1316–25. https://doi .org/10.1021/es2020499.

Statistik Austria. 2018. "Agricultural and Forestry Register." Database. http://www.statistik .at/web_en/statistics/Economy/agriculture_and_forestry/agricultural_and_forestry _register/index.html.

USAID (United States Agency for International Development). 2016. *Guide to the Use of Digital Financial Services in Agriculture*. Washington, DC: USAID.

Wiggins, S., and S. Keats. 2014. "Future Diets: Under- and Over-Nutrition in Developing Countries." Commonwealth Health Partnerships, Cambridge, UK. http://www.common wealthhealth.org/wp-content/uploads/2014/05/6-Future-diets-Wiggins-.pdf.

World Bank. 2018. *The Role of Digital Identification in Agriculture: Emerging Applications*. Washington, DC: World Bank.

PART THREE

Securing Gains from the Digital Transformation of the Agrifood System

CHAPTER SIX

Data's Possibilities and Risks

KEY MESSAGES

- Massive amounts of data are now relevant to and generated in the agrifood system.
- Through digital technologies, these data can be processed and analyzed to increase production efficiency, support more equitable access to markets, and incentivize sustainable practices.
- Realizing the full potential of these data requires building trust in the collection, sharing, utilization, and governance of the data.

DATA'S PROMISE FOR DIGITAL TRANSFORMATION OF THE AGRIFOOD SYSTEM

Access to data enables innovation in the digital agrifood system and offers the benefits of greater efficiency, enhanced equity, and improved environmental sustainability. As discussed in chapter 1, it is the ability to collect, use, and analyze massive amounts of machine-readable data about practically every aspect of the agrifood system that holds the promise of its transformation. Unlocking the potential of data, however, depends on the level of access available to various stakeholders in the agrifood system. In this chapter, we discuss the importance of data for enabling innovations in the digital agrifood system, with a particular focus on open data (box 6.1) as well as data-related challenges to achieving efficient, equitable, and environmentally sustainable outcomes with particular attention to open data.

BOX 6.1 Open Data Definition

Data are open if "they can be freely used, modified, and shared by anyone for any purpose" (Open Knowledge Foundation n.d.). But they must be legally and technically open (World Bank n.d.):

- Data are legally open if they have been placed in the public domain or are under liberal terms of use with minimal restrictions.
- Data are technically open if they are published in electronic formats that are machine readable and nonproprietary, enabling anyone to access and use them with freely available software. The data must also be publicly available, without password or firewall restrictions.

Legally and technically unrestricted access to data (that is, open data) can generate large financial benefits for the economy as a whole. The private sector benefits because open data facilitate skill sharing to increase workers' productivity and boost productivity by providing benchmarks, market data, and best practice information. Open data can also generate efficiency gains for the economy. For example, the US government, which does not charge for Landsat data, generated an estimated benefit of about $1.8 billion for users, thanks to the 2.38 million images they downloaded (Loomis et al. 2015). McKinsey Global Institute analyzed the economic potential of open data across seven sectors: education, transportation, consumer products, electricity, oil and gas, health care, and consumer finance. It estimated the value added enabled by the use of open data across these seven sectors at $3 trillion (Manyika et al. 2013).

Access to data, particularly open data, can enhance the efficiency of public sector support for the food system, at a time when more than a half trillion dollars are invested annually in countries tracked by the Organisation for Economic Co-operation and Development (OECD). Open data are sharable between different public agencies, improving the performance of public processes and increasing the efficiency of providing public services. Greater transparency also improves the accountability of public officials. Open data can make information about sectoral progress toward targets and best practices more transparent, prompting behavioral change by producers, regulators, and consumers in agrifood chains. In 2020, the EU28 are expected to save €1.7 billion in public administration costs thanks to the use of open data (European Data Portal 2020). Open data can also encourage innovative public service delivery—nongovernmental organizations and public agencies could use open data to develop new mobile applications to better serve the population (Ubaldi 2013). Data from farmers can be used to promote food safety and sustainable production and better land use (Maru et al. 2018). And data from downstream and upstream in the value chain can lead to a more efficient and targeted response to epidemics, better environmental protection, and more accurate market monitoring (European Commission 2018).

Access to data also supports innovation and entrepreneurship. Better access to data on weather, commodity prices, and agronomic research can be transformed by digital technologies to provide innovative solutions for farmers and other actors along the value chain. For example, the Global Agricultural Trial Repository (AgTrials) compiles and makes public information on agronomic and plant breeding trials. Scientists have used 250 AgTrials open datasets to build West Africa–specific crop models to predict the local impacts of climate change and to adapt breeding practices accordingly (Open Data Institute 2015). Business-to-business data sharing also stimulates innovation. For example, raw data from internet of things (IoT) devices could be less costly for IoT providers and thus more suitable for sharing with start-ups in a precompetitive space. In addition, having free access to data greatly reduces production costs and the riskiness of business for start-ups, a savings that encourages them to innovate. There is evidence that start-ups relying on open data attract more investors than their competitors (Iyengar and Bergemann 2018).

Access to data could improve the efficiency of farms and of firms up and down the value chain. Firms can learn about customer preferences and tailor their products accordingly. One study found that firms using big data are 3–6 percent more productive and experience higher returns on equity than firms that do not (Brynjolfsson, Hitt, and Kim 2011). Open data integrated with tracing systems can also increase transparency and accountability in food systems. Tracing systems integrated with public systems alert consumers over digital platforms and speed product recalls when food hazards are discovered (Potter et al. 2012). Traceability, as a part of food safety systems, limits costly outbreaks of foodborne illnesses (Hoffmann, Batz, and Morris 2012) and reduces the financial and reputational risks tainted food pose to grocery stores and fast food restaurants (Antle 1999; Hammoudi, Hoffman, and Surry 2009). Finally, open data on weather patterns can improve on-farm decision-making. For example, the Aclímate Colombia project—led by the International Center for Tropical Agriculture with private sector industry groups and government actors participating—uses open data sources to extend information to farmers on how to navigate shifting weather patterns due to climate change. It has accelerated knowledge transfer from research centers to the field. Farmers receive site-specific temperature data to maximize rice yields and support banana planting decision-making, rainfall frequency data to increase irrigation efficiency, and solar radiation information to improve rice ripening. The improvements to farmers' decision-making led to estimated savings of $3.6 million in the first year of the project (Young and Verhulst 2017).

Access to data can narrow the information divide between small firms and larger players in the food system. Freely available satellite data enable entrepreneurs in Africa to provide agricultural insurance. World Cover, an insurance provider in Ghana, uses freely available satellite data to monitor rainfall and trigger automatic payouts. Actors with low bargaining power, such as farmers, cannot provide such data in other ways, so using satellite data mitigates the risk of depending on expensive providers. Esoko, another Ghanaian company, increases data equity in price negotiations between farmers and buyers by providing information on the market prices of 58 commodities in 42 markets countrywide, collected at markets daily, as well as weather forecasts, crop price bids, and crop production protocols—all from open data sources. Farmers using that information received 10 percent more for maize and 7 percent more for groundnuts than farmers who did not (van Schalkwyk, Young, and Verhulst 2017).

Access to data can create environmental benefits and make sustainability goals easier to achieve. It increases the ability to monitor the use and depletion of natural resources, improve land management, and support environmental policy making. For example, remote-sensing methods, increasingly available and affordable, permit routine monitoring of natural resources by providing concise data and a readily available collection of imagery. Remote-sensing data also help build management tools, such as landscaping approaches, to limit the adverse consequences of land used for agricultural purposes and amplify cobenefits (Denier et al. 2015). Landscape approaches are rooted in the notion that separately owned parcels of land can share a common ecology and social heritage. They map the boundaries of landscape ecology and inventory its natural resources—advances in remote sensing allow researchers and planners to accomplish this quickly and accurately (Antrop 2000; Gallant 2015; Lopez and Frohn 2017). Remote-sensing data also help researchers model landscape hydrology and ecosystem services. Finally, data collected through remote sensing or precision equipment might allow policy makers to attribute current multisource pollution problems to more easily managed single-source polluter problems. For example, data from precision spreaders could verify compliance with nutrient runoff management protocols (Sisung 2016). Globally, soils have the potential to remove significant amounts of carbon from the atmosphere (Barker et al. 2007; Sommer and Bossio 2014). Still, soil chemistry is complex, which makes it hard to quantify the actual mitigation impact of projects speeding soil carbon sequestration. As a consequence, project financing available through such programs as the Clean Development Mechanism or California's cap-and-trade program is hard to tap (Larson, Dinar, and Frisbie 2011; Dinar, Larson, and Frisbie 2012). Better data on how soil management affects soil carbon could make this easier. One company, Indigo Ag, is building a detailed dataset to assess how soil management practices affect soil characteristics by paying farmers to adopt practices expected to boost soil carbon levels (Indigo Ag 2020).

DATA-RELATED CHALLENGES TO ACHIEVING THE PROMISE OF DIGITAL TECHNOLOGIES

Several data-related technical, social, and legal challenges must be addressed to take advantage of the full potential of data in food systems. The challenges include uncertainty on data ownership, access, and control; issues of data protection and security; veracity, validation, and liability; and unbalanced value chains.

Facing such challenges, farmers are often reluctant to share their data or adopt digital technologies. Despite the potential benefits of using data-aggregating precision technology, many farmers remain reluctant to make their data available (Poppe et al. 2015). For example, in a 2017 survey of grain farmers in Saskatchewan, Canada, farmers were more likely to share their data with researchers and less likely to share their data with the government, and only 36 percent of farmers were willing to hypothetically join a big data platform at all. That willingness increases with small financial or nonfinancial benefits, such as prescription yield and input-use benchmarks and maps to assess crop health and nutrition needs in different parts of a field (Turland and Slade 2019). In a 2017 survey of 1,000 Australian farmers, 56 percent of respondents indicated feeling uncomfortable with service and technology providers having access to their data, while only 24 percent felt comfortable or extremely comfortable (Leonard et al. 2017). And 67 percent of 400 US farmers surveyed in 2016 expressed concern about third-party entities accessing their farm data (American Farm Bureau Federation 2016). The underlying source of reluctance lies in the lack of trust between farmers and third-party actors who collect, aggregate, and share data. Farmers are particularly concerned that competitors or input companies will use their data to discriminate against them in pricing (Brown 2017). Addressing this lack of trust requires open dialogue, improved data governance, and education and awareness training (Wiseman et al. 2019).

Uncertainty about Data Ownership, Access, and Control Rights Down the Line

Clarifying individual versus aggregate ownership, access, and control rights over data is critical for both farmers and digital technology providers. Defining ownership rights is important for two main reasons.

1. *Data have economic value.* Data generated by digital technologies can generate monetary value, and this value increases as the data are collected from several farmers, aggregated, and shared with other users such as digital technology providers. Acquiring, trading, or selling data is a direct way of generating monetary value. Creating new products or services by leveraging farm data, even without selling it, is an indirect way of generating monetary value. For example, technology providers could reuse e-extension data, even if anonymous, to showcase successes to new clients (Rasmussen 2016). Further reuses and combination with other datasets also add economic value to the data collected from farmers.
2. *Unclearly defined data rights could discourage technology adoption.* Unclearly defined data ownership, access, and control rights could lead to data misuse, eroding farmers' trust in digital technologies and discouraging their adoption.

However, defining farm data ownership is difficult. First, data are intangible, so data ownership is different from house or truck ownership. Data generated by digital technologies are also nonrival because one's ability to access data (farmers or firms) does not alter someone else's ability to use it (Griffin 2016). Unlike patents, trademarks, or copyrights, data generation and collection do not involve a creative element, and so data do not qualify as intellectual property. And because digital technologies collect, aggregate, and process farm data and transfer them to other users, the high number of users further complicates defining data ownership, access, and control rights.

Views diverge on whether farmers should be data owners. The European Parliamentary Research Service and the German Agricultural Society clearly state that the farmer owns the data originating from his or her farm (DLG e.V. 2018; European Parliamentary Research Service 2017). But other experts think that data should not belong to farmers because of the following reasons:

- Farm data could be treated under dataset intellectual property right laws. According to this argument, the intellectual work of creating the database determines ownership. So the company processing the data would become the owner of the resulting dataset. But the protection of databases as intellectual property requires a substantial investment. Since the cost of building datasets has come down dramatically, this argument lost its effectiveness in the EU (van der Wees 2017).
- Database copyright seems to apply mainly to aggregated data, considered the property of the company responsible (see, for example, Rasmussen 2016). But in an aggregated dataset, the farmer has limited control over the data about his farm.
- Other established ownership-like rights apply to data before and irrespective of any contractual statement of ownership. These rights include copyright, database rights, technical protection measures, trade secrets and patents, plant breeders' rights, privacy, and even tangible property rights (de Beer 2017).
- Data cannot be owned, and ownership is not a useful concept when data move and change structure across systems. So ownership is not the most crucial aspect. Rights of access to and use and reuse of data are much more critical (COPA-COGECA 2018; van der Wees 2017).

In addition, laws addressing the ownership of data from digital agriculture are either missing or inadequate. No legislation currently addresses the ownership of data from digital agriculture in the EU. Elsewhere, when these laws exist, they tend to be fragmented and not systematic (World Bank 2019). The legal uncertainty about data ownership may lead to resistance to data sharing and to contractual agreements that need to be negotiated. This outcome is problematic for farmers, who tend to have less negotiating power than the actors to whom they send their data.

Furthermore, portability, a prerequisite for data access, is not guaranteed by legislation. Aggregated and transformed data can no longer be retrieved or changed by the farmer (European Parliamentary Research Service 2017). Regulations typically recognize the right to data exchange for personal data (as in the EU general data protection regulation). This right is associated with the freedom to switch providers and thus with fair competition and low entry barriers in the digital economy. But currently, there are no obligations to guarantee even a minimum level of data portability for nonpersonal data such as those generated by farmers (and related requirements of interoperability and standards) (European Commission 2017). The IoT is an example of digital technologies that deprive farmers of using the data they contribute.

In practice, the definitions of ownership, access, and control rights are currently left to contractual agreements, which are not perfect safeguards of farmers' rights over their data. Most contracts recognize the farmer's ownership. But they are much less clear about access and control rights over data once processed, which makes ownership quite meaningless. In addition, contract law varies by country, and in some countries contracts are not valid for third parties that may be involved in secondary and tertiary data reuse (César, Debussche, and Van Asbroeck 2017). Such arrangements can disproportionally harm farmers, who tend to have very little bargaining power in contractual negotiations (de Beer 2017).

Data Protection and Security

Digital technologies collect new types and large amounts of geotagged farm data, making it difficult to separate personal data (protected by data privacy law) from nonpersonal data (not protected). For example, the location of the farm is also the personal address of the farmer. So geotagged datasets make it possible to obtain the exact address of farms. And data on farm profitability reveals information on the financial situation of the farmer. Other sensitive data currently lack legal protection, such as farming techniques and other sensitive business data revealed by hi-tech farm equipment. Combining datasets about the farm from different sources—satellite imagery, census data, and geospatial data—allows third parties to obtain information about a farm and its activities, even without the farmer's active consent (European Parliamentary Research Service 2017). In data-driven agrifood chains using blockchain technology, methods such as zero knowledge-proof and ring signatures have been developed to improve farmers' privacy by reducing the transparency of transactions. But these methods are not entirely successful, since it is impossible hide the sender, the receiver, and the amount at the same time (Zhao et al. 2019).

Agrifood chains cross borders, and the data protection regimes are heterogeneous across countries. Legal uncertainty about data protection limits the use of data-driven technologies provided by foreign companies. National authorities, even in a homogeneous region like the EU, do not trust cross-border data storage and prescribe local limits for specific services. This issue also affects cloud services and represents a form of vendor lock-in (European Parliament 2018). Data policies need to be harmonized internationally.

Current data-sharing practices inadequately protect farmers' data. Farm data could be aggregated in open public datasets, such as farm registries or geospatial datasets. But linking several datasets could enable the reidentification of farmers. So trusting data protection policies that prescribe anonymous open data is difficult (Pollock and Lämmerhirt 2019). In addition, providers of digital technologies for agriculture rarely implement the principle of purpose limitation for farm data, a key element of (personal) data protection law. The principle prevents the use of personal data in ways that are incompatible with the original purpose of collecting the data. For example, data collected from hospitals cannot be sold to advertising agencies. This principle applies to personal data and is gaining ground for nonpersonal data. But it is rarely observed for agricultural data.

Veracity, Validation, and Liability

Data-driven agrifood chains can be weakened by incorrect or intentionally manipulated data. And there are risks related to the legal value even of the data managed with specific technology risks (Toulon 2018). Today, several digital technologies overrely on cloud computing and IoT computing. As a result, data quality remains a concern in the uptake and proper utilization of digital agriculture. Of the seven data quality dimensions defined by the OECD, accuracy and coherence are thought to be of greatest relevance to digital agriculture. Gaps in accuracy due to user error or a lack of functionality in devices are not uncommon: industry personnel in the United States have witnessed yield monitor errors of up to 10 percent for a variety of reasons, including improper maintenance of flow meters and calibration errors. Additionally, the proliferation of digital agriculture machinery manufacturers developing their own types of data has led to incompatibility and incoherence (Keogh and Henry 2016). One incorrect decision based on incomplete or incorrect data could harm consumers and society (van der Wees 2017). For example, farmers may find an incentive to tamper with and manipulate data in the presence of environmental regulations on water and nutrient usage. The result of inaccuracies in data of this sort could lead to an underestimation of environmental impacts, inflicting potentially significant costs on society (Keogh and Henry 2016). The liability of digital technology producers is beyond the specific concerns of the agricultural sector since it is sector blind. But the liability of farmers for data produced by digital technologies on their farm or for their data in aggregated datasets may be serious for farmers—for their liability is not covered or transparent in most digital agriculture contracts. Evidence from Australia indicates that the vast majority of farmers do not know much about terms and conditions relating to data collection in their agreement with service providers due to lengthy and complex standard-form license agreements (Wiseman et al. 2019). This is worrisome for farmers due to the possibility of user or machine error, poor legal support, and an increasingly stringent regulatory environment around food safety and production methods, wherein data can be viewed as evidence of compliance with legislation (Cho 2018).

Unbalanced Value Chains, Data Asymmetries, and Concentrations of Power

Digital technologies could increase information asymmetries along the value chain. Agricultural data could make farmers much more transparent than other value chain actors since farmers using digital technologies tend to share disproportionally more of their data. For example, EU farmers should share their data with the government, preferably through digital technologies, to demonstrate their compliance with standards and regulations. For traceability, transparency, certification, and access to markets, farmers also need to share a lot of potentially business-sensitive data with other actors in the value chain. Those imbalances are greater in value chains comprising unorganized small-holder farmers and concentrated upstream and downstream markets—further decreasing farmers' bargaining power.

Fragmented and smallholder farmers may not gain insights into the market if accompanying measures are not taken to level the playing field (Agricultural Markets Task Force 2016). Their data can also be exploited in different ways to deny services, gain unfair advantages (Maru et al. 2018), or lock farmers into "exclusive data exploitation arrangements" (European Commission 2017). Banks could obtain more information about farmers, which may or may not increase their access to loans. Farmers can also be more exposed to criticism and retaliation from environmental groups, competing farmers, or even digital technology providers (Rasmussen 2016).

This risk is high in value chains with vertically integrated upstream and downstream operators. Traditional agrifood value chains are long and more or less evenly distributed with many nodes—producers, collectors, aggregators, wholesalers, public markets, processors, product wholesalers, retailers, and consumers. But the most common type of value chain today has smallholder farmers and, in the other segments, more concentrated vertical corporations. By quickly transferring high volumes of data, digital technologies could increase power and vertical concentration in the entire food supply chain, with harmful effects. And data's increasing returns to scale could lead to market concentration among digital providers and create barriers to entry. Indeed, incumbents in the data economy are earning large profits, and several digital markets are highly concentrated, a consequence of hoarding customer data, which creates a barrier to entry for smaller firms (Furman 2019).

Algorithms to process data could further increase information asymmetries. Algorithms are opaque, so farmers cannot control decision-making (European Parliamentary Research Service 2017). With proprietary systems and data not portable from one system to another, farmers can get locked in to one technology provider. If not specified in their data contracts, the lack of possibility to transfer this data effectively prevents farmers from changing service provider or combining services from various providers, unless they are ready to lose all their historical data. The risk of lock-in could be significant if the provision of agronomic advice becomes dominated by data-driven technologies sold by the private sector. Independent, unbiased advisory services linked to public bodies or cooperatives, which could counter this domination, are not well organized (European Parliamentary Research Service 2017).

Contractual frameworks can reduce the capacity of farmers to choose providers for the servicing of their farm machinery, an issue referred to as the *right to repair*. As digital farm machinery and equipment now have sophisticated software programs embedded, the terms of use of the technology contracts that accompany the software often prevent farmers from being able to access the software for the purposes of repair (Solon 2017; Gasser 2006). There are potentially significant competition issues where agriculture machinery providers tie farmers into service agreements with authorized service agents and prevent access to third party repair services (Keogh 2017). This can be an important issue in remote areas where farmers have limited access to authorized service technicians. Conversely, farmers might feel they have a limited choice of agricultural machinery providers to choose from.

Farmers are the originators of data, but there is no practical method for sharing financial benefits with them. Monetizing data raises two concerns. First, farmers should consent to the secondary use of their data. Second, the financial benefit should be shared with the farmer, but this would, in turn, raise two additional concerns. First, while the total value of all farm data from all farmers is high, the value of data from the individual farmer would probably be small. Second, this practice could be inequitable since poor farmers would be willing to sell their data to earn additional income. In contrast, wealthier farmers would be able to keep and control their data. A potential solution is to create collective platforms for farm data sharing and selling that have a critical mass and are governed transparently. But there does not seem to be a market yet (Bloch 2018). So far, only two platforms—for the cloud in the United States (Farmobile n.d.) and blockchain in Canada (mPowered 2019)—enable the control and sale of farm data.

REFERENCES

Agricultural Markets Task Force. 2016. "Agricultural Markets Task Force Presents Recommendations on Farmers in the Food Supply Chain." European Commission, Brussels, November 14, 2016. https://ec.europa.eu/commission/presscorner/detail/en /IP_16_3658.

American Farm Bureau Federation. 2016. *Farm Bureau Survey: Farmers Want to Control Their Own Data.* Washington, DC: American Farm Bureau Federation. https://www .farms.com/news/farm-bureau-survey-farmers-want-to-control-their-own-data-107354 .aspx.

Antle, J. M. 1999. "Benefits and Costs of Food Safety Regulation." *Food Policy* 24 (6): 605–23.

Antrop, M. 2000. "Background Concepts for Integrated Landscape Analysis." *Agriculture, Ecosystem and Environment* 77 (1-2): 17–28.

Barker, T., I. Bashmakov, A. Alharthi, M. Amann, L. Cifuentes, J. Drexhage, et al. 2007. "Mitigation from a Cross-sectoral Perspective." In *Climate Change 2007: Mitigation: Contribution of Working Group III to the Fourth Assessment Report of the Intergovernmental Panel on Climate Change*, edited by B. Metz, O. R. Davidson, P. R. Bosch, R. Dave, and L. A. Meyer. Cambridge, UK: Cambridge University Press.

Bloch, S. 2018. "If Farmers Sold Their Data Instead of Giving It Away, Would Anybody Buy?" *Counter*, September 19, 2018. https://thecounter.org/farmobile-farm-data/.

Brown, E. 2017. "Why Big Data Hasn't Yet Made a Dent on Farms." *Wall Street Journal*, May 15, 2017. https://www.wsj.com/articles/why-big-data-hasnt-yet-made-a-dent-on-farms-1494813720.

Brynjolfsson, E., L. M. Hitt, and H. Kim. 2011. "Strength in Numbers: How Does Data-driven Decision-making Affect Firm Performance?" *SSRN*. http://dx.doi.org/10.2139/ssrn.1819486.

César, J., J. Debussche, and B. Van Asbroeck. 2017. "Supplementary Paper: Data Ownership—A New EU Right in Data." London: Bird & Bird.

Cho, G. 2018. "The Australian Digital Farmer: Challenges and Opportunities." *IOP Conference Series: Earth and Environmental Science*, 185.

COPA-COGECA (Comité des organisations professionnelles agricoles–Comité général de la coopération agricole de l'Union européenne/Committee of Professional Agricultural Organisations-General Confederation of Agricultural Cooperatives). 2018. EU Code of Conduct on Agricultural Data Sharing by Contractual Agreement, COPA-COGECA, Brussels.

de Beer, J. 2017. "Ownership of Open Data: Governance Options for Agriculture and Nutrition." GODAN (Global Open Data for Agriculture and Nutrition). https://www.godan.info/sites/default/files/documents/Godan_Ownership_of_Open_Data_Publication_lowres.pdf.

Denier, H. A. C., R. Bergstrom, C. Fountoukis, C. Johansson, S. N. Pandis, D. Simpson, and A. J. H. Visschedijk. 2015. "Particulate Emissions from Residential Wood Combustion in Europe: Revised Estimates and an Evaluation." *Atmospheric Chemistry and Physics* 15: 6503–19.

Dinar, A., D. F. Larson, and J. A. Frisbie. 2012. "Clean Development Mechanism Agricultural Methodologies Could Help California to Achieve AB 32 Goals." *California Agriculture* 66 (4).

DLG e.V. 2018. "Digital Agriculture: Opportunities, Risks, Acceptance." A DLG Position Paper, Frankfurt, DLG. https://www.dlg.org/en/agriculture/topics/a-dlg-position-paper/.

European Commission. 2017. "Building a European Data Economy." Communication from the Commission to the European Parliament, the Council, the European Economic and Social Committee and the Committee of the Regions, European Commission, Brussels.

European Commission. 2018. "Towards a Common European Data Space." Communication from the Commission to the European Parliament, the Council, the European Economic and Social Committee and the Committee of the Regions, European Commission, Brussels.

European Data Portal. 2020. "What Is Open Data?" updated June 6, 2020. Publications Office of the European Union, Luxembourg. https://www.europeandataportal.eu/en/training/what-open-data.

European Parliament. 2018. Regulation (EU) 2018/1807 of the European Parliament and of the Council of 14 November 2018 on a Framework for the Free Flow of Non-Personal

Data in the European Union (Text with EEA relevance.) PE/53/2018/REV/1. European Parliament, Brussels. https://www.legislation.gov.uk/eur/2018/1807/introduction.

European Parliamentary Research Service. 2017. "Precision Agriculture in Europe: Legal, Social, and Ethical Considerations." European Union, Brussels. https://www.europarl .europa.eu/thinktank/en/document.html?reference=EPRS_STU(2017)603207.

Farmobile. n.d. "Creating ROI for Farmers." Farmobile Leawood, KS. https://www.farmobile .com/data-store/.

Furman, J. 2019. *Unlocking Digital Competition: Report of the Digital Competition Expert Panel.* London: HM Treasury. https://assets.publishing.service.gov.uk/government/uploads /system/uploads/attachment_data/file/785547/unlocking_digital_competition_furman _review_web.pdf.

Gallant, A. L. 2015. "The Challenges of Remote Monitoring of Wetlands." *Remote Sensing* 7: 10938–50. doi:10.3390/rs70810938.

Gasser, U. 2006. "Legal Frameworks and Technological Protection of Digital Content: Moving Forward towards a Best Practice Model." *Fordham Intellectual Property, Media and Entertainment Law Journal* 17 (1): 39–113.

Griffin, T. 2016. "Adoption of Precision Agricultural Technology in Kansas. Kansas State University Department of Agricultural Economics Extension Publication." KFMA Research Paper, Manhattan, KS. http://www.agmanager.info/adoption-precision-agricultural -technology-kansas.

Hammoudi, A., R. Hoffmann, and Y. Surry. 2009. "Food Safety Standards and Agrifood Supply Chains: An Introductory Overview." *European Review of Agricultural Economics* 36 (4): 469–78.

Hoffmann, S., M. B. Batz, and J. G. Morris. 2012. "Annual Cost of Illness and Quality-adjusted Life Year Losses in the United States Due to 14 Foodborne Pathogens." *Journal of Food Protection* 75: 1292–302.

Indigo Ag. 2020. "Indigo Launches the Terraton Initiative to Remove One Trillion Tons of Carbon Dioxide from the Atmosphere." Indigo, Boston, MA. https://www.indigoag.com /pages/news/indigo-launches-terraton-initiative.

Iyengar, S., and P. Bergemann. 2018. "The Entrepreneurial Impact of Open Data." February 8. *MacArthur Foundation Research Network on Opening Governance Blog.* https://opening -governance.org/blog/the-entrepreneurial-impact-of-open-data.

Keogh, M. 2017. "Consolidation in Agriculture: Impacts to the Farm, Research, and Agribusiness." Paper presented at the UWA Institute of Agriculture-Industry Forum, Perth, Australia, July 18, 2017. https://www.accc.gov.au/speech/consolidation-in-agriculture -impacts-to-the-farm-research-and-agribusiness.

Keogh, M., and M. Henry. 2016. *The Implications of Digital Agriculture and Big Data for Australian Agriculture.* Sydney, Australia: Australian Farm Institute.

Larson, D., A. Dinar, and J. A. Frisbie. 2011. "Agriculture and the Clean Development Mechanism." Policy Research Working Paper 5621, World Bank, Washington, DC.

Leonard, E., R. Rainbow, A. Laurie, D. Lamb, R. Llewellyn, E. Perrett, J. Sanderson, A. Skinner, T. Stollery, L. Wiseman, and T. Wood. 2017. *Accelerating Precision Agriculture to Decision Agriculture.* Narrabri, New South Wales, Australia: Cotton Research and Development Council.

Loomis, J., S. Koontz, H. Miller, and L. Richardson. 2015. "Valuing Geospatial Information: Using the Contingent Valuation Method to Estimate the Economic Benefits of Landsat Satellite Imagery." *Photogrammetric Engineering & Remote Sensing* 81 (8): 647–56.

Lopez, R. D., and R. C. Frohn. 2017. *Remote Sensing for Landscape Ecology: New Metric Indicators.* Boca Raton, FL: CRC Press.

Manyika, J., M. Chui, D. Farrell, S. Van Kuiken, P. Groves, and E. Almasi Doshi. 2013. *Open Data: Unlocking Innovation and Performance with Liquid Information.* London: McKinsey Global Institute.

Maru, A., D. Berne, J. de Beer, P. Ballantyne, V. Pesce, S. Kalyesubula, N. Fourie, C. Addison, A. Collett, and J. Chaves. 2018. *Digital and Data-Driven Agriculture: Harnessing the Power of Data for Smallholders.* Rome: Global Forum on Agricultural Research and Innovation.

mPowered. 2019. "Take Control of Your Data." mPowered, Guelph, Ontaria, Canada. https://www.mpowered.io.

Open Data Institute. 2015. "How Can We Improve Agriculture, Food and Nutrition with Open Data?" Working Paper, Open Data Institute, London. https://theodi.org/article/improving-agriculture-and-nutrition-with-open-data.

Open Knowledge Foundation. n.d. "Open Definition: Defining Open in Open Data, Open Content and Open Knowledge" (accessed August 11, 2020). Open Knowledge Foundation, London. http://opendefinition.org.

Pollock, R., and D. Lämmerhirt. 2019. "Open Data around the World: European Union." In *The State of Open Data: Histories and Horizons*, edited by T. Davies, S. Walker, M. Rubinstein, and F. Perini. Cape Town, South Africa and Ottawa, Canada: African Minds and International Development Research Centre.

Poppe, K. J., J. Wolfert, C. N. Verdouw, and A. Renwick. 2015. "A European Perspective on the Economics of Big Data." *Farm Policy Journal* 12 (1): 11–19.

Potter, A., J. Murray, B. Lawson, and S. Graham. 2012. "Trends in Product Recalls within the Agri-food Industry: Empirical Evidence from the USA, UK and the Republic of Ireland." *Trends in Food Science & Technology* 28: 77–86.

Rasmussen, N. 2016. "From Precision Agriculture to Market Manipulation: A New Frontier in the Legal Community." *Minnesota Journal of Law, Science & Technology* 17 (1).

Sisung, Theresa. 2016. "Soil TESTING and Nutrient Application Practices of Agricultural Retailers in the Great Lakes Region." PhD dissertation, Kansas State University, Manhattan, KS.

Solon, O. 2017. "It's Digital Colonialism: How Facebook's Free Internet Service Has Failed Its Users." *Guardian*, July 27, 2018. https://www.theguardian.com/technology/2017/jul/27/facebook-free-basics-developing-markets.

Sommer, R., and D. Bossio. 2014. "Dynamics and Climate Change Mitigation Potential of Soil Organic Carbon Sequestration." *Journal of Environmental Management* 144: 83–87.

Toulon, N. 2018. "The Blockchain: Opportunities and Challenges for Agriculture." *ICT Update* 09, Issue 88. https://ictupdate.cta.int/en/article/the-blockchain-opportunities-and-challenges-for-agriculture-sid065ec1d7b-8031-4fb5-ba75-d7c3b8333a7d.

Turland, M., and P. Slade. 2019. "Farmers' Willingness to Participate in a Big Data Platform." *Agribusiness* 31 (1): 20–36.

Ubaldi, B. 2013. "Open Government Data: Towards Empirical Analysis of Open Government Data Initiatives." OECD Working Papers on Public Governance 22, OECD Publishing, Paris.

van der Wees, A. 2017. "Cross Fertilisation through Alignment, Synchronisation and Exchanges for IoT" H2020 Work Progamme 2016–2017: H2020—CREATE-IoT Project, Deliverable 05.05, Legal IoT Framework (Initial), European Large-Scale Pilots Program. https://european-iot-pilots.eu/wp-content/uploads/2018/02/D05_05_WP05_H2020_CREATE-IoT_Final.pdf.

van Schalkwyk, F., A. Young, and S. Verhulst. 2017. "Ghana: Esoko—Leveling the Information Playing Field for Smallholder Farmers." Open Data's Impact. http://odimpact.org/files /case-esoko.pdf.

Wiseman, L., J. Sanderson, A. Zhang, and E. Jakku. 2019. "Farmers and Their Data: An Examination of Farmers' Reluctance to Share Their Data through the Lens of the Laws Impacting Smart Farming." *NJAS–Wageningen Journal of Life Sciences* 90–91 (December 2019).

World Bank. n.d. "Data: Open Data Essentials" (database). World Bank, Washington, DC, August 11, 2020. http://opendatatoolkit.worldbank.org/en/essentials.html.

World Bank. 2019. *Future of Food: Harnessing Digital Technologies to Improve Food System Outcomes*. Washington, DC: World Bank.

Young, A., and S. Verhulst. 2017. *Aclímate Colombia: Open Data to Improve Agricultural Resiliency*. Open Data's Impact. http://odimpact.org/files/case-aclimate-colombia.pdf.

Zhao, G., S. Liu, C. Lopez, H. Lu, S. Elgueta, H. Chen, and B. J. Boshkosha. 2019. "Blockchain Technology in Agrifood Value Chain Management: A Synthesis of Applications, Challenges and Future Research Directions." *Computers in Industry* 109: 83–99.

CHAPTER SEVEN

Policies to Maximize the Gains Made through Digital Technologies

KEY MESSAGES

- How much digital technologies can accelerate transformation of the agrifood system will be determined by the commitment of governments around the world to creating an enabling environment for digital transformation and maximizing its efficiency, equity, and environmental sustainability.
- The primary role of the public sector is to create an enabling environment for private sector investments to ensure the development of key digital transformation enablers.
- The role of the government is also to ensure that the outcomes of digital transformation are equitable and environmentally sustainable.
- Instruments for this strategy will include legal and regulatory measures as well as appropriate public investments.

POLICY FRAMEWORK FOR FOSTERING DIGITAL TRANSFORMATION OF THE AGRIFOOD SYSTEM

For digital technologies to optimally enhance efficiency, equity, and environmental sustainability in the agrifood system, the private and public sectors need to work together to create a thriving digital agriculture ecosystem. Creating an enabling environment for digital transformation in the food system requires a variety of interconnected elements to be put in place. A policy framework (figure 7.1) guiding a public policy response aimed at maximizing the efficiency, equity, and environmental sustainability gains of such a transformation should be structured along

a. Policies to enable digital transformation of the agrifood system

Tier 1 enablers
- Enabling availability and accessibility of digital infrastructure
- Enabling availability of physical infrastructure
- Strengthening government capacity to foster digital innovation

Tier 2 enablers
- Enabling access to data in agriculture
- Designing legal and regulatory framework conducive to digital innovations
- Enabling competition in digital markets
- Supporting development of digital payment systems
- Supporting digital skills development
- Fostering digital entrepreneurship ecosystems

Policies for adoption
- Strengthening knowledge and skill development of farmers
- Supporting customization of digital tools
- Reducing the cost of adopting digital technologies
- Building trust in digital applications

b. Policies to maximize equity and environmental sustainability gains of digital transformation

Equity
- Improving access to and use of digital technologies by marginalized groups
- Addressing data access asymmetries
- Adopting compensatory measures for potential losers of digital transformation in agrifood system

Environmental sustainability
- Strengthening digital environmental monitoring
- Incentivizing use of digital technologies for environmental sustainability by producers
- Incorporating environmental sustainability goals in agricultural policies
- Influencing behavior of consumers and producers through e-education and information dissemination

Source: World Bank.

two pathways: (1) ensuring the enabling environment for digital transformation in the agrifood system to maximize the efficiency gains and (2) influencing the incentives and decisions of private agents with the goal of maximizing the equity and environmental sustainability impacts of the adoption of digital agriculture. The enabling environment for digital transformation can be achieved through supporting the development of tier 1 and tier 2 enablers as well as policies to support adoption of digital solutions. Tier 1 enablers include availability and accessibility of digital infrastructure, availability and accessibility of physical infrastructure, and governmental capacity to foster digital transformation. Tier 2 enablers include access to data, availability of digital platforms and digital payment systems, digital skills, and availability of a digital entrepreneurship ecosystem.

Since most of the interventions required for the tier 1 enablers lie outside of the competencies of the ministries of agriculture, this section only briefly mentions key public policy measures supporting their development. Instead, the focus of the section is on the role of the public sector in facilitating the broader development and adoption of digital agriculture technologies and ensuring equitable and environmentally sustainable distribution of their gains. It should also be noted that the categories within the proposed framework are not mutually exclusive and are often complementary. The framework offers a toolkit of key policy areas to enable digital transformation in agriculture. Prioritization of policy actions would often be country specific and depend on the level of development of both agriculture and digital technologies. Appendix A offers an assessment tool that can be used to evaluate the state of agricultural and digital development in a country and identify public policy entry points to maximize the efficiency, equity, and environmental sustainability of digital transformation in agriculture.

POLICIES FOR ENABLING DIGITAL TRANSFORMATION TO MAXIMIZE EFFICIENCY GAINS

Policies for Tier 1 (Foundational) Enablers of Digital Transformation

Enabling the availability and accessibility of digital infrastructure

Good quality, accessible mobile and internet networks are essential to maximize the efficiency, equity, and environmental sustainability gains from digital agriculture in the agrifood system. The set of digital technologies across farms, value chains, and public services requires different levels of mobile phone and internet connectivity (World Bank 2019a). For agricultural extension and farmer-to-farmer learning, digital videos can be provided off-line with no need for mobile or internet connections. For value chain traceability, distributed ledger technologies are best suited to environments with both high mobile coverage and high internet connectivity. On the continuum of requirements for connectivity between these extremes, the highest potential of digital agriculture to contribute to efficiency, equity, and sustainability in the agrifood system can be realized only with widespread and reliable mobile and internet coverage in rural areas.

Creating an enabling environment for telecom sector activity for expanding network coverage is a key precondition in rural areas. At lower population densities, unit costs of telecom service providers per user are higher, since rural areas often have higher installation and maintenance costs, greater distances from main roads, more uneven terrain, and lack of electricity. In such an environment of inherently high costs, it is especially important to use the available policy and regulatory levers to keep costs for network expansion as low as possible (box 7.1) (Buys et. al. 2009). That is why public policy entry points to expand rural coverage in developing countries need to create inviting enabling environments for the private sector and to spur competition. Examples include introducing flexible regulatory frameworks, lowering infrastructure taxes and import duties for equipment, and encouraging companies to expand coverage to underserved areas. Given the unique features and requirements of rural areas, ministries of agriculture need to be closely engaged in crafting regulations, even though the regulations will for the most part need to apply countrywide.

An important step in reducing investment risks and encouraging mobile coverage expansion in rural areas is to make the regulatory environment stable, flexible, predictable, and low cost. High quality and stable regulatory systems provide greater certainty for investors and are necessary for expanding digital infrastructure in rural areas. According to the World Bank's Enabling the Business of Agriculture (EBA) report, countries with higher quality information and communication technology regulations tend to also perform well on the GSMA Mobile Connectivity Index (World Bank 2017). In contrast, arbitrary regulatory changes create high transaction costs that drive up prices for end users in rural areas (Samarajiva and Zainudeen 2010). (It is beyond the purview of this report to describe in-depth design of regulatory frameworks that can facilitate investments in rural digital technology by operators—more information can be found in GSMA 2018.)

Tax policies should be crafted to reduce investment risks and support expansion in rural areas without creating inappropriate incentives. Fiscal and other policy instruments can be deployed in ways that encourage network expansion in rural areas. The most obvious policy advice is to refrain from imposing any taxes specific to digital activities or infrastructure, or if this is impractical, at least make them predictable and low. This would include import duties on necessary capital equipment. In Sub-Saharan African countries, evidence shows that there is a strong negative correlation between sector-specific tax rates and connectivity (GSMA 2018). Perhaps not quite so obvious is that how the tax base is defined affects the incentive to expand coverage. Taxes levied on profits, rather than on revenue, will encourage companies to reinvest.

In addition to taxes, countries have used a range of other subsidies and policies to try to encourage companies to expand coverage to underserved areas, generally rural. Experience with these schemes has been mixed, and any future programs should take the lessons into account (GSMA 2018). The programs fall into four basic classes:

The World Bank Group's Enabling the Business of Agriculture (EBA) project collects data that allow benchmarking of information and communication technology
(ICT) regulatory practices that enable access to digital technologies in rural areas in
80 countries.[a] Such regulatory practices encompass general authorization regimes,
efficient spectrum management, and infrastructure sharing.

General authorization regimes facilitate competition. Competition in the telecommunication sector is promoted through a general authorization regime that
allows mobile operators to start a business with license-exempt entry or a simple
notification submitted to the regulatory authority, as opposed to obtaining an individual operating license. According to the EBA findings, only 13 of 80 countries
studied have a general authorization regime that increases competition by reducing
barriers to entry and simplifying the regulatory process (Colombia, Denmark,
Georgia, Greece, Guatemala, Italy, the Netherlands, Poland, Romania, Serbia,
Spain, Ukraine, and the United States). The validity of the general authorization
is indefinite, which eliminates any uncertainty surrounding license renewal. And
administrative charges associated with general authorization regimes are publicly
available. In contrast, individual licenses are prone to regulatory uncertainty and
ambiguity over licensing fees and renewal conditions. Of the 67 countries that
impose individual licenses, 28 do not publish online the exact fees associated with
obtaining an operating license. In 49 countries, the renewal conditions of the operating licenses are not clearly stated in the regulations. In 14 countries, the validity
of the individual operating license is less than 15 years. Such uncertainties over fees,
renewal conditions, and relatively short license terms make infrastructure investments risky for mobile operators and thus deter investments in rural areas, which
are less viable commercially.

Spectrum management. The expansion of mobile networks to remote areas is
also influenced by spectrum management. Spectrum type and availability have a
direct impact on the access to digital services in rural areas and on the maximum
coverage and capacity of mobile base stations. They can thus determine the investments required to cover a certain area. Lower radio frequencies significantly reduce
the capital expenditures for base stations and provide greater coverage in rural
areas. For example, 18 countries never licensed spectrum lower than 900 megahertz for mobile operators, whereas all high-income countries allowed the use of
spectrum bands lower than 800 megahertz.

Good spectrum management also allows for voluntary spectrum trading, a
mechanism whereby rights to use spectrum and any associated obligations can
be transferred from one party to another in the market. This process can facilitate
more efficient allocation and use of scarce spectrum resources and foster innovation and the introduction of new services. Only 23 of the 80 countries allow this
practice, including 10 high-income economies of the Organisation for Economic
Co-operation and Development (OECD). In Sub-Saharan Africa only Angola and
Nigeria have implemented regulations allowing voluntary spectrum trading. No
low-income countries have allowed voluntary spectrum trading.

(Continued)

Infrastructure sharing. Infrastructure sharing fosters efficiency by significantly reducing capital expenditures required to provide digital services in rural locations. The benefits of infrastructure sharing include cost savings, improved service quality, and acceleration of network coverage in rural areas. It also has a positive impact on the environment while optimizing resources. Twelve countries still prohibit passive infrastructure sharing (sharing of space or physical supporting infrastructure) and only half the countries studied allow active infrastructure sharing (sharing of the active network layer elements).

a. For more details on the Enabling the Business of Agriculture project, methodology, and countries covered, refer to https://eba.worldbank.org/.

1. *Single wholesale networks.* These government-sanctioned monopolies can take advantage of economies of scale and are usually subsidized in one way or another. As monopolies, they suffer from reduced incentives to innovate and could abuse their market power, even if regulated. Once established, they may also preempt future competition that would become viable as market conditions change. On a practical level, the implementation record has been generally poor. A study of such networks in Kenya, Mexico, the Russian Federation, Rwanda, and South Africa found that none has so far been successful, and some were totally abandoned (GSMA 2018).

2. *Universal service funds.* These schemes collect levies on mobile service networks and are supposed to use the proceeds to fund government-selected connectivity programs. A study of 64 such schemes found that most were neither efficient nor effective in expanding coverage (GSMA 2018). More than a third continued to collect levies but had not yet disbursed any of the funds collected, effectively acting as a sector-specific tax and discouraging the kinds of investments they were supposed to encourage. Even so, not all such funds have been so unsuccessful, and GSMA (2018) includes a set of characteristics of the ones that show the greatest promise.

3. *Coverage obligations.* Some countries relying on coverage obligations to increase service in rural areas have been effective, although others have failed. To be successful, schemes need to be realistic in regard to expansion targets in light of actual market conditions and should allow companies to take the obligations into account when formulating business plans and bidding for spectrum.

4. *Subsidies.* These include both grants and more indirect subsidies, such as tax rebates. Some subsidy schemes have been effective when they

are well targeted, transparent, and simple to administer and monitor. Malaysia set up an effective scheme in 2014, when the government gave corporate tax rebates of up to 70 percent for capital investments in rural areas as well as import duty exemptions for last-mile connectivity equipment.

Enabling the availability of physical infrastructure

On the investment side, public expenditures in physical infrastructure can address supply constraints for providers of digital solutions in rural areas and make it feasible for them to invest in areas where costs would otherwise be too high. Lack of complementary rural infrastructure—such as roads, energy, postharvest storage, and logistics—can limit the adoption and impact of digital technologies in agriculture (Deichmann, Goyal, and Mishra 2016). For example, it is difficult to sell products on e-commerce platforms if there are no roads to markets or to sell high-quality fruits to online customers if there is no storage to preserve their freshness. A recent study in China indicated that poor storage and transportation, particularly for perishable products, was a factor in decisions not to sell products online (Huang and Zhi 2018).

Strengthening government capacity to foster digital innovation

The technological and human capacity of ministries of agriculture influences the extent of change they can bring to fostering digital development in the sector. To stay relevant in the fast-changing digital transformation of the agrifood system, ministries of agriculture need to continually adapt. Having the right skills and capacities is pivotal to design digital agriculture strategies and effectively implement them. Attracting new talent, providing dedicated training, and increasing awareness among civil servants can help improve human capacity at the ministerial level (OECD 2015). To play an efficient role in creating an enabling environment for digital development in the agricultural sector, ministries of agriculture need to have in place modern data infrastructure—the physical, digital, and institutional structures enabling and governing some aspects of agricultural data collection, transfer, storage, and analysis to produce knowledge and advice and to provide a feedback loop to farmers and decision-makers pertinent to the mandate of the ministries. Data infrastructure depends both on connectivity infrastructure (hard infrastructure) and the regulatory environment and institutional arrangements (soft infrastructure) (OECD 2019). Figure 7.2 sets out this data infrastructure, highlighting the flow of data at different stages and outlining how data are collected, combined, and analyzed. It also presents key policy and regulatory components that need to be in place for data infrastructure (OECD 2019). Availability of data infrastructure and human capacity would also be key for improving the efficiency of agricultural policies.

FIGURE 7.2 The Data Infrastructure for Agriculture

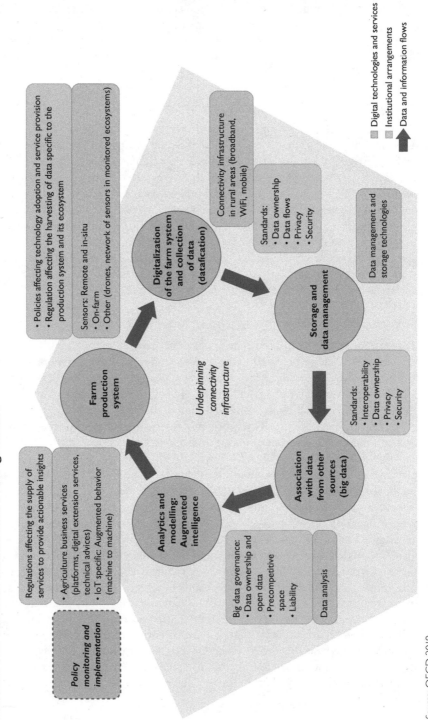

Source: OECD 2019.

Note: IoT = Internet of things.

Policies for Tier 2 Enablers of Digital Transformation

Enabling access to data in agriculture

Data are the fuel that drives the digital transformation of the agrifood system. Developers of digital innovations in agriculture are dependent on access to high-quality data to make their discoveries. The role of the public sector is in enabling access to various agriculture-related data. Governments can do this by investing in open data that have public-good characteristics, encouraging the private sector to share data in the public interest, improving the governance of data-sharing platforms, creating data interoperability standards, and putting in place data governance frameworks to address any risks associated with data use.

Investments in public, open databases and innovation platforms could be very effective in promoting the development of digital tools. Many types of data are quintessential public goods, so public investments in sources of open data can have high payoffs. These include agricultural statistics, agroclimatic data, and soil quality maps, which seem to be underappreciated potential drivers of the development by entrepreneurs of new digital applications to better meet the needs of smallholders. Making these data available would reduce the cost of developing and scaling up novel digital applications, because developers would not have to individually spend resources to collect them.

Similarly, data sharing between the public and private sectors and within the private sector is an important avenue for advancing innovation and increasing transparency and accountability in the agrifood system. Policy makers should assess the public-good nature of data held by private actors and identify ways of making the data available for public use. Several instruments can be employed, including providing a clear legal framework recognizing "a general principle of access to privately held data of public interest," claiming public interest based on the public or collective contribution to the value of certain private data assets, identifying and building on competitive spaces for sharing private sector data—where private actors realize the value of open data in promoting innovation, cost-sharing, and value chain efficiencies—and combining with other datasets for new insights. The public sector could also create public-private partnerships by, for example, cofinancing research and development with private sector firms.

Open access data, however, should not be confused with cost-free data, since making data available involves significant labor, service, and technology costs. Data resources can be very expensive, and demand is increasing for accurate and reliable sources of information. Many data resources do not have secure funding over the near future and depend on short-term grants. Dedicated funding is essential to curate and structure data to make it accessible and usable by the community. A data resource generally combines several revenue streams to differentiate income sources, such as public funding, academic user funding, third party funding, and commercial user funding (Gabella, Durinx, and Appel 2017). An ideal funding model would guarantee open access to and opportunity to use data, generate enough revenues to fully cover costs over time, derive them from transparent sources, and combine different revenue streams. The funding model for UniProt, a resource for protein sequences and functional informational knowledge, guarantees these criteria. It integrates funding from private and public agencies that pay directly for stewardship in contributions proportionate to grant volume. Called the "infrastructure model," it requires contributions of ~0.1 percent of total spending for life science research grants of five funding agencies and allows for the generation of up to €20 million in income.

To ensure the wide use of data, it is essential for it to be shared on large trusted platforms. Such platforms can be governed by the private or the public sector—what is essential is that the governance models for such platforms be grounded in transparency and respect for data privacy. Suggestions in this direction include the following:

- *Public sector–led data platforms.* The European Parliamentary Research Service proposes an ambitious European Union (EU)–wide independent, farmer-centric data repository under the governance of EU public authorities to guarantee security, interconnection, and interoperability and to avoid misuse of data. Such a repository would build on the data already collected in the framework of Common Agriculture Policy payments and on existing EU standards linked to this system, such as INSPIRE. It would support administrative simplification, both for farmers and for administrations, and it could enable synergies with different applications, such as the traceability of food and certification schemes (European Parliamentary Research Service 2017). Other public platforms could be regional, national, commodity-specific, or specific to value chain segments.
- *Stakeholder-led data platforms.* Trust can be built in nonpublic data platforms if they are governed by a trusted organization of network members. Data platforms can be governed by farmers' aggregations or consortia, including other value-chain actors, as in any form of "data cooperative" owned by its membership. The bodies governing these platforms should be recognized as "trust organizations" that verify, validate, and authenticate data flow and ensure fair, just, inclusive, and equitable data and information flows in the agrifood system (Maru et al. 2018).

The impact of open data is highly correlated with the frequency of use, so promoting data use is key. This can be done in several ways, including the following:

- Improving data standardization to allow for data portability and interoperability
- Promoting the FAIR data principles (see third paragraph that follows)
- Publishing data in ways that make them easily consumable by apps and digital technologies

- Allowing the use of open data to increase the efficiency of administrative processes (The regulatory framework should encourage the use of public data for administrative simplification, to demonstrate its usefulness. A promising example are the EU rules allowing the use of Sentinel data, remote sensing data collected by the European Space Agency's Copernicus Programme, as evidence of compliance with administrative requirements.)

Standards for handling data can particularly increase the benefits of and demand for digital technologies if they ensure consistency and interoperability. One area of data governance that is very important for developing e-agriculture is creating standards to harmonize the ways data are collected, processed, stored, and shared. To maximize the benefits of digital technology use, there needs to be some way to ensure the consistent collection, exchange, and dissemination of accurate information across boundaries, both sectoral and geographic. Without such consistency, there is a real risk of misinterpretation of information, and incompatibility of data structure and terminology (FAO and ITU 2016). The objective should be to ensure compatibility not only for e-agricultural applications, but also for other sectors, including e-governance, e-health, and e-education. For example, Estonia's e-government initiative contains the X-Road tool, which allows the nation's various databases and registers, both in the public and private sector, to connect and operate together, regardless of what platform they use. Many of these data are used in operations of web and mobile applications developed for farm management, such as VitalFields, eAgronom, and Terake.eu (Kärner 2017).

There is so far limited clarity about the appropriate role of public policy in setting standards, which is not necessarily a government function. Many kinds of standards are developed by industry groups and other nongovernmental organizations, internationally and (in high-income countries) nationally. If some nongovernmental organizations (international or national) are capable of promulgating standards appropriate for a developing country, it may be best to leave this function to them. If not, some governmental involvement may be required. Many of the data standards will not be solely or even mainly used by the agricultural sector, but some will. For example, terminology in information provided to farmers through e-agriculture applications should adhere to the Food and Agriculture Organization's AGROVOC standards to avoid confusion (AIMS 2020). What is needed is some general guidance for developing countries to help them gauge the need for nationally appropriate standards for information in agrifood markets, and to determine whether these are likely to be available from sources outside the country or will need to be developed locally. If locally, general guidelines are needed to assist countries in putting them in place, considering any special needs of the agrifood sector. One pitfall to avoid is a proliferation of different standards and regulations across countries. That could fragment markets and deter entry by international firms, as has sometimes been the case in agricultural input markets.

In addition, the governments should promote the FAIR data principles. First defined by Wilkinson et al. (2016), the principles for "good data management and stewardship" reflect findability, accessibility, interoperability, and reusability. *Findability* means that data and supplementary materials have sufficiently rich metadata and unique and persistent identifiers. *Accessibility* means that metadata and data are understandable to humans and machines. *Interoperability* means metadata use a formal, accessible, shared, and broadly applicable language for knowledge representation. *Reusability* means that data and collections have a clear usage license and provide accurate information on provenance. Ensuring that agricultural data meet FAIR principles requires standards that are in development but whose adoption is lacking, so further engagement by academic, federal, and nonprofit researchers is necessary. Policy makers can facilitate the adoption of FAIR data principles by supporting the infrastructure, resources, and access that allow real-time FAIR compliance, data curation, and preservation in a system that incentivizes team science and data sharing (Brouder et al. 2019).

Designing legal and regulatory framework conducive for digital innovations

The growing complexity of digital innovation ecosystems that underpin the digitization of food systems adds to the challenges for designing appropriate policy and regulatory systems to guide such ecosystems. Growing innovation and rapid market changes make regulations more complex yet quickly obsolete. And the existing policy and regulatory frameworks often are not suitable for addressing concerns about rapid digitization. All this results in higher likelihoods of regulatory uncertainty and higher compliance costs and hinders technology adoption. As one example, according to a recent PricewaterhouseCoopers survey, regulatory uncertainty around blockchain-based solutions was a major scale-up challenge across various sectors (PwC 2018). For the new regulatory frameworks to address this, regulations and regulatory institutions should be redesigned around the concept of functionality rather than technologies. Regulations should be dynamic and focus on enforcement of broad rules rather than detailed prescriptions. And new regulatory frameworks should recognize that many current regulations are outdated and that the new digital economy requires a clean slate approach to evaluate existing and new regulations (GSMA 2016).

New technologies used in some digital agriculture applications require a new legal framework in areas that may at first seem to be not very relevant for agriculture. Some of these are the use of unmanned aerial vehicles (or drones) as well as a global positioning system to collect data for precision agriculture. Data collection raises issues of privacy and data ownership. But beyond this, it creates the need to address safety and security concerns arising from the potential use of drones as weapons and harm to bystanders from crashes. Even high-income countries are grappling with appropriate responses, and issues and options are laid out in a recent EU Science and Technology Options Assessment dealing with precision agriculture (European Parliamentary Research Service 2017). This includes suggestions for special rules for small drones used in precision agriculture. The relevant regulations in this area will be promulgated and enforced by civil aviation or in some cases military authorities, but getting the rules right could have an important impact on the development of precision agriculture.

Enabling competition in digital markets

Given the tendency toward market concentration in digital markets, taxation, competition, and data sharing policies need to be adjusted. That tendency is not unique to digital transformation in the agrifood system, so the policy solutions are also not sector specific but revolve around changes to competition and taxation policies. Competition policy will be important in creating and capturing value in the digital economy (UNCTAD 2019). Existing frameworks need to be adapted to provide for competitive and contestable markets in the digital era and broadened to consider consumer privacy, personal data protection, consumer choice, market structure, switching costs, and lock-in effects. Taxation is another key instrument for sharing the economic gains from digital data. Many countries are rethinking how taxation rights should be allocated to prevent the undertaxation of major digital platforms in the fast-evolving digital economy. Additional proposals call for remunerating individuals who are sharing data with platforms through personal data markets or data trusts. Others call for collective data ownership and of digital data funds as a basis for a new "digital data commons." Antitrust regulation is an important instrument to ensure competition in the digital technology industry. A 2019 report to the United Kingdom Treasury, however, emphasized that conventional antitrust policies would be insufficient and that policies and regulations for data privacy, interoperability, and data use rights serve as significant factors in maintaining a competitive environment among digital platforms (Furman 2019). Additional policy instruments include investing in public research and development, facilitating access to intellectual property, and not creating unnecessary barriers to entry (OECD 2019).

Governments can also introduce their own digital transaction platforms as a service to the entire agrifood value chain, or they can provide seed financing for platforms where private funding is not furnished by the market. Countries in the developing world should not miss out on the benefits of an effective and accessible transaction platform for the agricultural sector despite a relative lack of private financing. Policy should focus on crowding in investment from the private sector or, when public investment is justified, using government and donor funds to develop digital agriculture transaction platforms. For example, India has developed its own digital transaction platform for the agricultural sector as part of its One Nation, One Market initiative. The platform, known as the Electronic National Agricultural Market (eNAM), consolidated 585 local produce markets in 14 states into one centralized website. A study from Reddy and Mehjabeen (2019) found that the eNAM platform had already yielded positive impacts only two years after its implementation in 2016. It found a statistically and economically significant positive impact on prices for pigeon peas and groundnuts received by farmers and moderately positive impacts on market arrivals for traders. The friendly posture of the Indian government toward digital technology (Digital India 2015) and its publication of open agricultural data has also allowed for the development of numerous other platforms linking producers and distributors, such as Mandi Trades. In Europe, the state-owned venture firm Portugal Ventures helped provide seed money for the digital agriculture platform AgriMarketplace with financing assistance from the European Regional Development Fund. The transaction platform aims to link farmers and producer organizations directly with counterparts in the agrifood value chain in order to facilitate transparency, fair trade, and access to the global market (Portugal Ventures 2019).

Supporting development of digital payment systems

Digital payments are an important element of digital transformation of the agrifood system. As e-commerce improves links between buyers and sellers in the value chains, digital payments are necessary to ensure that the transaction can take place in the virtual world. Digital payment systems, however, are successful only if there is sufficient interest and trust from both parties engaged in a transaction to use this form of payment. An appropriate consumer protection framework, robust digital networks, and banking and telecom policies that support digital financial services are all important components of a functioning digital payment system. In addition, targeted efforts are needed to support inclusion of the poor and disadvantaged in these payment systems to prevent inequality (World Bank 2019a).

Supporting digital skills development

Developing digital solutions for agriculture requires a certain set of skills. There is a significant need to build relevant skills and other capabilities to enable active participation of agrifood system stakeholders in the digital economy. With the expansion of various data-driven business models and solutions, companies and governments need to create and extract value from digital data. This requires a wide range of specialists, such as data scientists and data engineers. However, even in many industrialized countries, investment in more advanced computer science skills, such as those required to develop tools for machine learning, is insufficient to exploit the future opportunities of digitization (Hilbert 2016). Incorporating more digital technology content in the curriculum of agricultural universities and training institutes could help develop skill sets useful in digital development in the food system.

Fostering digital entrepreneurship ecosystems

How much digital entrepreneurship can serve as a key driver behind the increased supply of digital solutions in the agrifood system depends on the quality of surrounding ecosystems. Digital entrepreneurship refers to creating new ventures and transforming existing businesses by developing new digital technologies or experimenting with novel uses (Elio, Margherita, and Passiante 2020; Zhao and Collier 2016). The digital entrepreneurship ecosystem is the complex sociotechnical system in which distributed, heterogeneous actors participate and collaborate in digital entrepreneurship projects. The actors include potential customers and suppliers, universities and research centers, policy makers, private companies, and innovative start-ups and entrepreneurs (Cohen 2006; Isenberg 2010). The ecosystem's quality depends on the quality of its building blocks, including market accessibility, human capital availability, financial support, professional services, an explicit regulatory framework, a diffused culture, and a sensibility for education, innovation, and research (Drexler et al. 2014; Hwang and Horowitt 2012).

Effective policy responses are needed to address the digital entrepreneurship ecosystem's bottlenecks. Several bottlenecks, particularly prevalent in developing countries, can impair the quality and functioning of the digital entrepreneurship ecosystem and thus impede the supply of digital agriculture solutions (UNCTAD 2019). A common bottleneck in developing countries is the small size and scope of markets for digital solutions. Digital enterprises tend to focus their solutions on geographically narrow niche markets—often limiting their financial sustainability. Skill- and knowledge-intensive, digital enterprises rely on skilled software developers, designers, and data scientists, who are often rare in developing countries. Entrepreneurial knowledge—how to run and scale a digital enterprise—is also important but often limited. Access to finance is another critical determinant for forming an entrepreneurship ecosystem, but in developing countries, the financial sector remains generally underdeveloped. Policy makers have several entry points to support the development of quality digital entrepreneurship ecosystems in their countries.

Governments can support their agridigital entrepreneurs in scaling up their digital solutions through regional and market aggregation. Policy makers can provide incentives to support the creation of regional innovation platforms and ecosystems to deal with fragmented technological landscapes, such as those in many developing countries (UNCTAD 2019). They can incentivize different clusters within a region to develop complementary and deep technical knowledge bases, bringing together universities, research centers, and private firms. They can also offer support for scaling up promising digital solutions to attain financial viability. The greatest potential would be for digital products that are hard to replicate elsewhere, bring significant value locally or regionally, and can be easily adapted to local needs of the users. For example, the Chinese government created an initiative to establish agricultural technology parks to demonstrate new technologies, apply research and development (R&D) outputs, train human resources, and support new business plans. The National Agricultural Science and Technology Parks (NASTPs) were created to establish innovation hubs and an entrepreneurial chain to foster the transformation and incubation of agriculture science and technology innovation. By the end of 2015, 246 NASTPs were founded using both private and public funds (OECD 2018).

Improved access to financial services is another ingredient for the success of starting and taking to scale digital technology enterprises and for farmer uptake of e-agriculture. Early maturity enterprises need to rely mainly on financing from family or friends, venture capital, or commercial finance blended with concessional funding from a development partner. Notably, in some countries with flourishing digital agriculture scenes such as Brazil, the United Kingdom, and the United States, a mature venture capital ecosystem has provided the seed money for agritech start-ups (AgFunder 2018; AgFunder 2019; Radar AgTech Brazil 2019). In addition, a recent report from Disrupt Africa showed that investment in agricultural technology enterprises grew by 121 percent from 2016 to 2017 on the African continent (Disrupt Africa 2018). Nevertheless, finance inflows for digital entrepreneurship remain low, compared with other sectors in the economy. Governments can support the provision of grants to digital entrepreneurs.

Like digital skills, entrepreneurial skills are important for fostering a digital entrepreneurial ecosystem. Mentoring and business advisory programs for enterprise development tend to be more effective than one-off training (World Bank 2019a). Twiga Foods, launched in Kenya in 2014, uses a technology platform to improve the supply chain from farmers to markets—and has benefited from mentorship programs (Google Launchpad and GSMA Ecosystem). According to the United Nations Conference on Trade and Development, governments might do less on hackathons, boot camps, and high-profile technology parks and more on fostering entrepreneurial knowledge through mentorship programs, vocational training, apprenticeships, and internships (UNCTAD 2019). Policy support could also be provided to create exchange programs to build the knowledge and skills of entrepreneurs. For example, an entrepreneurship exchange program between three African countries and the United States was associated with a significant increase in participants' entrepreneurial knowledge and skills, as well as broadening new business ideas, increasing confidence to expand their business, and applying new technologies and work ethics to improve the efficiency of their business (Jayaratne et al. 2017).

Agricultural R&D is an important element of the digital innovation ecosystem. Digital solutions in agriculture rely on a large body of research, often funded by the public sector. For example, companies that produce tailormade seeds can use artificial intelligence and advanced analytics to determine a plant's genetic traits as a good match to a given soil quality. Such endeavors require surveying the existing research on plant genetics and soil quality. This kind of information has the character of a public good, and a typical task of publicly funded agricultural projects is to make this information available. But countries around the world spend less than a quarter of state support to agriculture on public goods, such as agricultural innovation systems (R&D, agricultural extension, training, and education), food safety and quality inspection systems, and physical infrastructure. And the share is much lower in developing countries. Redirecting state support to fund more R&D would improve the enabling environment for digital entrepreneurship. Note, however, that the private and public sectors need to cooperate closely in R&D in agriculture, while public funding of research centers should be driven largely by the commercial applicability of the research.

Policies Targeted at Improving Adoption of Digital Agriculture Technologies

Strengthening knowledge and skill development

Capacity building and skill development programs can stimulate demand for digital technologies from farms. A lack of understanding of how to take advantage of the benefits digital technologies offer can undermine their adoption. Investments to increase digital literacy and knowledge can resolve this (World Bank 2016). Extension and advisory services can deliver support to farmers, with different forms of learning having differing impacts on rural women (Vasilaky and Islam 2018). Governments can also facilitate farmers' education in the use of these technologies by organizing farmers into groups to promote digital literacy (FAO and ITU 2016). In addition, public-private partnerships can help farmers understand and gain a presence on e-commerce platforms. For example, technical support was provided to melon farmers in the Xinjiang region in China to improve the quality of melons, support online promotion, and manage logistics shipments to clients (World Bank 2019a).

Supporting customization of digital tools

To ensure greater inclusion of benefits from these technologies will also require developing relevant, customized digital tools of appropriate design and in relevant languages targeted to disadvantaged groups. To correctly identify potential user needs requires participatory approaches in digital agriculture initiatives (Treinen and van der Elstraeten 2018). For example, in a needs assessment at the Kubere Center in Uganda, women indicated that their main interest was in farming techniques, market prices for farm produce, and health and education issues (World Bank, FAO, and IFAD 2009). Consequently, this information was provided through radio and by mobile phone, which were used by women. Language is also important in product design, and the public sector can help ensure that products meet customer needs in this dimension. In Ghana, Talking Books reached a high adoption rate by providing 140 hours of audio content to illiterate people on agriculture and other rural issues in local languages and dialects on a low-cost audio computer. From 2008 to 2015, the number of

Talking Books users increased from 1,000 to 175,000 in Ghana alone. In 2012, the average harvest of farmers who used Talking Books increased by 36 percent after one year (Treinen and van der Elstraeten 2018). And in Rwanda, reasons for the low uptake rates of the e-wallet initiative among farmers was attributed to receiving text messages in English rather than in Kinyarwanda (Grossman and Tarazi 2014).

Reducing the cost of adopting digital technologies

Reducing the cost of digital technology adoption will also promote inclusion. The price farmers pay for digital services seems to matter for adoption, with a lower willingness to pay by women, a difference that may reflect differential access to resources (Palloni et al. 2018). Technology can be expensive, and this problem can be exacerbated if technology companies do not understand farmers' needs but overdesign the products they are marketing (UN 2017). In some cases, it may be useful for ministries of agriculture to bring together farmers and tech companies to make sure this does not happen. The public-good nature of some digital services needs to be reflected in its price for farmers. Information is a classic public good, so it could be provided for free or at minimal cost. Public subsidies should not displace private activity, but for true public goods, for which the benefits are not appropriable by the provider because they are not excludable (for instance, information), there may be no displacement because the private sector would not provide such goods in any case.

Apart from finance for technology development and diffusion, the lack of finance to enable farmers and agribusinesses to invest in these technologies can also be a limiting factor. Finance for agriculture through commercial banks is still limited, and the sector attracts credit well below its contribution to gross domestic product. For example, only about 1 percent of commercial credit in Africa goes to agriculture. Enabling inclusive access to finance through credit and insurance could allow farmers and agribusinesses to invest in digital solutions. Microfinance institutions in several countries serve rural households, but at relatively high costs. Digital innovations in themselves can also solve the problems of access to finance. (Relevant public policy entry points to solve constraints on adopting digital technologies for agricultural finance are discussed in detail in chapter 4.)

In some instances, the public sector can support private and cooperative providers of apps and digital platforms technically and financially. Both private contractors and farmer cooperatives provide digital services to farmers. For example, private contractors generally own machinery and provide services for ploughing, spraying, harvesting, and so on to farmers for a payment. Digital tracking devices, by reducing transaction costs in the machinery rental market, enhance smallholder farmers' access to machinery. Digital technologies have considerable cost advantages for contractors—for example, software tools are available that help manage agricultural machinery—so it is not surprising that large-scale contractors providing machinery services to farmers are at the forefront of using digital agricultural technologies. But many smallholder farmers are still not able to access such services. Farmer cooperatives may provide digital services. For example, a dairy cooperative might collect breeding performance information or provide an app with information on feeding and management. The public sector, jointly with the private sector and farmer associations, can identify areas where additional technical or financial support may be provided to ensure that marginalized producers can benefit from such services, while ensuring that public sector support does not substitute for private sector investments.

Building trust in digital applications

Lack of information on technology and lack of trust in its promised benefits constrain farmers' adoption of digital technologies. Governments can facilitate adoption by reducing constraints, including through generating knowledge and evidence about digital technologies' effectiveness, organizing field trips and shows where farmers can directly observe improvements achieved by early adopters, improving the skills of farmers to use such technologies, ensuring privacy of their data, and, in some cases, providing monetary incentives for technology use.

Generating knowledge and evidence about digital technologies' effectiveness can lower the risk aversion that delays adoption. Choosing new technologies often requires absorbing considerable information. Individuals tend to learn from the experience of members of their community and adopt the practices used by successful individuals. Such information sharing or farmer-to-farmer learning has been common, but digital tools allow spreading information more widely. To reduce uncertainty about a practice's effectiveness, the public sector can support piloting and knowledge exchange through farmers' schools. And public extension agents equipped with smartphones or tablets can document interesting innovations that farmers propose and share the information with other farmers.

Strengthening extension services to promote and support analysis using digital support tools with new data streams provides a new and productive direction for governments to support the uptake of digital technologies by farmers. Advanced communications provide an opportunity for remote assistance to farmers whereby advisory staff could present from remote locations, provide analytic results and advice, check on data quality and content, and interact visually with farmers in the field. The change of emphasis and realignment of required skills for advisory staff provide an entry point for government action and a mechanism for substantially more cost-effective delivery of services. Integrating digital agriculture into the curriculum for extension agents and developing training programs for staff already in service are key activities. Training that uses digital tools already available, such as apps and platforms for farmers and for extension agents, will be most effective. Governments can support training by developing training materials in agricultural ministries and agencies. The provision of extension services does not need to be provided by governments in that digital economy training programs for farmers can be supplied by the service economy, while the entry points for public policy are associated with the enabling environment. The role of the government would shift from developer and provider of farmer training to director of curriculum, overseer of standards of delivery, and monitor of outcomes. The changed role would enable private providers to develop and deliver materials and charge either the government or trainees for the training.

In addition, the public sector could support the development of generic extension management software that national extension services could adapt to their specific needs. As an example, Uganda's national agricultural extension service is piloting an electronic diary (e-diary) for agricultural extension agents that facilitates planning and reporting daily extension activities. The e-diary also improves accountability by giving the agents' supervisor access to their documentation of activities, such as photos of meetings with farmers. The pilot has been promising (Namenya, Rwamigisa, and Birner 2019).

Cooperatives, as well as private entrepreneurs, can provide digital services to farmers and indirectly facilitate the adoption of digital technologies by them. In addition, digitally savvy cooperatives can help the smallest and most isolated producers reduce transaction costs and boost bargaining power. The role of the government lies in ensuring a business environment favorable for cooperatives, including ensuring that the regulatory framework allows for digitally enabled governance mechanisms. In addition, the public sector could work with cooperatives in training farmers on using digital technologies.

Government can act to build the trust of farmers in e-commerce. With a reported target of reducing transaction costs and providing an alternative route to the consumer, e-commerce confronts problems of trust among farmers. Various entry points for public policy appear and represent developments on existing policy roles. They include the establishment and enforcement of the quality standards and nomenclature used to describe products and recognition of specific product certifications. Regulatory mechanisms are needed to specify the quality of inputs and monitor them to ensure they are unadulterated and correctly labeled. In addition, given the paperless nature of e-transactions, it is crucial to find mechanisms for the identification of parties and the authentication of commercial transactions. In this sense, a central issue is the legal recognition of electronic and digital signatures, so that both parties can be assured of the validity of their transactions (World Bank 2019b). Similarly, the lack of or inadequate enforcement of rules on electronic payments may diminish trust in e-commerce. Digital transaction laws on e-signatures and payments are needed to limit the potential distrust of farmers in e-commerce solutions.

POLICIES TARGETED AT MAXIMIZING EQUITY OUTCOMES OF DIGITAL TRANSFORMATION

Addressing Data Access Asymmetries in the Agrifood System

Asymmetry of information and misalignment of incentives about the use and business value of data create new roles for governments to ensure equitable distribution of value creation in digital economy. The data-heavy character of digital agriculture has raised concerns over data privacy, security, and sovereignty (Bronson and Knezevic 2016; Carolan 2017; Wolfert et al. 2017). So an important role for the government is putting in place a legal and regulatory framework to address any risks associated with data use. Efforts to ensure appropriate data privacy should be based on three underlying principles. First, collecting data should be transparent (individuals should know if someone is collecting their data). Second, individuals should know and have a voice in how their data is being used. And third, the models for data sharing should work for both the suppliers of the data (individuals) and the users of the data (enterprises). Data governance arrangements should build the confidence and trust of users of digital technologies, such as farmers and agribusinesses, and help facilitate development of digital applications that can benefit them, such as improving access to finance.

Some good practices arising around the world aim to ensure data privacy, security and sovereignty. As of 2014, 107 countries had privacy laws in place (FAO 2019). Several international organizations—including the OECD, the United Nations, and the African Union—have principles or guidelines for governance of data collection, use, and flows. But even in developed countries, the legal and regulatory frameworks for agricultural data ownership remain piecemeal and provisional. In Canada and the United States, the law does not recognize agricultural data as physical or intellectual property. So, data ownership is not clearly defined. Countries have also been experimenting with different approaches to address data ownership. Agricultural sectors in New Zealand and the United States have been using voluntary industry standards to establish an understanding between farmers and service providers who use farm data on data ownership. In 2018, a coalition of agrifood associations in the EU introduced a joint EU Code of Conduct on agricultural data sharing. The EU has also issued a Science and Technology Options Assessment dealing with precision agriculture, which includes a comprehensive discussion of many legal and ethical issues raised by data collection and use in e-agriculture, and options for dealing with them (European Parliamentary Research Service 2017).

Governments also have a role in ensuring interoperability and promoting standards to ensure compatibility of digital tools across brands. Data incompatibility and nontransferability across digital platforms and the equipment of different service providers could create difficulties in changing providers, path dependencies, power asymmetries between agribusinesses and farmers, and a loss of farmer bargaining power. The imbalance could amplify if agribusiness companies know a farmer's yields from sensors on harvesters, along with crop price data and input data, in order to extract the highest price for services or equipment the farmer will accept. The risk of imbalance depends partly on whether digital agriculture solutions are based on closed proprietary systems or open and flexible systems (Wolfert et al. 2017). One such closed system would be John Deere's, in which digital locks keep farmers from accessing some data their machines collect (Bronson 2019). So far, industry self-regulation by developing common standards has kept this problem in check. For tractors and implements, the ISOBUS (ISO 11783) standard has been established, and for precision livestock farming, the ISOAgriNet standard (Jungbluth, Büscher, and Krause 2017, 48). If industry initiatives turn out insufficient, antitrust regulation is possible. As in the software industry (for example, in the famous 2001 Microsoft antitrust case), regulators may require agricultural companies to make their software systems for equipment and farm management compatible so that farmers can combine hardware and software from different providers.

Similarly, governments can encourage interoperability between mobile operators and financial institutions to improve the financial inclusion of smallholder farmers. Interoperability is the ability of mobile money operators to connect to each other and to the banking system. For smallholder farmers, this means that they can send money across mobile money networks to a savings account or to a receiver in real time. Two examples of interoperability are worth highlighting. Equitel, a partnership between Equity Bank and Airtel, is the first. This service allows customers to maintain cash in a savings account, send money from their account to any bank account in Kenya, and obtain loans. M-Shwari, a partnership between Safaricom and the Commercial Bank of Africa in Kenya, is a second example. The technology that allows interoperability is straightforward since mobile networks are already interoperable. But mobile network operators, especially large incumbents, may not necessarily find interoperability attractive since they would rather keep their large market share. One option would be for the public sector to design a central switch or automated clearinghouse and request that all operators connect to it. A regulator ensures that the central switch does not harm national interests. For example, the Bank of Ghana set up a subsidiary, the Ghana Interbank Payment and Settlement Systems, with the mandate of establishing and operating a national switch (Beck and Maimbo 2012).

Improving the Access and Use of Digital Technologies by Marginalized Groups

Policies and public expenditures need to ensure that digital agriculture does not create or add to existing inequities. This includes expanding network coverage to more remote rural areas, supporting youth and women entrepreneurs with mentoring and technical support, improving the skills of smallholder farmers to take advantage of digital technologies, and fostering the development of digital technologies, including government e-services, customized to the needs and general skills of small farmers.

Securing farmers' rights to their land is necessary to mitigate the digital divide between large and small farms. Digital technologies risk eroding the competitive advantage of small family farms over large ones. To avoid unfair competition, family farms' rights to their land must be secured and corporate farms kept from disregarding labor and environmental standards. At the international level, the World Committee on Food Security has developed two policy instruments to address this problem: the Voluntary Guidelines on the Responsible Governance of Tenure of Land, Fisheries, and Forests in the Context of National Food Security and the principles for Responsible Investment in Agriculture and Food Systems. Even though these instruments were not developed specifically for digitization, the large corporate farms' digitization creates an additional rationale for governments to ensure that they are observed.

The smallest and most isolated producers can reduce transaction costs and boost bargaining power by digitally empowered collective action, but the regulatory framework needs to catch up to enable digitally enabled governance mechanisms. New cooperative laws will be needed to extend cooperatives' principle of shared ownership and benefits of use to data assets. Cooperatives' equity-conscious governance entails shared ownership. Collaborative models that rely on a "digital commons" and access to the sharing economy for services require several new elements of cooperative governance and public policy treatment of farmer collaboration. Ownership of data and the hardware and service elements of a functioning digital resource all pose challenges to existing cooperative law and the emerging interface between the cooperative and the data it uses, generates, and shares. Cooperative law and operating principles generally refer to the allocation of benefits through use: members benefit not from ownership of the cooperative's assets but from their use (ICA 2018). Public policy toward cooperatives would need to identify data and services associated with cooperative operations and relate them to members' use. This is made more complex by the likely appearance of new business models using cooperative principles (Proctor and Vorley 2008).

An increase in the volume and speed of cooperative marketing will also require new cooperative laws and digitally enabled governance mechanisms. The further development of cooperatives as data-driven organizations offers the opportunity for government to provide demand-side stimulus to farmers in relation to the downstream food value chain. Virtual cooperative organizations will be associated with online collaboration within and beyond their membership, weak ties to any specific location, and diversification in commodities, markets, and member types. These characteristics depart from much existing cooperative law and practice, so they would need new cooperative legislation. Internal management and control mechanisms, such as price pooling and the establishment of interim and final payments would ideally be supported by digital tools, and the implementation of governance would be linked to the same information systems. Public policy has a role in defining and verifying the efficacy of such digital oversight, providing links to cooperative regulation, and aligning activities with cooperatives' stated purpose and bylaws. This allows the government to take advantage of new data streams and their capacity for integration.

Programs can be designed to target women effectively. In Bihar, India, recent support connected women farmers with agricultural market platforms. The project organized women farmers into their own producer company and supported them with daily commodity price information via mobile phones. It used digital scales and electronic moisture meters to challenge traders' manipulated equipment. It connected farmers to an online commodity exchange to sell anywhere in the country. And it improved their access to storage and warehousing so they could sell when prices were better. These interventions increased the product prices the women farmers received. Beyond individual programs, digital innovations should be mainstreamed into national strategies in a gender-sensitive way to advance the social inclusion of women. There is also a need to collect gender-disaggregated data to analyze how women and men access digital tools and use them for agricultural activities—and how access for women can be improved.

Improving Smallholders' Access to Mobile Payments and Digital Credit

Mobile money and digital credit positively contributes to the financial inclusion of smallholder farmers. It not only helps households deposit and withdraw their savings in formal institutions, it also allows them to tap into their savings or credit resources in times of need. But the fast-evolving world of mobile money risks harming end users. Therefore, the public sector should create appropriate policies and regulations and use them to protect smallholder interests. This objective could be achieved as follows:

- *Building the capacity of financial institutions serving smallholder farmers to provide services in a digital format.* Mobile money operators are increasingly innovating in the services they provide. To keep pace and cooperate effectively with mobile money operators, financial institutions, especially those serving smallholder farmers, need strong in-house information technology capacities, which the public sector could provide. Smallholder farmers face their own needs, given the seasonality of their activities and vulnerability to weather shocks. Therefore, the capacity of financial institutions should also be strengthened, through a combination of grants and trainings, to address the needs of smallholder farmers and learn to assess the bankability of agricultural projects.
- *Raising awareness and providing specialized technical support for marginalized customers, including smallholder farmers.* The public sector should design

complementary, supportive policies that ensure the inclusion of the marginalized smallholders in digital credit. Examples include providing technical resources to navigate bureaucratic systems, or in some cases, overcome basic literacy constraints. In addition, the public sector could support (financially and technically) the development of products tailored to women. Products that provide women (and other social and economic groups) greater control and privacy are promising for women's economic empowerment, although the specific embodiment of those principles may vary from place to place (Buvinic, Furst-Nichols, and Pryor 2013; Karlan et al. 2016).

• *Financing databases that the private sector can use to assess the creditworthiness of marginalized groups.* Mistaken predictions through digital credit scores, especially for marginalized populations, are likely. Model outputs tend to skew toward individuals who associate with people there is information about. Further data collection efforts for marginalized groups are beginning—such as the GSM Association's piloting of approaches to detect transactions by women—under the premise that distinguishing marginalized groups in transaction data can lead to policies removing barriers to their participation. The public sector could financially support this data collection effort and build the data infrastructure. Credit predictions will, however, need to avoid using digital footprint information that reflects characteristics whose use might be considered discriminatory under fair lending acts.

Empowering Female Digital Entrepreneurs

Broadening opportunities for women entrepreneurs in digital agriculture can bridge the gender-induced digital divide. Several forms of financial and technical support could be considered by governments and donor organizations. Mentoring, networking, and exposure to role models can help overcome gender biases or cultural norms that limit women's ability to confidently start or sustain projects in e-commerce and data-driven technology. The G20 has made bridging the digital gender divide a priority and provided examples of policy interventions. For example, France introduced in October 2017 a new partnership between the bank Caisse d'épargne, the agency Caisse des dépôts, and the state to increase the number of women entrepreneurs in France by at least 40 percent in 2020. Germany's Frauenunternehmen encourages women to consider entrepreneurship or self-employment as a viable career option by providing them with role models (OECD 2019). Donor organizations such as the Canadian International Development Research Centre have supported initiatives in developing countries to broaden digital opportunities for female entrepreneurs, notably the Improving Prospects for Digitally Enabled Livelihoods project in the Arab Republic of Egypt, which aims to pilot and develop localized high-quality training content mainly for women to develop the skills needed to profit from job and entrepreneurship opportunities in the digital economy (OECD 2019). While these interventions are not specific to agriculture, they can be adapted for the needs of entrepreneurship in digital agriculture. Another approach is to support new networks of women leaders in e-commerce in different developing regions (UNCTAD 2019). The African Women Agribusiness Network in Kenya does just that, supporting women in agriculture entering global markets by organizing leadership and management trainings, as well as networking opportunities (CTA 2019). Broader dialogue among policy makers, private enterprise, and civil society on empowering women to take advantage of digital transformations in agriculture should be encouraged locally, nationally, and internationally

Adopting Compensatory Measures for the Potential Losers in Digital Transformation of the Agrifood System

Public policy should ensure that winners compensate losers emerging from digital transformation through transfer payments or paying for their unemployment compensation and training programs. The net outcome of digital transformation on the agricultural sector will likely be contextual, depending on the level of sector and country development, production and market structures, and skills and technological capabilities. It will also depend on policy actions taken to manage the technological transition. Education, training, social protection measures, and labor market policies could mitigate the negative impact of digital transformation on those unable to reap its benefits. Most of these policies are not specific to agriculture, but ministries of agriculture can support the development of training programs that would allow agricultural workers to transition to higher value jobs within the agrifood system. Similarly, ministries of agriculture need to be champions of coherence between social protection and agriculture. Social protection measures could be designed to encourage recipients to take advantage of the changing realities of digital transformation in the agrifood system.

POLICIES TARGETED AT MAXIMIZING ENVIRONMENTAL SUSTAINABILITY OUTCOMES OF DIGITAL TRANSFORMATION

Strengthening Digital Environmental Monitoring in the Agrifood System

Digital technologies can strengthen monitoring of the environmental impacts of the agrifood system. Digital technologies can improve the monitoring, cataloging, interpreting, and dissemination of data about the status and trends of agroecosystems to ensure that agricultural products are delivered with smaller environmental footprints and their prices reflect the life-cycle costs of production (Zaks and Kucharik 2011). In general, modern agroecological monitoring systems require physical monitoring systems (remote sensing and ground-based monitoring with real-time, smart, wireless, internet-connected sensor webs). They also require data analysis systems that transform raw data streams into useful information for decision-making (Adamchuk et al. 2004; Hale and Hollister 2009; McLaren et al. 2009; Rundel et al. 2009). Environmental field data most often collected include quantifying soil, water, greenhouse gases, and nutrient cycling. But environmental data collection methods in agroecological landscapes vary based on the scale of interest and intended purpose. They are rarely consistently integrated with crop production data.

Stronger monitoring of environmental impacts can provide incentives for creating and integrating environmental and production data streams and directing them to decision-makers. Many technologies and data for environmental monitoring are already available but have seldom been incorporated systematically (Gebbers and Adamchuk 2010). Governments can introduce policies and economic incentives that bring together academia, private industries, and farmers to deliver monitoring data to decision-makers. This would require a robust system to collect, analyze, and disseminate data on the functioning of the agricultural system (Zaks and Kucharik 2011). Putting these data in the hands of decision-makers—producers, scientists, or policy makers—could reduce environmental impact while increasing the efficiency of production.

Digital technologies can support more efficient monitoring of compliance with agrienvironmental policies. Advances in remote sensing, precision agriculture, and automation algorithms hold promise for monitoring policy compliance. Communication technologies and high-resolution agricultural data can also improve farmers' awareness of environmental issues and their contribution to them. Digital communication tools—increasing transparency on compliance but also on the impacts of policies—can support better engagement by farmers. Digitally enabled results-based policies could thus be an opportunity to improve policy participation with the goal of improving the environmental performance of agriculture.

Public datasets can support natural resource management policies. Although data collected by precision agriculture technologies could help policy makers monitor on-farm decisions that affect the environment, such data are owned by the technology provider and are subject to confidentiality conditions. But the public sector, in programs paying farmers based on ecosystem services, could ask farmers to share their data to verify compliance with the programs.

Incorporating Environmental Sustainability Goals in Agricultural Policies

Agricultural policy and support should incentivize farmers to adopt digital technologies with environmental benefits. Digital technologies, however, cannot substitute for sound policies and coordinated efforts to safeguard natural resources. Digital technologies do not, by themselves, directly address the market failures that devalue natural resources. And some agricultural policies may discourage farmers from using digital solutions. For example, when governments provide subsidized fertilizers and determine the type of fertilizer and the time it is provided, farmers have no incentive to invest in digital agriculture, few of them will use digital advisory services, and fertilizer firms have limited incentives to offer farm management services or improved fertilizers. Similarly, government regulation of drone use is often not adapted to agriculture, leaving cumbersome procedures that effectively prevent it (Reger, Bauerdick, and Bernhardt 2018). Governments could incentivize using digital technologies that promote environmental sustainability by repurposing distortive support toward digital technologies with environmental cobenefits, such as precision agriculture equipment or tractor rental through digital platforms (the latter since renting has a lower environmental footprint than buying). Support could be provided, for example, as a matching grant to cofinance equipment purchases or, for the poorest farmers, e-vouchers to subsidize machinery rentals.

Incentivizing Development of Green Digital Technologies

Government can also support access to finance for local entrepreneurs who develop green digital technologies. Entrepreneurs in developing countries often lack access to finance. At the same time, financing mechanisms created to support climate-friendly projects could benefit digital technologies with the potential to reduce greenhouse gas emissions. Although various opportunities exist for finance at preferential rates for climate-friendly projects, entrepreneurs have little knowledge of them and so fail to access them. Maintaining a central repository of such opportunities and public sector advertising of them when they are available may improve entrepreneurs' access to finance.

Influencing Consumer Behavior and Agrifood Markets

Informed consumers can shift agrifood markets toward greater environmental sustainability through changes in their purchasing and consumption habits. Environmentally sustainable consumer behavior could include voluntarily reducing or simplifying consumption of a product, choosing products with sustainable sourcing, production, and features, and using more sustainable modes of food waste disposal (White, Habib, and Hardisty 2019). Digital technologies also offer opportunities for governments to influence consumer behavior by delivering information and education about sustainable consumer practices. For example, the US Department of Agriculture (USDA n.d.) has a Food Loss and Waste Portal with information on the importance of reducing food waste and on initiatives, activities, strategies, and USDA partnerships to reduce waste for upstream and downstream firms and individuals—with links for farmers, businesses, consumers, and schools. In Hong Kong SAR, China, the government is using a range of technologies, from social media to mobile apps, to increase the consumption of sustainable food by its citizens.

Digital decision tools also offer significant advances in the development and presentation of value chain performance measures concerned with environmental sustainability. These analytic devices would become required content under a code of practice where government at all levels would require reporting and in return supply its own data for use in the support tools. Sanderson, Wiseman, and Poncini (2018) evaluate two such national level codes of practice for agricultural data (in New Zealand and the United States), which both focus on "consent, disclosure, transparency and, ultimately, the building of trust" (p. 3). In both cases, upward communication to higher level policy was emphasized by links to laws on business operation and privacy, while downward links enabled the use of a trademark by commercial firms certified according to the code of practice.

REFERENCES

Adamchuk, V., J. Hummel, M. Morgan, and S. Upadhyaya. 2004. "On-the-go Soil Sensors for Precision Agriculture." *Computers and Electronics in Agriculture* 44: 71–91.

AgFunder. 2018. "AgFunder AgriFood Tech Investing Report, 2018." AgFunder, San Francisco, CA. https://agfunder.com/research/agrifood-tech-investing-report-2018/.

AgFunder. 2019. "AgFunder AgrifoodTech Investing Report, 2019." AgFunder, San Francisco, CA. https://agfunder.com/research/agfunder-agrifood-tech-investing-report-2019/.

AIMS (Agriculture Information Management Standards Portal, FAO). 2020. "AGROVOC." FAO, Rome. http://aims.fao.org/vest-registry/vocabularies/agrovoc.

Beck, Thorsten, and Samuel Munzele Maimbo, eds. 2012. *Financial Sector Development in Africa: Opportunities and Challenges.* Washington DC: World Bank. https://doi .org/10.1596/978-0-8213-9628-5.

Bronson, K. 2019. "Looking through a Responsible Innovation Lens at Uneven Engagements with Digital Farming." *NJAS–Wageningen Journal of Life Sciences* 90–91 (December): 100294.

Bronson, K., and I. Knezevic. 2016. "Big Data in Food and Agriculture." *Big Data & Society* 3 (1): 1–5.

Brouder, S., A. Eagle, N. Fukagawa, J. McNamara, S. Murray, C. Parr, and N. Tremblay. 2019. "Enabling Open-source Data Networks in Public Agricultural Research." Council for Agricultural Science and Technology, Ames, IA. https://www.cast-science.org/wp -content/uploads/2019/05/QTA2019-1-Data-Sharing.pdf.

Buvinic, Mayra, Rebecca Furst-Nichols, and Emily Courey Pryor. 2013. "A Roadmap for Women's Economic Empowerment." UN Foundation, New York. http://www .womeneconroadmap.org/sites/default/files/WEE_Roadmap_Report_Final.pdf.

Buys, P., S. Dasgupta, T. Thomas, and D. Wheeler. 2009. "Determinants of a Digital Divide in Sub-Saharan Africa: A Spatial Econometric Analysis of Cell Phone Coverage." *World Development* 37 (9): 1494–505.

Carolan, M. 2017. "Publicising Food: Big Data, Precision Agriculture, and Co-experimental Techniques of Addition." *Sociologia Ruralis* 57 (2): 135–54.

Cohen, B. 2006. "Sustainable Valley Entrepreneurial Ecosystems." *Business Strategy and the Environment* 15 (1): 1–14.

CTA (Technical Center for Agriculture and Rural Cooperation). 2019. *The Digitalization of African Agriculture Report.* Wageningen, the Netherlands: CTA. https://doi.org/10.1093 /oxfordjournals.afraf.a094187.

Deichmann, U., A. Goyal, and D. Mishra. 2016. "Will Digital Technologies Transform Agriculture in Developing Countries?" *Agricultural Economics* 1 (47): 21–33.

Digital India. 2015. "How Digital India Will Be Realized: Pillars of Digital India." Ministry of Electronics and IT, New Delhi. https://digitalindia.gov.in/content/programme-pillars.

Disrupt Africa. 2018. "Agrinnovating for Africa 2018." Disrupt Africa. https://gumroad.com/l/pExaF.

Drexler, M., M. Eltogby, G. Foster, C. Shimizu, S. Ciesinsik, A. Davila, S. Z. Hassan, et al. 2014. *Entrepreneurial Ecosystems around the Globe and Early-stage Company Growth Dynamics: Industry Agenda.* Geneva: World Economic Forum.

Elio, G., A. Margherita, and G. Passiante. 2020. "Digital Entrepreneurship Ecosystem: How Digital Technologies and Collective Intelligence Are Reshaping the Entrepreneurial Process." *Technological Forecasting and Social Change* 150: 119791.

European Parliamentary Research Service. 2017. *Precision Agriculture in Europe: Legal, Social, and Ethical Considerations.* Brussels: European Union.

FAO (Food and Agriculture Organization of the United Nations). 2019. "Digital Technologies in Agriculture and Rural Areas: Briefing Paper." FAO, Rome. http://www.fao.org/3/ca4985en/ca4985en.pdf.

FAO (Food and Agriculture Organization of the United Nations) and ITU (International Telecommunication Union). 2016. *E-agriculture Strategy Guide: Piloted in Asia-Pacific Countries.* Bangkok: FAO and ITU.

Furman, J. 2019. *Unlocking Digital Competition: Report of the Digital Competition Expert Panel.* London: HM Treasury. https://assets.publishing.service.gov.uk/government/uploads/system/uploads/attachment_data/file/785547/unlocking_digital_competition_furman_review_web.pdf.

Gabella, C., C. Durinx, and R. Appel. 2017. "Funding Knowledge Bases: Towards a Sustainable Funding Model for the UniProt Use Case." F100 Research 6 (ELIXIR): 2051. Swiss Institute of Bioinformatics, Lausanne, Switzerland.

Gebbers, R., and V. Adamchuk. 2010. "Precision Agriculture and Food Security." *Science* 327 (5967).

Grossman, J., and M. Tarazi. 2014. "Serving Smallholder Farmers: Recent Developments in Digital Finance." Focus Note 94, Consultative Group to Assist the Poorest, Washington, DC.

GSMA. 2016. *A New Regulatory Framework for the Digital Ecosystem.* London: GSMA. https://www.gsma.com/publicpolicy/wp-content/uploads/2016/09/GSMA2016_Report_NewRegulatoryFrameworkForTheDigitalEcosystem_English.pdf.

GSMA. 2018. *State of the Industry Report on Mobile Money: 2018.* London: GSMA.

Hale, S. S., and J. W. Hollister. 2009. "Beyond Data Management: How Ecoinformatics Can Benefit Environmental Monitoring Programs." *Environmental Monitoring and Assessment* 150: 227–35.

Hilbert, M. 2016. "Big Data for Development: A Review of Promises and Challenges." *Development Policy Review* 34 (1): 135–74. https://doi.org/10.1111/dpr.12142.

Huang, J., and H. Zhi. 2018. "The Uses of ICT in Agriculture and E-commerce in Rural China: The Evidence from Village and Household Surveys." Background paper, World Bank, Washington, DC.

Hwang, V. W., and G. Horowitt. 2012. *The Rainforest: The Secret to Building the Next Silicon Valley.* Scotts Valley, CA: Createspace Independent.

ICA (International Co-operative Alliance). 2018. "Cooperative Identity, Values and Principles." ICA, Brussels. https://www.ica.coop/en/cooperatives/cooperative-identity.

Isenberg, D. J. 2010. "How to Start an Entrepreneurial Revolution." *Harvard Business Review* (June 2010).

Jayaratne, K., L. Taylor, M. C. Edwards, D. Cartmell, C. Watters, and S. Henneberry. 2017. "Evaluation of an International Entrepreneur Exchange Program: Impacts, Lessons Learned, and Implications for Agricultural Development." *Journal of International Agricultural and Extension Education* 24 (2): 50–64. doi:10.5191/jiaee.2017.24204.

Jungbluth, T., W. Büscher, and M. Krause. 2017. *Technik Tierhaltung*, 2nd ed.. Stuttgart: Eugen Ulmer.

Karlan, Dean, Jake Kendall, Rebecca Mann, Rohini Pande, Tavneet Suri, and Jonathan Zinman. 2016. "Research and Impacts of Digital Financial Services." National Bureau of Economic Research, Cambridge, MA. https://www.nber.org/system/files/working_papers/w22633/w22633.pdf.

Kärner, E. 2017. "The Future of Agriculture is Digital: Showcasing e-Estonia." *Frontiers in Veterinary Sciences* 21 (September). https://doi.org/10.3389/fvets.2017.00151.

Maru, A., D. Berne, J. de Beer, P. Ballantyne, V. Pesce, S. Kalyesubula, N. Fourie, C. Addison, A. Collett, and J. Chaves. 2018. *Digital and Data-Driven Agriculture: Harnessing the Power of Data for Smallholders*. Rome: Global Forum on Agricultural Research and Innovation.

McLaren, C. G., T. Metz, M. van den Berg, R. M. Bruskiewich, N. P. Magor, and D. Shires. 2009. "Chapter 4 Informatics in Agricultural Research for Development." *Advances in Agronomy* 102: 135–57.

Namenya, A., P. Rwamigisa, and R. Birner. 2019. "Using a Diary to Strengthen Accountability in Agricultural Extension Services." Unpublished manuscript, University of Hohenheim, Stuttgart, Germany.

OECD (Organisation for Economic Co-operation and Development). 2015. *OECD Public Governance Reviews: Estonia and Finland. Fostering Strategic Capacity across Governments and Digital Services across Borders*. Paris: OECD.

OECD. 2018. *Innovation, Agricultural Productivity and Sustainability in China*. OECD Food and Agricultural Reviews. Paris: OECD. https://doi.org/10.1787/9789264085299-en.

OECD. 2019. *Digital Opportunities for Better Agricultural Policies*. Paris: OECD. https://doi.org/10.1787/571a0812-en.

Palloni, G., J. Aker, D. Gilligan, M. Hidrobo, and N. Ledlie. 2018. *Paying for Digital Information: Assessing Farmers' Willingness to Pay for a Digital Agriculture and Nutrition Service in Ghana*. Washington, DC: International Food Policy Research Institute.

Portugal Ventures. 2019. "Agrimarketplace." Portugal Ventures, Porto, Portugal. https://www.portugalventures.pt/en/portfolio/agrimarketplace/.

Proctor, F. J., and B. Vorley. 2008. "Innovation in Business Models and Chainwide Learning for Market Inclusion of Smallholder Producers." *BANWA: A Multidisciplinary Journal* 8 (2): 1–17.

PwC (PricewaterhouseCoopers). 2018. "Global Blockchain Survey." PwC, London (accessed August 10, 2020). https://www.pwc.com/blockchainsurvey. Accessed 10 August 2020.

Radar AgTech Brazil. 2019. "Mapeamento das startups do setor agro brasileiro." https://www.radaragtech.com.br.

Reddy, A. A., and Mehjabeen. 2019. "Electronic National Agricultural Markets, Impacts, Problems and Way Forward." *IIM Kozhikode Society & Management Review* 8 (2): 143–155.

Reger, M., J. Bauerdick, and H. Bernhardt. 2018. "Drones in Agriculture: Current and Future Legal Status in Germany, the EU, the USA and Japan." *Landtechnik* 73 (3): 62–79. https://doi.org/10.15150/lt.2018.3183.

Rundel, P. W., E. A. Graham, M. F. Allen, J. C. Fisher, and T. C. Harmon. 2009. "Environmental Sensor Networks in Ecological Research." *New Phytologist* 182 (3): 589–607.

Samarajiva, R., and A. Zainudeen. 2010. "Regulatory Reform and Rural Roll-Out of Information and Communication Technologies (ICTs)." In *Information Technology and Communications Resources for Sustainable Development*, edited by A. Jhunjhunwala. UNESCO Encyclopedia Life Support Systems. Paris: UNESCO.

Sanderson, J., L. Wiseman, and S. Poncini. 2018. "What's behind the Ag-Data Logo? An Examination of Voluntary Agricultural Data Codes of Practice." *International Journal of Rural Law and Policy* 1: 1–21.

Treinen, S., and A. van der Elstraeten. 2018. *Gender and ICTs: Mainstreaming Gender in the Use of Information and Communication Technologies (ICTs) for Agriculture and Rural Development*. Rome: FAO.

UN (United Nations). 2017. *United Nations Global Compact Progress Report 2017: Business Solutions to Sustainable Development*. New York: UN.

UNCTAD (United Nations Conference on Trade and Development). 2019. *Digital Economy Report 2019: Value Creation and Capture: Implications for Developing Countries*. Geneva: UNCTAD.

USDA (US Department of Agriculture). n.d. "Food Loss and Waste." USDA, Washington, DC. https://www.usda.gov/foodlossandwaste.

Vasilaky, K. N., and A. M. Islam. 2018 "Competition or Cooperation? Using Team and Tournament Incentives for Learning among Female Farmers in Rural Uganda." *World Development* 103: 216–25.

White, K., R. Habib, and D. Hardisty. 2019. "How to SHIFT Consumer Behaviors to be More Sustainable: A Literature Review and Guiding Framework." *Journal of Marketing* 83 (3): 22–49.

Wilkinson, M. D., M. Dumontier, I. J. Aalbersberg, G. Appleton, M. Axton, A. Baak, N. Blomberg, et al. 2016. "The FAIR Guiding Principles for Scientific Data Management and Stewardship." *Scientific Data* 2016 (3): 160018. doi:10.1038/sdata.2016.18.

Wolfert, S., L. Ge, C. Verdouw, and M.-J. Bogaardt. 2017. "Big Data in Smart Farming: A Review." *Agricultural Systems* 153 (May): 69–80.

World Bank. 2016. *World Development Report 2016: Digital Dividends*. Washington, DC: World Bank.

World Bank. 2017. *Enabling the Business of Agriculture 2017*. Washington, DC: World Bank. http://pubdocs.worldbank.org/en/251961534213553996/EBA17-Reports-Highlight17 .pdf.

World Bank. 2019a. *Future of Food: Harnessing Digital Technologies to Improve Food System Outcomes*. Washington, DC: World Bank.

World Bank. 2019b. *Unleashing E-commerce for South Asian Integration*. Washington, DC: World Bank.

World Bank, FAO (Food and Agriculture Organization of the United Nations), and IFAD (International Fund for Agricultural Development). 2009. *Gender in Agriculture Sourcebook*. Washington, DC: World Bank.

Zaks, D., and C. Kucharik. 2011. "Data and Monitoring Needs for a More Ecological Agriculture." *Environmental Research Letters* 6 (1). https://doi.org/10.1088/1748-9326/6/1/014017.

Zhao, F., and A. Collier. 2016. "Digital Entrepreneurship: Research and Practice." Paper presented at the 9th Annual Conference of the EuroMed Academy of Business, September 2016, Warsaw, Poland.

PART FOUR

Appendixes

The Digital Agriculture Profiling Tool

Prioritizing policy actions for accelerating digital transformation of the agrifood system depends on the specific characteristics of a country and the levels of its agricultural and digital development. The Digital Agriculture Profiling Tool offers an assessment framework with which to evaluate the state of agricultural and digital development in a country and identify public policy entry points to maximize the efficiency, equity, and environmental sustainability (EEE) of digital transformation of the agrifood system. The tool assesses digital development in a country (tier 1 and tier 2 enablers), key constraints to EEE in agriculture, and the *progress*, *policy* and enabling environment, and *potential* impact and replicability (PPP) of the technologies suggested as a solution to EEE shortcomings. The assessment is done by analyzing existing data, reviewing the literature, and consulting with stakeholders. Based on the results, a policy agenda is outlined for the digital transformation of the agrifood system.

ASSESSMENT OF DIGITAL DEVELOPMENT IN A COUNTRY (TIER 1 AND TIER 2 ENABLERS)

Tier 1 Enablers

To measure the tier 1 (foundational) enablers for digital transformation in agriculture, the report introduces the Agriculture Digitalization Index (ADI). Using the index, stakeholders can evaluate countries in terms of the state of development of key foundations; it enables countries to identify opportunities for accelerating the digital transformation in the agrifood system. The ADI is not meant to be comprehensive but to serve as an entry point for identifying key foundational strengths and weaknesses of the enabling environment for digital agriculture development and its contribution to agricultural transformation. It can be supplemented by additional metrics. The ADI comprises three subindexes.

The *Digital Agriculture Availability Subindex* estimates the share of farmland in a country with mobile coverage (map A.1). It is constructed by comparing maps of farmland against maps of mobile coverage and calculating how much they overlap (see appendixes B, C, and D for more details). The subindex differentiates across 2G, 3G, and 4G coverage. The type of network available influences the type of digital applications that can be used. For example, second generation (2G) networks are more suited for voice and text messaging, while third (3G), fourth (4G), and now fifth generation (5G) networks allow for a much broader set of digital devices and applications.

The *Digital Affordability Subindex* uses the GSMA mobile connectivity index (GSMA Intelligence 2019) that measures the availability of mobile services and devices at price points that reflect the level of income across a national population. It includes metrics for mobile tariffs, handset price, mobile-specific tax, and inequality in income (see appendixes B and D for more details).

The *Nondigital Enabling Environment Subindex* is based on the fact that complementary investments are required to realize the potential benefits of digital technologies, especially in developing countries, and to address the multiple constraints faced by farmers. It includes four metrics of the level of development of nondigital enablers and governmental capacity to support digital innovation (see appendixes B and D for more details): market access, access to electricity, basic skills level, and the Online Services Index.

Tier 2 Enablers

As mentioned in chapter 2, in addition to tier 1 enablers, innovation ecosystems need to include tier 2 enablers such as the availability of open datasets, digital platforms, digital payment systems, and digital skills to incentivize the development and adoption of digital solutions in agriculture. Assessment of the state of each component under tier 2 enablers in any given country should combine the available indicators and qualitative assessment grounded in stakeholder consultations. For some components, such as digital payment systems and digital entrepreneurship, there are several indicators and methodologies that may guide assessment, such as those presented in the World Bank Global Findex (Demirgüç-Kunt et al. 2018) and the World Bank report *Scaling up Disruptive Agricultural Technologies in Africa* (World Bank 2020b), respectively. For other enablers under tier 2, such as the state of open data development or digital platforms, there are no existing indicators with a comprehensive global coverage as of now, so the assessment needs to be qualitative and should focus on both the state of development of these enablers in a country and the policy and regulatory environment for their development. Chapter 6 outlines best practices for policies and regulations for the use of data in agriculture and can guide the above assessment.

IBRD 45528 | JANUARY 2021

0
0.2
0.4
0.6
0.8
1.0

Source: World Bank.

ASSESSMENT OF EEE IN THE AGRIFOOD SYSTEM

This step of the assessment aims at understanding the key shortcomings in efficiency, equity, and environmental sustainability in agriculture. Where possible, the assessment should be conducted across the entire food system and in each of its hubs (figure A.1) and use the existing indicators and data as well as the inputs from stakeholder consultations.

FIGURE A.1 Food System Hubs

Input   Production   Distribution   Consumption

Across the food system

Tables A.1, A.2. and A.3 present examples of indicators that can be used to analyze EEE. The underlying causes of scoring low on indicators should be analyzed and listed.

TABLE A.1 Efficiency Indicator Examples

Indicator	Source
Yields for key commodities (compared with comparator countries)	FAOSTAT, USDA PSD
Yield gap	Global Yield Gap Atlas
Agricultural total factor productivity growth indexes	USDA ERS
Agriculture value added per worker	FAOSTAT
Agricultural machinery—tractors per 100 square kilometers of arable land	WBI
Fertilizer consumption (kilograms per hectare of arable land)	FAOSTAT
Fertilizer nutrient use efficiency on arable and permanent crops	FAOSTAT
EBA scores regarding seed, water, fertilizer, machinery, finance, markets, transport, and water	World Bank EBA
Trade potential for key commodities	ITC
Food loss index—food losses that occur from production up to (but not including) the retail level	SDGs
Food waste index—food waste that occurs at the retail and consumption levels	National database

Source: World Bank.
Note: The food loss measures the changes in percentage losses for a basket of 10 main commodities by country in comparison with a base period. EBA = Enabling the Business of Agriculture; ERS = Economic Research Service; FAOSTAT = Food and Agriculture Organization of the United Nations Statistics; ITC = International Trade Centre; PSD = Production, Supply, and Distribution; SDGs = Sustainable Development Goals (United Nations); USDA = US Department of Agriculture; WBI = World Bank Indicators.

TABLE A.2 Equity Indicator Examples

Indicator	Source
Median farm size or share of smallholder producers in total number of producers	National data
Employment in agriculture, female (percent of female employment) (modeled ILO estimate)	ILOSTAT
Rural poverty gap at national poverty lines (percent)	World Bank
Prevalence of undernourishment	FAOSTAT
Prevalence of obesity	FAOSTAT
Percentage of people with ownership or secure rights over agricultural land (out of total agricultural population), by sex	Demographic surveys, SDGs
Share of women among owners or rights bearers of agricultural land, by type of tenure	Demographic surveys, SDGs

Source: World Bank.
Note: FAOSTAT = Food and Agriculture Organization of the United Nations Statistics; ILOSTAT = International Labour Organization Statistics; SDGs = Sustainable Development Goals (United Nations).

TABLE A.3 Environmental Indicator Examples

Indicators	Source
Greenhouse gas emissions from the key agricultural categories such as enteric fermentation, manure management, rice cultivation, synthetic fertilizers, manure applied to soils, manure left on pasture, crop residues, cultivation of organic soils, burning of savannas, burning of crop residues, and energy use in CO_2 equivalent per year.	FAOSTAT, national inventories, UNFCCC reports
Area (in hectares or percent) of productive land lost to soil erosion, degradation	National data, scientific literature, LDN profiles
Water use efficiency in irrigated agriculture—the value added per cubic meter of water withdrawn, expressed in dollars per cubic meter over time	FAO and SDGs
Level of water stress: freshwater withdrawal as a proportion of available freshwater resources, that is, the ratio between total freshwater withdrawn by major economic sectors and total renewable freshwater resources, after taking into account environmental water requirements	SDGs
Rate of deforestation due to agricultural land use expansion; rate of deforestation	National data, scientific literature
Pollution (for example, because of fertilizers)	National data, scientific literature
Biodiversity loss due to the agrifood sector	National data, scientific literature

Source: World Bank.
Note: FAO = Food and Agriculture Organization of the United Nations; FAOSTAT = Food and Agriculture Organization of the United Nations Statistics; LDN = Land Degradation Neutrality; SDGs = Sustainable Development Goals (United Nations); UNFCCC = United Nations Framework Convention on Climate Change.

ANALYSIS OF PPP IMPACT AND REPLICABILITY

Following the EEE analysis, a set of technologies that can help address existing challenges in the agriculture sector can be identified using a PPP framework, comprising, as noted, an assessment of progress, policy and enabling environment, and potential impact and replicability of each technology suggested. The PPPs are defined as follows:

- *Progress.* Current degree of development, use, maturity, scaling, uptake, and profitability of the technology
- *Policy and enabling environment.* Degree to which policy, programs, and investments enable further development, adoption, and impact of the technology
- *Potential impact and replicability.* Assessment of transformational impact of the technology in terms of its potential for replication and scale-up.

Each technology is assessed and scored across six dimensions: efficiency, equity, environmental sustainability, progress, policy and enabling environment, and potential impact, including replicability and scale-up (figure A.2). Each question is rated on a scale of 1–5 by a group or an individual. Within each category, an average of the questions rated is then calculated.

POLICY FRAMEWORK DEVELOPMENT

As a result of the analysis, a policy framework for each country can be drafted outlining policy interventions for developing and strengthening tier 1 and tier 2 enablers, as well as identifying the most promising digital technologies to address the existing weaknesses in EEE in the country. These should be grounded in national and regional development objectives.

ORGANIZING STAKEHOLDER CONSULTATIONS

To develop an actionable and relevant policy framework for the digital transformation of agriculture, digital agriculture profiling needs to be undertaken in close cooperation with relevant stakeholders involved in the digital agriculture ecosystem. Engaging with and properly understanding the perspective of different stakeholders involved in the digital agriculture ecosystem is essential for effectively capturing their considerations. Key steps for organizing stakeholder consultations are as follows.

Step 1: Stakeholder Mapping
Stakeholders cover a broad range of actors, including government agencies (departments and regulators), the private sector, media, farmers, development agencies, business associations, research institutes, academia, experts, nongovernmental

FIGURE A.2 Example of EEE and PPP Framework Application

	Challenge	Technology	Outcome	Analysis
Input and producer hub	Lack of financial and decision support	**Advanced analytics for accurate market information**	Consolidates current market information to give farmers negotiation leverage	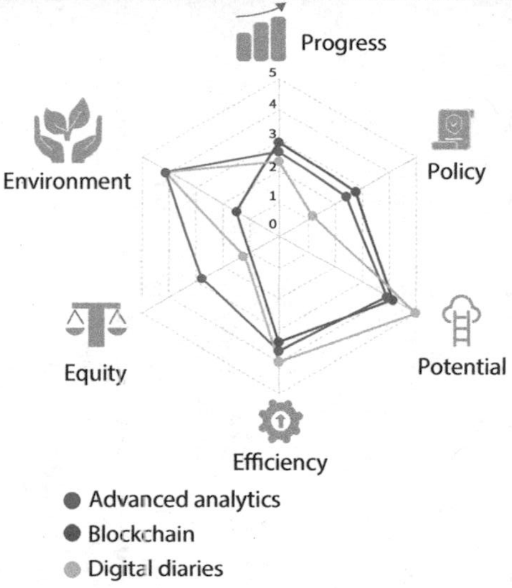
		Blockchain for traceability	Enables e-contracts and e-finance, which reduce processing times and improve transparency and security	
		Digital diaries for financial decision support	Improves input efficiency and provides advisories and information to support decision-making	

Source: World Bank 2020a.

Note: EEE = efficiency, equity, and environmental sustainability; PPP = progress, policy and enabling environment, and potential impact and replicability.

organizations, and other entities. Receiving the inputs, engagement, and endorsement of this diverse range of stakeholders is crucial to correctly analyze the potential of digital technologies in the country. The priorities and interests of strategic stakeholders should be considered in order to align the vision with stakeholder interests and expectations, as well as with broader national development goals.

A stakeholder mapping should be conducted, considering the inclusion of the following potential actors:

- Public sector representatives: policy makers and administrators (such as representatives from the ministries of agriculture, finance, environment, planning, infrastructure, and digital development)
- Smallholders and large-scale farmers, fisherfolk, and forest dwellers (female and male) and their organizations
- Value chain actors (such as processors, transporters, wholesalers, and retailers)
- Digital entrepreneurs: start-ups and ag-tech incubators
- Agriculture, forestry and fisheries research, extension, or development institutions
- Civil society organizations
- International developmental partners
- National and international financing agencies

Step 2: Consultation with Individual Experts

- Conduct semistructured interviews using the EEE categories with national experts over telephone, by email, or in face-to-face interviews to decide whom to invite to the workshop.
- Identify people who should be consulted directly and be part of a consultation workshop.
- Invite experts to a two to three day consultation workshop.

Step 3: Consultation through Workshop and Interviews with Key Experts

Goal of the consultation:

- Validate and finalize the development objectives and constraints to be considered.
- Present the set of technologies identified.
- Prioritize one to three technologies per constraint.
- Conduct EEE and PPP analysis for each technology.

Workshop structure:

- First and second days: Conduct focus groups and semistructured interviews with a broad range of actors.

- Third day: Present and validate the identified development objectives, constraints, and digital solutions tackling these constraints.
- Discuss necessary policies, the role of the public and private sectors, and the financing options available to support the promotion of the most promising technologies.

Step 4: Analyze Data and Share with Stakeholders for Final Validation

- Analyze the data.
- Share a preliminary draft with stakeholders.
- Conduct validation through peer review, by workshop, or by phone.
- Outline policy recommendations.

Step 5: Dissemination and Outreach

Generated knowledge can be disseminated through national workshops, bilateral meetings with relevant national entities, online events, social media channels (Twitter, LinkedIn, email lists), and so on. A targeted and efficient dissemination needs a communication strategy that includes communication objectives and a detailed plan. The communication plan should indicate the target audience, goals, schedule, format (in-person, online webinar, social media channels, workshops, conferences, bilateral meetings), and clear responsibilities.

REFERENCES

Demirgüç-Kunt, Asli, Leora Klapper, Dorothe Singer, Saniya Ansar, and Jake Hess. 2018. *The Global Findex Database 2017: Measuring Financial Inclusion and the Fintech Revolution.* Washington, DC: World Bank.

GSMA Intelligence. 2019. *Mobile Connectivity Index: Methodology.* London: GSMA.

World Bank. 2020a. *Digital Agriculture Profile for Vietnam.* Washington, DC: World Bank.

World Bank. 2020b. *Scaling Up Disruptive Agricultural Technologies in Africa.* Washington, DC: World Bank.

APPENDIX B

The Agriculture Digitalization Index

TABLE B.1 Agriculture Digitalization Index

Country	Agriculture Digitalization Index	Availability				Affordability					Enabling environment				
		2G coverage (%)	3G coverage (%)	4G coverage (%)	Digital Agriculture Availability Subindex	Mobile tariffs	Handset price	Mobile-specific tax	Inequality	Digital Affordability Subindex	Market Access Index	Access To electricity	Basic skills	Online Services Index	Nondigital Enabling Environment Subindex
Afghanistan	38.3	49.9	12.2	0.0	14.9	32.7	3.5	67.9	85.5	41.5	68.0	98.7	26.7	41.2	58.7
Albania	74.4	99.8	99.6	35.1	73.8	53.0	45.4	75.0	79.5	60.4	99.0	100.0	72.6	84.1	88.9
Algeria	57.2	100.0	53.6	2.9	42.6	50.3	32.9	74.3	84.0	56.6	99.5	100.0	62.5	27.7	72.4
Angola	32.5	30.2	2.7	0.4	7.3	45.1	31.6	82.9	40.3	47.6	40.8	43.3	37.6	48.8	42.6
Argentina	55.1	68.5	24.3	7.3	26.3	57.0	54.3	19.5	48.0	46.9	96.9	100.0	86.5	84.7	92.0
Armenia	76.4	98.4	92.0	81.2	89.0	52.2	49.4	54.3	69.0	55.1	97.8	100.0	73.0	70.0	85.2
Australia	86.6	51.4	96.9	88.8	84.6	82.5	100.0	87.5	69.3	86.1	65.0	100.0	97.2	94.7	89.2
Austria	90.5	100.0	96.2	96.1	96.9	90.2	75.0	75.0	72.8	79.1	99.9	100.0	86.9	94.7	95.4
Azerbaijan	65.7	91.6	76.7	0.7	49.3	61.3	52.8	68.2	90.3	65.9	94.7	100.0	62.3	70.6	81.9
Bahamas, The	50.3	46.3	24.1	21.7	27.6	63.7	71.2	50.3	51.3	60.8	14.5	100.0	67.9	67.7	62.5
Bahrain	85.2	100.0	100.0	100.0	100.0	57.1	73.3	93.1	52.8	68.3	99.7	100.0	70.1	78.8	87.2
Bangladesh	53.2	99.4	52.7	0.1	41.0	66.1	39.4	0	73.3	46.3	99.7	85.2	43.4	61.2	72.4
Barbados	73.7	100.0	100.0	86.2	94.5	40.8	56.0	49.1	28.5	44.5	98.9	100.0	71.3	57.7	82.0
Belarus	70.1	100.0	99.9	3.4	61.3	59.9	49.1	50.5	85.5	59.9	99.7	100.0	85.8	70.6	89.0
Belgium	90.5	100.0	100.0	99.9	100.0	70.4	100.0	73.8	84.0	82.7	99.9	100.0	90.1	65.9	89.0
Belize	50.9	92.6	80.0	7.4	53.5	27.2	44.6	53.2	17.8	35.7	69.0	99.5	58.7	26.5	63.4
Benin	37.8	64.2	32.0	0.2	25.7	24.7	14.5	76.9	32.5	33.6	92.4	41.5	31.2	51.2	54.1
Bhutan	49.6	94.3	19.3	1.6	27.2	48.9	39.4	75.0	62.5	54.0	65.8	100.0	35.8	68.2	67.5
Bolivia	46.2	44.5	15.4	7.7	18.1	46.6	39.0	73.4	38.3	48.0	72.5	95.6	63.5	58.2	72.4

(Continued)

TABLE B.1 Agriculture Digitalization Index (Continued)

Country	Agriculture Digitalization Index	Availability				Affordability					Enabling environment				
		2G coverage (%)	3G coverage (%)	4G coverage (%)	Digital Agriculture Availability Subindex	Mobile tariffs	Handset price	Mobile-specific tax	Inequality	Digital Affordability Subindex	Market Access Index	Access To electricity	Basic skills	Online Services Index	Nondigital Enabling Environment Subindex
Bosnia and Herzegovina	64.3	100.0	98.8	3.9	61.1	46.0	47.9	57.0	62.0	52.0	99.9	100.0	65.6	53.5	79.7
Botswana	44.6	82.9	13.9	0.4	22.3	51.7	66.4	85.0	0	52.5	78.5	64.9	56.5	36.5	59.1
Brazil	52.1	67.3	33.1	8.3	30.0	60.8	63.4	0.9	20.8	41.6	86.0	100.0	66.2	87.1	84.8
Brunei Darussalam	81.2	96.6	95.3	90.7	93.7	59.7	71.0	97.5	54.6	69.6	94.0	100.0	63.2	63.5	80.2
Bulgaria	74.5	100.0	99.9	29.4	71.7	67.1	57.0	75.0	52.7	62.8	99.4	100.0	79.3	77.1	88.9
Burkina Faso	40.0	96.1	32.1	0	32.1	31.4	16.8	80.5	69.3	44.4	94.7	14.4	19.0	46.5	43.6
Burundi	30.6	74.5	12.0	3.9	21.3	11.9	0	51.4	60.3	25.9	99.6	11.0	32.6	35.3	44.6
Cambodia	71.6	99.7	97.8	77.6	90.1	48.6	36.8	76.2	76.8	56.2	96.3	91.6	40.9	45.3	68.5
Cameroon	51.7	92.6	87.2	2.9	54.6	40.5	38.0	63.4	22.8	40.8	84.3	62.7	45.1	47.1	59.8
Canada	84.6	75.1	95.8	93.7	90.8	79.1	84.3	60.3	67.0	74.5	85.8	100.0	84.1	84.1	88.5
Chad	17.9	73.3	6.3	0	17.2	12.9	0	0	41.5	12.2	52.5	11.8	12.7	20.0	24.2
Chile	73.4	90.5	90.1	37.0	68.9	65.7	66.0	74.3	30.8	60.5	94.8	100.0	83.3	85.3	90.8
China	59.6	62.9	12.1	14.5	23.2	78.7	63.7	86.9	44.0	68.9	91.5	100.0	64.7	90.6	86.7
Colombia	54.8	73.3	37.7	9.5	33.5	54.1	54.8	59.5	22.0	49.0	83.7	99.9	67.4	76.5	81.9
Costa Rica	64.7	93.1	73.7	26.0	58.5	69.1	58.8	39.5	32.0	52.7	93.7	100.0	70.1	68.2	83.0
Croatia	85.9	100.0	99.6	97.1	98.7	88.3	51.5	68.8	74.5	70.6	99.8	100.0	78.3	75.3	88.4
Cyprus	79.4	100.0	98.7	47.8	78.6	54.3	68.6	76.3	76.8	67.5	99.7	100.0	81.2	87.1	92.0

(Continued)

Country	Agriculture Digitalization Index	Availability				Affordability					Enabling environment				
		2G coverage (%)	3G coverage (%)	4G coverage (%)	Digital Agriculture Availability Subindex	Mobile tariffs	Handset price	Mobile-specific tax	Inequality	Digital Affordability Subindex	Market Access Index	Access To electricity	Basic skills	Online Services Index	Nondigital Enabling Environment Subindex
Czech Republic	88.5	100.0	99.4	98.3	99.1	75.4	74.7	73.8	89.5	77.7	99.9	100.0	83.1	72.4	88.8
Denmark	90.1	100.0	100.0	98.8	99.5	78.6	66.0	68.8	84.0	73.9	99.7	100.0	90.6	97.1	96.8
Dominican Republic	64.6	97.6	89.0	24.0	64.7	51.8	58.4	11.3	42.3	43.8	98.0	100.0	66.6	76.5	85.3
Ecuador	58.8	86.3	41.9	4.9	36.0	53.7	51.8	85.0	36.3	55.9	90.6	100.0	66.1	81.2	84.5
Egypt, Arab Rep.	59.2	95.7	80.6	4.5	53.2	85.4	47.1	18.8	21.3	47.7	97.7	100.0	51.9	57.1	76.7
El Salvador	63.2	99.7	74.2	38.6	65.1	40.4	45.3	52.5	54.5	47.1	99.5	100.0	52.3	57.7	77.4
Estonia	90.3	100.0	100.0	100.0	100.0	74.4	78.2	75.0	73.8	75.5	98.4	100.0	83.7	99.4	95.4
Ethiopia	33.0	31.4	6.8	0.1	9.0	20.2	16.3	81.3	79.0	43.0	82.8	45.0	24.0	36.5	47.1
Fiji	53.5	67.7	39.4	16.5	35.9	36.7	42.6	97.5	56.0	54.5	58.6	99.6	71.2	50.6	70.0
Finland	90.9	100.0	100.0	100.0	100.0	79.4	81.1	70.0	86.5	79.5	83.7	100.0	92.7	97.1	93.4
France	86.0	100.0	98.6	77.6	90.5	67.9	84.5	75.0	76.5	76.0	99.6	100.0	78.5	88.2	91.6
Gabon	34.2	30.4	6.7	3.2	10.0	57.1	41.6	4.9	59.5	42.5	19.5	93.0	55.9	32.4	50.2
Gambia, The	33.9	100.0	10.3	0.8	24.4	17.1	7.6	78.1	33.8	29.8	98.4	60.3	28.4	2.9	47.5
Georgia	67.6	97.9	84.4	29.7	65.2	59.3	41.0	65.1	53.5	53.8	96.1	100.0	79.9	58.8	83.7
Germany	89.6	100.0	99.1	97.4	98.6	96.1	74.0	76.3	68.3	79.9	99.9	100.0	87.5	73.5	90.2
Ghana	50.9	95.7	33.9	1.2	33.2	61.4	38.7	42.5	49.3	48.4	92.4	82.4	46.1	63.5	71.1
Greece	77.3	99.9	99.3	70.2	87.8	63.0	70.7	11.1	63.8	55.1	98.0	100.0	88.1	70.6	89.2

(Continued)

TABLE B.1 Agriculture Digitalization Index (Continued)

Country	Agriculture Digitalization Index	Availability				Affordability					Enabling environment				
		2G coverage (%)	3G coverage (%)	4G coverage (%)	Digital Agriculture Availability Subindex	Mobile tariffs	Handset price	Mobile-specific tax	Inequality	Digital Affordability Subindex	Market Access Index	Access To electricity	Basic skills	Online Services Index	Nondigital Enabling Environment Subindex
Guatemala	52.0	84.0	43.5	21.8	42.9	29.7	50.6	85.0	24.0	45.9	78.1	94.7	45.3	51.2	67.3
Guinea	33.9	44.7	3.7	0	10.4	44.8	33.3	50.0	69.8	47.4	89.9	44.0	20.3	21.8	44.0
Guyana	37.3	46.5	8.3	0	12.6	34.1	45.7	55.3	49.8	45.0	25.7	91.8	53.1	46.5	54.3
Haiti	36.1	86.9	44.5	0.9	35.5	29.7	21.2	44.8	0	24.2	95.0	45.3	35.4	18.8	48.6
Honduras	48.2	87.2	53.7	10.0	42.9	12.5	27.1	79.4	25.3	32.8	89.6	91.9	47.4	46.5	68.9
Hungary	87.4	100.0	99.2	99.8	99.6	81.1	70.3	77.8	72.3	75.4	99.9	100.0	74.6	74.7	87.3
India	62.3	87.2	35.1	17.6	38.5	71.8	61.8	66.3	65.5	66.4	99.6	95.2	48.0	85.3	82.0
Indonesia	56.4	62.6	48.5	11.7	36.6	64.0	37.9	85.9	62.3	60.2	64.1	98.5	59.3	68.2	72.5
Iran, Islamic Rep.	57.5	89.9	26.1	9.5	32.2	67.3	31.2	84.1	63.3	59.0	94.7	100.0	71.7	58.8	81.3
Iraq	50.1	97.1	18.4	16.3	33.3	42.7	43.2	25.0	80.8	46.9	97.1	99.9	50.1	33.5	70.2
Ireland	90.7	100.0	98.1	86.6	93.9	95.5	95.4	71.3	75.0	86.5	99.9	100.0	89.2	77.1	91.5
Israel	86.0	100.0	99.9	89.9	95.9	89.0	72.3	69.1	53.3	72.9	99.8	100.0	81.7	74.7	89.1
Italy	82.9	100.0	100.0	85.9	94.4	87.2	83.9	7.1	59.2	64.6	99.9	100.0	76.4	82.9	89.8
Jamaica	58.7	100.0	96.6	2.6	59.7	38.3	62.8	27.9	32.5	42.4	99.7	98.9	59.1	38.8	74.1
Japan	83.6	3.4	93.0	90.6	74.1	72.9	87.1	87.5	96.8	84.8	99.0	100.0	77.6	90.6	91.8
Jordan	71.6	99.5	97.7	72.9	88.1	38.7	42.8	73.5	67.8	52.7	97.8	99.9	62.8	35.9	74.1
Kazakhstan	57.6	40.3	8.2	1.3	11.9	86.6	59.1	85.0	86.8	78.0	63.5	100.0	76.3	92.4	83.0
Kenya	48.8	89.2	42.9	6.0	37.4	45.1	33.1	44.3	29.8	38.2	97.0	75.0	43.8	67.7	70.9

(Continued)

WHAT'S COOKING: DIGITAL TRANSFORMATION OF THE AGRIFOOD SYSTEM

TABLE B.1 Agriculture Digitalization Index (Continued)

Country	Agriculture Digitalization Index	Availability				Affordability					Enabling environment				
		2G coverage (%)	3G coverage (%)	4G coverage (%)	Digital Agriculture Availability Subindex	Mobile tariffs	Handset price	Mobile-specific tax	Inequality	Digital Affordability Subindex	Market Access Index	Access To electricity	Basic skills	Online Services Index	Nondigital Enabling Environment Subindex
Korea, Rep.	83.1	11.6	98.9	99.9	81.8	71.0	68.1	81.4	62.0	70.4	99.9	100.0	88.8	100.0	97.2
Kuwait	85.1	100.0	100.0	100.0	100.0	59.7	77.5	99.2	37.0	68.4	99.9	100.0	64.0	84.1	87.0
Lao PDR	50.2	84.8	70.0	14.7	50.8	40.0	40.2	46.9	61.8	45.8	55.8	97.9	42.7	19.4	54.0
Latvia	84.0	100.0	100.0	97.9	99.2	62.4	65.7	73.8	66.3	66.4	99.9	100.0	88.0	58.2	86.5
Lebanon	68.1	100.0	87.1	57.8	78.0	36.3	52.2	86.3	37.5	51.3	99.6	100.0	58.3	41.8	74.9
Lesotho	46.6	98.5	85.6	0.9	54.3	15.8	19.6	87.5	9.8	30.1	98.5	47.0	41.0	35.3	55.5
Liberia	29.7	96.2	14.5	1.5	25.6	7.5	18.2	20.4	55.8	22.9	80.5	25.9	30.6	24.7	40.4
Libya	41.4	98.0	15.7	0	25.9	39.0	40.1	42.9	51.2	42.6	93.8	67.0	57.9	4.1	55.7
Lithuania	82.2	100.0	95.8	61.3	82.8	82.6	67.0	73.8	58.0	71.2	99.9	100.0	85.1	85.3	92.6
Luxembourg	90.2	100.0	100.0	100.0	100.0	100.0	83.6	78.8	71.0	85.0	99.4	100.0	66.4	76.5	85.5
Madagascar	18.2	15.6	2.3	0.4	4.2	7.3	15.4	25.0	61.5	24.1	12.4	25.9	38.5	28.8	26.4
Malawi	28.2	66.3	15.5	1.9	20.2	4.9	0.9	38.6	31.5	15.7	98.5	18.0	35.5	42.4	48.6
Malaysia	75.9	87.7	83.9	78.7	82.6	69.3	45.1	93.2	38.8	60.7	85.5	100.0	66.7	85.3	84.4
Mali	33.6	32.5	3.8	0	8.0	30.2	29.0	76.9	74.0	48.0	77.0	50.9	16.5	34.7	44.8
Malta	84.4	100.0	100.0	100.0	100.0	58.5	62.3	59.3	81.3	64.4	99.3	100.0	75.0	81.2	88.9
Mauritania	24.6	54.1	1.2	0	11.3	46.9	45.7	8.4	51.0	39.7	9.2	44.5	26.9	10.0	22.7
Mauritius	82.0	100.0	99.7	98.0	99.1	57.4	56.8	81.3	67.0	63.9	99.3	97.5	65.6	70.0	83.1
Mexico	58.2	63.3	36.1	16.3	33.6	54.4	72.1	80.0	21.8	58.3	85.1	100.0	63.8	82.4	82.8

(Continued)

TABLE B.1 Agriculture Digitalization Index (Continued)

Country	Agriculture Digitalization Index	Availability				Affordability					Enabling environment				
		2G coverage (%)	3G coverage (%)	4G coverage (%)	Digital Agriculture Availability Subindex	Mobile tariffs	Handset price	Mobile-specific tax	Inequality	Digital Affordability Subindex	Market Access Index	Access To electricity	Basic skills	Online Services Index	Nondigital Enabling Environment Subindex
Moldova	66.8	100.0	97.9	12.2	64.0	41.9	39.9	55.6	77.5	51.2	99.7	100.0	66.1	75.3	85.3
Mongolia	37.9	8.7	1.6	0.2	2.5	49.8	22.4	83.9	73.3	53.1	7.8	98.1	73.9	52.9	58.2
Montenegro	80.2	99.9	97.1	91.5	95.4	57.7	52.4	73.8	76.0	63.0	99.9	100.0	75.3	54.1	82.3
Morocco	58.9	99.2	44.9	18.5	45.2	47.4	52.1	74.2	58.3	56.3	98.8	100.0	49.1	52.4	75.3
Mozambique	36.3	68.9	22.4	0	22.7	27.6	18.4	73.1	41.5	36.7	86.3	31.1	29.1	51.8	49.6
Myanmar	44.1	39.1	19.8	0.8	16.1	61.7	37.8	89.6	62.8	60.3	92.0	66.3	39.7	25.9	56.0
Namibia	33.1	61.9	12.9	0.1	17.6	49.6	43.2	59.7	0	39.8	9.6	53.9	52.3	52.4	42.0
Nepal	49.0	88.4	53.7	0.6	39.4	44.6	16.8	58.1	71.8	44.4	80.2	93.9	39.1	40.0	63.3
Netherlands	90.9	100.0	100.0	99.4	99.8	79.8	76.4	73.8	82.3	78.0	99.8	100.0	88.9	90.6	94.8
New Zealand	88.7	82.5	91.3	93.1	90.3	78.4	93.8	81.3	71.5	82.2	90.4	100.0	90.7	92.9	93.5
Nicaragua	40.3	59.1	21.7	2.2	21.4	19.1	34.0	63.6	39.5	36.6	55.9	88.1	52.9	54.7	62.9
Niger	25.4	82.6	1.4	0	17.1	5.2	0	55.9	71.5	27.0	71.2	17.6	9.7	29.4	32.0
Nigeria	46.2	92.3	9.0	0.6	22.3	49.2	47.5	88.0	42.0	55.0	97.9	56.5	38.9	51.8	61.3
Norway	80.2	94.5	77.4	61.7	74.5	94.3	79.7	68.8	80.8	82.1	58.3	100.0	89.6	87.7	83.9
Oman	72.2	92.9	69.2	39.8	62.2	66.0	67.9	90.8	62.3	70.8	83.5	100.0	66.1	85.3	83.7
Pakistan	46.2	85.6	17.7	3.2	25.5	60.7	35.3	28.9	69.5	48.5	93.9	71.1	30.5	62.9	64.6
Panama	62.1	85.0	74.0	22.3	55.5	57.6	70.7	52.8	21.3	53.3	81.0	100.0	66.5	62.4	77.5

(Continued)

TABLE B.1 Agriculture Digitalization Index (Continued)

Country	Agriculture Digitalization Index	Availability				Affordability					Enabling environment				
		2G coverage (%)	3G coverage (%)	4G coverage (%)	Digital Agriculture Availability Subindex	Mobile tariffs	Handset price	Mobile-specific tax	Inequality	Digital Affordability Subindex	Market Access Index	Access To electricity	Basic skills	Online Services Index	Nondigital Enabling Environment Subindex
Papua New Guinea	34.8	58.1	4.2	0.3	13.4	27.8	46.3	87.5	61.3	52.0	37.1	59.0	37.1	22.4	38.9
Paraguay	50.0	57.4	23.9	3.2	22.3	51.5	49.8	86.9	27.5	53.3	69.0	100.0	57.9	70.6	74.4
Peru	56.0	58.7	22.3	9.5	24.5	72.7	59.9	77.5	41.8	63.6	77.6	95.2	71.5	75.3	79.9
Philippines	59.9	88.0	57.0	14.1	46.0	43.8	46.1	85.0	42.3	52.4	94.9	94.9	62.2	72.9	81.2
Poland	88.1	100.0	100.0	99.6	99.8	74.0	68.6	71.3	76.5	72.4	99.9	100.0	82.6	85.9	92.1
Portugal	85.2	100.0	99.8	93.2	97.2	64.2	73.3	71.3	67.3	69.0	99.9	100.0	74.4	83.5	89.4
Qatar	88.1	100.0	100.0	100.0	100.0	82.4	100.0	98.8	45.7	83.6	100.0	100.0	56.4	65.9	80.6
Romania	76.1	100.0	99.9	31.7	72.6	74.5	66.2	76.3	60.8	69.6	99.8	100.0	71.7	72.4	86.0
Russian Federation	74.5	97.0	85.6	22.1	62.5	79.6	73.5	75.0	65.8	74.1	81.8	100.0	84.0	81.8	86.9
Rwanda	51.4	96.9	24.8	87.5	64.3	34.0	18.3	58.6	21.5	31.7	99.6	34.7	36.4	61.8	58.1
Saint Lucia	58.0	100.0	96.3	48.9	78.1	35.6	56.0	56.2	44.0	47.5	0	99.5	56.3	38.2	48.5
Samoa	42.9	90.2	24.2	3.9	29.3	26.9	39.0	81.3	78.3	51.7	0	100.0	64.7	26.5	47.8
Saudi Arabia	68.6	93.7	69.6	21.6	55.2	78.7	44.6	93.8	54.0	66.5	90.1	100.0	77.3	68.8	84.1
Senegal	41.0	69.3	15.6	0.3	20.2	45.2	37.1	56.2	43.3	44.6	90.1	67.0	26.3	49.4	58.2
Serbia	79.9	100.0	99.5	69.2	87.5	67.1	49.0	78.1	63.3	63.1	99.8	100.0	77.3	79.4	89.1
Sierra Leone	38.0	66.5	32.2	9.1	29.8	14.4	17.0	79.5	68.3	39.0	96.9	26.1	27.4	30.6	45.2
Slovenia	89.3	100.0	100.0	100.0	100.0	79.8	61.3	72.5	89.8	74.8	99.9	100.0	86.9	85.3	93.0

(Continued)

Country	Agriculture Digitalization Index	Availability				Affordability					Enabling environment				
		2G coverage (%)	3G coverage (%)	4G coverage (%)	Digital Agriculture Availability Subindex	Mobile tariffs	Handset price	Mobile-specific tax	Inequality	Digital Affordability Subindex	Market Access Index	Access To electricity	Basic skills	Online Services Index	Nondigital Enabling Environment Subindex
Solomon Islands	28.5	11.7	7.8	0	5.5	7.1	38.7	86.7	64.0	43.9	0	66.7	46.1	32.4	36.3
South Africa	65.0	99.7	92.3	13.2	62.1	58.3	59.9	81.3	0	51.7	99.4	91.2	59.4	74.7	81.2
Spain	81.7	100.0	99.5	53.2	81.1	68.6	78.8	73.8	57.8	70.5	99.7	100.0	85.0	88.8	93.4
Sri Lanka	80.6	99.6	94.5	93.0	94.9	81.5	45.3	68.5	60.0	63.7	99.6	99.6	62.1	71.8	83.3
Sudan	28.0	71.8	4.8	0	16.3	40.1	16.0	15.1	30.0	25.9	48.8	59.8	28.6	30.6	41.9
Sweden	89.4	100.0	99.2	97.0	98.5	89.6	71.7	68.8	80.0	78.1	89.8	100.0	86.3	90.0	91.5
Switzerland	91.7	99.9	99.3	97.9	98.9	88.3	84.3	90.4	76.3	85.1	99.6	100.0	82.4	82.9	91.2
Tajikistan	55.3	98.0	89.8	0.1	55.6	20.4	25.9	41.4	76.3	37.4	99.2	99.3	62.0	31.8	73.1
Tanzania	37.0	95.1	15.2	1.6	25.7	32.4	37.0	10.5	56.5	34.2	78.2	35.6	34.7	55.3	51.0
Thailand	84.2	99.8	99.7	99.6	99.7	74.6	53.4	91.3	53.0	67.3	99.0	100.0	64.5	79.4	85.7
Timor-Leste	44.5	73.9	12.4	0.4	19.9	29.2	47.5	56.2	78.5	49.9	82.1	85.6	43.1	44.1	63.7
Togo	37.4	63.0	8.5	0.1	16.0	5.3	30.6	76.9	49.8	36.1	99.6	51.3	39.5	50.0	60.1
Trinidad and Tobago	70.7	100.0	96.6	38.9	74.2	35.6	57.1	82.7	57.8	55.9	99.7	100.0	67.6	61.2	82.1
Tunisia	63.6	100.0	93.6	7.3	60.4	62.2	35.5	43.8	65.3	51.1	99.2	99.8	56.1	62.4	79.4
Turkey	65.6	98.8	84.9	14.8	59.6	70.7	44.8	0	56.0	45.8	98.7	100.0	80.6	85.9	91.3
Uganda	41.0	93.7	36.4	0.9	33.7	25.4	31.2	25.3	50.3	32.1	87.8	42.7	40.1	58.2	57.2
Ukraine	64.6	100.0	44.6	17.1	44.7	70.4	34.4	58.9	91.3	61.5	99.9	100.0	81.9	68.2	87.5

(Continued)

TABLE B.1 Agriculture Digitalization Index (Continued)

Country	Agriculture Digitalization Index	Availability				Affordability					Enabling environment				
		2G coverage (%)	3G coverage (%)	4G coverage (%)	Digital Agriculture Availability Subindex	Mobile tariffs	Handset price	Mobile-specific tax	Inequality	Digital Affordability Subindex	Market Access Index	Access To electricity	Basic skills	Online Services Index	Nondigital Enabling Environment Subindex
United Arab Emirates	81.5	99.5	80.0	58.1	75.1	79.6	83.7	91.2	63.4	79.9	99.2	100.0	68.8	90.0	89.5
United Kingdom	91.2	99.9	97.2	93.5	96.3	85.2	93.6	75.0	70.0	82.7	99.8	100.0	83.5	95.9	94.8
United States	86.1	92.8	87.6	84.9	87.6	80.1	100.0	69.3	46.0	77.1	90.5	100.0	89.5	94.7	93.7
Uruguay	74.5	99.6	97.1	14.0	64.4	79.5	72.6	71.6	57.5	71.5	92.2	100.0	73.8	84.1	87.5
Uzbekistan	52.1	99.3	18.3	0.2	27.3	62.4	13.0	49.3	62.3	44.9	99.2	100.0	59.3	78.2	84.2
Vanuatu	30.5	33.4	6.2	1.6	9.8	28.8	36.0	67.1	63.3	45.5	0	61.9	48.8	33.5	36.0
Vietnam	69.7	93.7	85.3	45.4	71.0	56.2	33.1	91.3	67.3	58.5	95.7	100.0	57.3	65.3	79.6
Yemen, Rep.	33.3	90.3	1.2	0	18.5	0.3	14.2	69.0	58.0	29.8	82.2	62.0	29.9	32.4	51.6
Zambia	30.3	62.4	9.5	0.5	16.5	43.7	41.2	8.9	0	27.3	70.2	39.8	52.3	25.9	47.0
Zimbabwe	29.4	56.1	4.6	0.4	13.2	2.4	9.2	30.0	45.0	18.5	84.5	41.0	47.6	52.4	56.4

Source: World Bank.

Note: In order to ensure consistent units of measurement, all indicators have been normalized to have a value within a range of 0 to 100, with a higher score representing stronger performance. ■ = score above 75; ■ = score between 50 and 74.9; ■ = score between 25 and 49.9; ■ = score between 0 and 24.9.

Mobile Coverage in Rural Areas

MAP C.1   South Asia

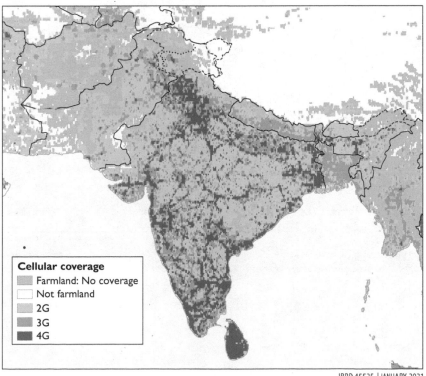

Cellular coverage
- Farmland: No coverage
- Not farmland
- 2G
- 3G
- 4G

IBRD 45525 | JANUARY 2021

Sources: World Bank using GSMA Intelligence (2019) for data on cellular network coverage, and Geo-Wiki data retrieved from Fritz et al. (2017) for cropland data.

MAP C.2 Sub-Saharan Africa

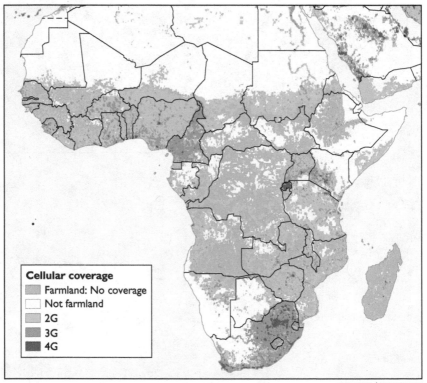

Cellular coverage
- Farmland: No coverage
- Not farmland
- 2G
- 3G
- 4G

IBRD 45526 | JANUARY 2021

Sources: World Bank using GSMA Intelligence (2019) for data on cellular network coverage, and Geo-Wiki data retrieved from Fritz et al. (2017) for cropland data.

MAP C.3 Europe and Central Asia

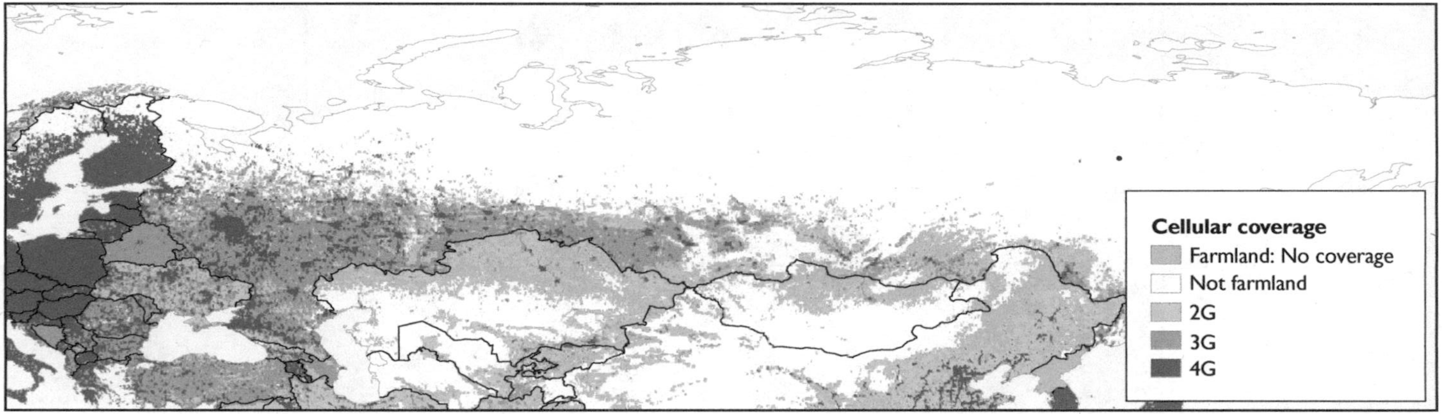

Cellular coverage

Farmland: No coverage
Not farmland
2G
3G
4G

IBRD 45522 | JANUARY 2021

Sources: World Bank using GSMA Intelligence (2019) for data on cellular network coverage, and Geo-Wiki data retrieved from Fritz et al. (2017) for cropland data.

MAP C.4 Latin America and the Caribbean

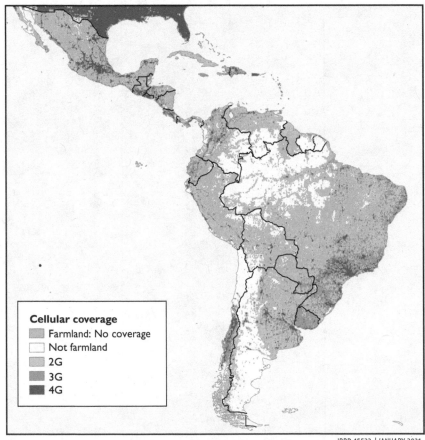

IBRD 45523 | JANUARY 2021

Sources: World Bank using GSMA Intelligence (2019) for data on cellular network coverage, and Geo-Wiki data retrieved from Fritz et al. (2017) for cropland data.

MAP C.5 Middle East and North Africa

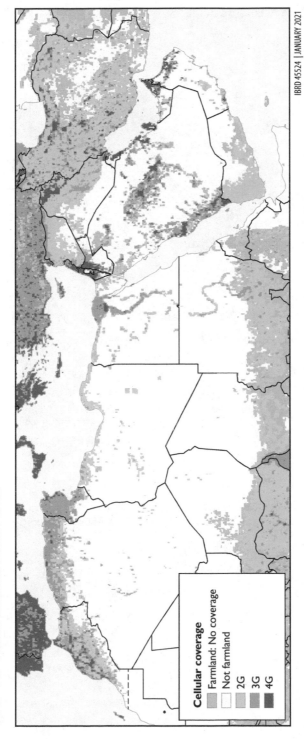

Cellular coverage

- Farmland: No coverage
- Not farmland
- 2G
- 3G
- 4G

IBRD 45524 | JANUARY 2021

Sources: World Bank using GSMA Intelligence (2019) for data on cellular network coverage, and Geo-Wiki data retrieved from Fritz et al. (2017) for cropland data.

MAP C.6 East Asia and Pacific

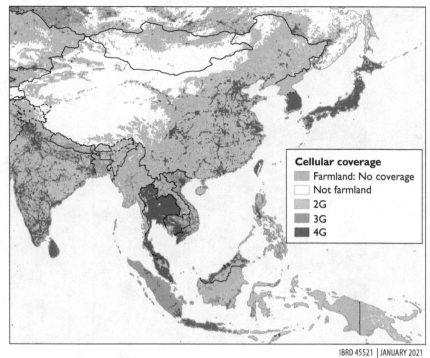

Cellular coverage
- Farmland: No coverage
- Not farmland
- 2G
- 3G
- 4G

IBRD 45521 | JANUARY 2021

Sources: World Bank using GSMA Intelligence (2019) for data on cellular network coverage, and Geo-Wiki data retrieved from Fritz et al. (2017) for cropland data.

REFERENCES

Fritz, S., L. See, C. Perger, I. McCallum, C. Schill, D. Schepaschenko, M. Duerauer, et al. 2017. "A Global Dataset of Crowdsourced Land Cover and Land Use Reference Data." *Scientific Data* 4: 170075.

GSMA Intelligence. 2019. *Mobile Connectivity Index: Methodology.* London: GSMA.

Agriculture Digitalization Index Methodology

INTRODUCTION

The Agriculture Digitalization Index (ADI) evaluates countries on the state of development of three foundations of the enabling environment for digital transformation of the agrifood system—availability of mobile coverage, affordability of mobile services, and nondigital enablers. The ADI is not meant to be comprehensive, but rather serves as an entry point into identifying key foundational strengths and weaknesses (tier 1 enablers) for the enabling environment for digital agriculture development and its contribution to agricultural transformation.

To calculate the ADI, a simple, unweighted average was taken of three subindexes: the Digital Agriculture Availability Subindex, the Digital Affordability Subindex, and the Nondigital Enabling Environment Subindex (table D.1).

TABLE D.1 Summary of Agricultural Digitalization Index

Subindex (weight in total)	Indicator (weight in total)	Indicator description	Source
Digital Agriculture Availability Subindex (33%)	2G coverage (20%)	% farmland receiving 2G coverage	Original calculations for this publication
	3G coverage (40%)	% farmland receiving 3G coverage	Original calculations for this publication
	4G coverage (40%)	% farmland receiving 4G coverage	Original calculations for this publication
Digital Affordability Subindex (33%)	Mobile tariffs (30%)	Average monthly cost of 100MB, 500MB, and 1GB	2019 GSMA Mobile Connectivity Index
	Handset price (30%)	Cost of entry-level, internet-enabled handset	2019 GSMA Mobile Connectivity Index
	Mobile-specific tax (20%)	Cost of overall and mobile-specific taxation	2019 GSMA Mobile Connectivity Index
	Inequality (20%)	Inequality in income, Atkinson measure	2019 GSMA Mobile Connectivity Index
Nondigital Enabling Environment Subindex (33%)	Market access index (25%)	% of farmland within four hours of a settlement of at least 100,000 people	Original calculations for this publication
	Access to electricity (25%)	% of country population with access to electricity	2018 World Bank World Development Indicators
	Basic skills index (25%)	Level of skills of the adult population	2019 GSMA Mobile Connectivity Index
	Online services index (25%)	Use of ICTs by governments in delivering public services at the national level	2020 United Nations E-Government Survey

Source: World Bank.

Note: GB = gigabyte; ICT = information and communication technology; MB = megabyte.

THE DIGITAL AGRICULTURE AVAILABILITY SUBINDEX

This subindex estimates the share of farmland in a country with mobile coverage. It is constructed by comparing maps of farmland against maps of mobile coverage and calculating how much they overlap. In each country, as noted in appendix A, the amount of farmland was calculated that receives each of 2G, 3G, and 4G cell phone coverage, and those amounts divided by the total farmland in the country. The result of these calculations was three percentages, indicating the percentage of farmland in each country that has each of the three levels of coverage. Following GSMA's mobile connectivity index methodology (GSMA Intelligence 2019), 2G coverage was multiplied by 0.2, 3G coverage by 0.4, and 4G coverage by 0.4 and the sum of these weighted 2G, 3G, and 4G coverages represents the Digital Agriculture Availability Subindex for each country.

For cropland data, Geo-Wiki land cover data were used, available globally as gridded data with a resolution of 300 meters per pixel (Fritz et al. 2017). Values range from 0 to 100, indicating what percentage of each pixel can be considered cropland. Geo-Wiki data combine remote-sensing observations with crowdsourced contributions to arrive at an estimate of different land cover types. Validation information and accuracy metrics can be found in Comber et al. (2013).

To verify the accuracy of Geo-Wiki data, an identical analysis was conducted with a different land cover dataset, that of Copernicus Global Land Service (Buchhorn et al. 2019). This dataset is similar to the Geo-Wiki data in that it is a globally available gridded dataset, with finer resolution at 100 meters. An identical analysis to the Geo-Wiki analysis was performed to arrive at country-level indexes for 18 sampled countries with the Copernicus data. Although not identical, ADI values calculated with Copernicus and Geo-Wiki data are very similar, with a Pearson's correlation coefficient of 0.969.

THE DIGITAL AFFORDABILITY SUBINDEX

This index uses the affordability subindex of the GSMA mobile connectivity index (GSMA Intelligence 2019) to measure the availability of mobile services and devices at price points that reflect the level of income across a national population. The affordability of digital solutions for agriculture is critical since the capacity for uptake of these solutions is largely determined by their accessibility. It includes metrics for mobile tariffs, handset price, and mobile-specific tax. Data for selected Digital Affordability Subindex indicators were retrieved for represented countries from the 2019 GSMA Mobile Connectivity Index dataset (Bahia and Agnoletto 2020).

Mobile tariffs measure the average cost of 100 megabytes (MB), 500MB, and 1 gigabyte of data for a country, expressed as a percentage of monthly gross domestic product per capita. These data were produced by the GSMA using three defined baskets based on usage allowance, contract, and technology, taking into account historic trends in data consumption across countries, a selection of allowances currently offered by operators, and baskets used in other mobile pricing benchmark studies. These costs were measured in local currency and converted into dollars using exchange rates as of the first quarter (Q1) 2017, Q1 2018, and Q1 2019 (Bahia and Agnoletto 2020).

Handset price reflects the average prices of entry-level mobile handsets that allow for internet connectivity. These prices were produced by the GSMA by researching the lowest-priced phone available on the websites of all mobile network operators (MNOs) in each country. Phones qualify as having access to the internet if they are either 3G or 4G capable. 2G and wireless application protocol (WAP) were not considered for these prices. The prices were measured in local currency and converted into dollars using exchange rates as of Q1 2017, Q1 2018, and Q1 2019 (Bahia and Agnoletto 2020).

Mobile-specific tax indicates the cost of mobile specific taxes as percentage of total cost of mobile ownership (TCMO). TCMO was calculated based on three elements: handset price, the activation and connection price or any other charges incurred to connect to the MNO's network, and the price related to use (Bahia and Agnoletto 2020).

Inequality reflects the Atkinson index, which represents the percentage of total income a country would have to sacrifice in order to achieve greater equality (Atkinson 1970; UNDESA 2015). GSMA uses the United Nations' Atkinson estimates (Bahia and Agnoletto 2020).

The Digital Affordability Index was generated using a weighted average of the indicators, using the same methodology used by the GSMA Mobile Connectivity Index. The weights were distributed as follows: mobile tariffs, 30 percent; handset price, 30 percent; mobile-specific tax, 20 percent; and inequality, 20 percent. These are the same weights used by the GSMA when calculating the Affordability Enabler in the Mobile Connectivity Index.

NONDIGITAL ENABLING ENVIRONMENT SUBINDEX

As noted in appendix A, complementary investments are required to realize the potential benefits of digital technologies, especially in developing countries, and to address the multiple constraints faced by farmers. This subindex includes five metrics to measure the level of development of nondigital enablers and governmental capacity to support digital innovation.

Market access index measures the share of farmland in a country located within four hours of travel time to a settlement of at least 100,000 people.

To construct a measure for market access, two geographical datasets were compared. The first is a dataset that provides a gridded map of travel distance for every point on the globe at approximately one kilometer resolution (Nelson et al. 2019). Using geographic data of transportation networks, Nelson et al. use a friction, or "cost surface"–based model, in which each pixel is assigned a time value defining the time needed to travel across it. The estimated travel time calculated for each pixel is the sum of "costs" between that pixel and settlements of different sizes.

The second dataset contains gridded cropland estimates from Geo-Wiki— the same dataset described for the Digital Availability Subindex (Fritz et al. 2017). Following previous publications, market access was defined as being located within four hours from a settlement of at least 100,000 people (Dorosh et al. 2010; Stifel and Minten 2008; World Bank 2016).

For each pixel of farmland in the Geo-Wiki dataset, an indicator variable was constructed that denoted whether or not that pixel was within four hours of a settlement of 100,000 or more. Two sums were calculated at the country level: the amount of farmland within four hours of a settlement of 100,000 people or more and the total area of farmland in the country. The market access index is calculated as the total farmland within four hours of a settlement divided by the total farmland in the country.

Access to electricity measures the percentage of a country's population with access to electricity. The data for access to electricity were retrieved from the 2018 World Development Indicators.

Basic skills index measures the level of skills of the adult population calculated based on adult literacy levels, school life expectancy, total years of schooling, and tertiary enrollment rate. The index, produced by GSMA, uses an unweighted average of the four components.

Online services index measures the use of information and communication technologies by governments in delivering public services at the national level, with scores ranging from 0 (lowest) to 100 (highest). Data for the Online Service Index were retrieved from the 2020 United Nations E-Government Survey (UN 2020).

The Nondigital Enabling Environment Subindex was calculated using a simple, unweighted mean of the market access index, access to electricity, basic skills index, and online services index.

REFERENCES

Atkinson, A. B. 1970. "On the Measurement of Inequality." *Journal of Economic Theory* 2 (3): 244–63.

Bahia, K., and F. Agnoletto. 2020. *Connected Society: Methodology: Mobile Connectivity Index 2020*. London: GSMA.

Buchhorn, M., B. Smets, L. Bertels, M. Lesiv, N. E. Tsendbazar, M. Herold, and S. Fritz. 2019. "Copernicus Global Land Service: Land Cover 100m: Epoch 2015: Globe." Dataset of the global component of the Copernicus Land Monitoring Service 2019. https://land .copernicus.eu/global/products/lc.

Comber, A., L. See, S. Fritz, M. Van der Velde, C. Perger, and G. Foody. 2013. "Using Control Data to Determine the Reliability of Volunteered Geographic Information about Land Cover. *International Journal of Applied Earth Observation and Geoinformation* 23: 37–48.

Dorosh, P., H. G. Wang, L. You, and E. Schmidt. 2010. "Crop Production and Road Connectivity in Sub-Saharan Africa: A Spatial Analysis." Policy Research Working Paper 5385, World Bank, Washington, DC.

Fritz, S., L. See, C. Perger, I. McCallum, C. Schill, D. Schepaschenko, M. Duerauer, et al. 2017. "A Global Dataset of Crowdsourced Land Cover and Land Use Reference Data." *Scientific Data* 4: 170075.

GSMA Intelligence. 2019. *Mobile Connectivity Index: Methodology*. London: GSMA.

Nelson, A., D. J. Weiss, J. van Etten, A. Cattaneo, T. S. McMenomy, and J. Koo. 2019. "A Suite of Global Accessibility Indicators." *Scientific Data* 6 (266). https://doi.org/10.1038 /s41597-019-0265-5.

Stifel, D., and B. Minten. 2008. "Isolation and Agricultural Productivity." *Agricultural Economics* 39 (1): 1–15.

UN (United Nations). 2020. *UN E-Government Survey 2020.* New York: UN. https://public administration.un.org/egovkb/en-us/Reports/UN-E-Government-Survey-2020.

UNDESA (United Nations Department of Economic and Social Affairs). 2015. "Inequality Measurement." *Development Issues* 2 (December 2015). https://www.un.org/en/develop ment/desa/policy/wess/wess_dev_issues/dsp_policy_02.pdf.

World Bank. 2016. *Transport and ICT.* Washington, DC: World Bank.

APPENDIX E

Maximizing the Finance for Development Approach to Assess the Public Sector Role in Facilitating Broader Development and Adoption of Digital Technologies

TABLE E.1 Potential Entry Points for Public Sector Actions

Maximizing finance for development questions	Supply-side factors		Demand-side factors
	Expand digital infrastructure	**Develop digital agriculture solutions**	**Facilitate adoption of digital technologies in food system**
Is the private sector doing it?	Current status: • More than 90 percent coverage in high-income countries • Fifty percent coverage in low-income countries (even lower for 3G or faster networks)	Current status: • Rapid increase in ag-tech investment over the past 10 years • Significant variations across countries	Higher farmer adoption of digital technologies in high-income countries than in low-income countries

(Continued)

Maximizing finance for development questions	Supply-side factors		Demand-side factors
	Expand digital infrastructure	**Develop digital agriculture solutions**	**Facilitate adoption of digital technologies in food system**
If not, are they limited by policy and regulatory weaknesses or gaps?	• Adopt spectrum management that boosts connectivity. • Lower infrastructure taxes and duties. • Allow infrastructure sharing. • Reduce policy and regulatory uncertainty.	• Improve policy and regulatory environment for business development. • Create data interoperability standards. • Develop governance arrangements for open data. • Clarify data ownership.	• Develop data governance arrangements that build users' confidence and trust in digital technologies • Strengthen land ownership rights.
If not, can public sector investment help crowd in private investment?	• Invest in complementary infrastructure. • As a last resort, subsidize service providers to offset the higher costs of rolling out rural coverage.	• Invest in open data that have public-good characteristics. • Support skills development. • Improve access to finance for start-ups and early maturing ag-tech enterprises. • Support increased use of digital payments. • Support development of digital platforms. • Invest in complementary infrastructure and research and development.	• Support skills development, including digital. • Reduce cost of technology adoption. • Improve access to finance for digital tech adoption. • Invest in complementary infrastructure. • Reevaluate agricultural policies.

Source: World Bank. 2019. *Future of Food: Harnessing Digital Technologies to Improve Food System Outcomes.* Washington, DC: World Bank.

GLOSSARY

agricultural transformation. The structural change in a country's economy that entails a declining share of agriculture in gross domestic product (GDP) (and employment) and a rising share of industry and services as GDP per capita rises. Agricultural transformation is key to reducing poverty and improving livelihoods in the rural space.

application (app). A software program or groups of programs enabling users to perform particular operations. They consist of systems software (operating systems for managing computer resources, for example) and programs such as those for data processing, word processing, and a multitude of functions that run on systems software. An information technology application for managing dairy cooperatives, for example, relies on numerous kinds of applications running on the operating systems of any number of devices and the internet. See http://www .webopedia.com/TERM/A/application.html.

artificial intelligence (AI). In computer science, the theory and development of computer systems able to perform tasks that normally require human intelligence. Sometimes called *machine intelligence*, artificial intelligence may include visual perception, speech recognition, decision-making, translation, crop and soil monitoring, weather forecasting, disease and pest identification, and predictive analytics.

big data. Extremely large volumes of both structured and unstructured data—too large or complex to be processed by traditional data-processing techniques—that may be analyzed to reveal patterns, trends, and associations.

blockchain. A digital public ledger, which is a record of online transactions, containing information that can be simultaneously used and shared via a large decentralized, publicly accessible network. For example, blockchain is the core technology for cryptocurrencies such as bitcoin; it ensures the integrity of cryptocurrencies by encrypting, validating, and permanently recording transactions. Blockchain provides a secure way to store and manage data, facilitating the traceability of information throughout the agrifood system.

broadband network. Telecommunications networks that include wide bandwidth data transmissions of audio, data, still images, or full-motion video and that flexibly allocate transmission capacity over multiple-point connections.

cloud computing. On-demand availability of remote computing services such as servers, storage, databases, networking, software, analytics, and intelligence over the internet in a commercial provider's data center, known as the *public cloud*, without direct active management by the user. Cloud computing offers faster innovation, flexible resources, and economies of scale.

crowdsourcing. Shorthand for leveraging mass collaboration through information and communication technologies by distributing tasks to or requesting information from a large group of people or community ("crowd") through an open call or message.

data. Quantities, characteristics, symbols, or information, usually numerical, that are collected through observation and used as a basis for reasoning, discussion, or calculation.

database. Structured collections of data, stored and accessed electronically from an accessible computer system.

decision-support system (DSS). Collect, process, and provide data from various sources to support human decision-making under different circumstances. A DSS consists of three main components: sophisticated database management capabilities with access to internal and external data, powerful modeling functions accessed by a model management system, and powerful user interface designs that enable interactive queries, reporting, and graphing functions. A DSS can employ big data and AI, and they can be made available through smartphone apps.

digital agriculture. The collection of tools that collect, store, analyze, optimize, and share digital information along the entire food value chain, from farm to fork. It encompasses the links of a diversifying and rapidly expanding spectrum of digital technologies across different value chain segments and is anchored around data generation and (often interrelated) data systems.

digital divide. The differences in the capacity to access and use information and communication technologies (ICTs) among individuals, men and women, households, geographic areas, socioeconomic groups, ethnic groups, and so forth.

The capacity to access ICTs encompasses physical access as well as access to the resources and skills to participate effectively as digital citizens.

digital goods. Also *electronic* or *e-goods*, defined as intangible products stored, sold, and delivered electronically: for example, over the internet. Some examples of digital goods include digital media, internet coupons, and electronically traded financial instruments.

digitalization. The use of digital technologies and digitized data and information to change businesses models by providing new revenue opportunities. Digitalization may also refer to the restructuring of social life around digital communication and media infrastructures.

digital payments. Also *electronic* or *e-payments*, conducted over the internet and mobile channels. Payers and payees both use digital modes to send and receive money.

digital platforms. A place that brings together stakeholders in the agrifood system to exchange information, goods, and services through digital technologies, such as mobile phones, computers, internet kiosks, and so on. Common features of digital platforms include network effects and a large scale (or scale-up potential).

digital services. Services (transactions devices in which no physical goods are transferred from the seller to the buyer) delivered via the internet or electronic network across platforms. Digital services typically require little to no human intervention.

digital technologies. Tools that collect, store, analyze, and share information digitally, including mobile phones and the internet. These technologies range from simple off-line farmer advisory digital videos to complex systems requiring higher levels of mobile phone and internet connectivity, such as distributed ledger technologies for value chain traceability and some forms of precision agriculture. Digital technologies have significant potential to improve efficiency, equity, and environmental sustainability in the food system.

digital transformation. The integration of people-centric, cross-cutting, core organizational changes in a business, economy, or society that leverages digital technologies. Digital transformation must be backed by leadership and encourages businesses to experiment frequently and challenge the status quo.

digitization. The material process of converting individual analog data into digital bits. Digitization can result in internal optimization and cost reduction.

distributed ledger technology. Digital and distributed transaction ledger that stores blocks of data shared across a network of computer nodes. Each block of the ledger contains data about transactions that have been executed on the platform. To add a block to the ledger, every computer node of the network needs to verify and validate it. Thanks to this verification, the system does not need an intermediary to check transactions.

e-commerce. Also *electronic commerce*, the activity of electronically buying or selling goods or services using the internet, and the transfer of data and money to execute the transactions. E-commerce can also describe any kind of commercial transaction facilitated by the internet. E-commerce in agriculture is technologically divided into two general modes of operation: via a website direct to buyers and via a third-party-operated platform. E-commerce has a variety of business models (business-to-business, online-to-online, online-to-off-line, and so on).

e-government. Also *electronic government*, a government's use of information and communication technologies to enhance public services.

e-learning. Also *electronic learning*, the use of electronic technologies to deliver, facilitate, and enhance both formal and informal learning and knowledge sharing at any time, in any place, and at any pace.

e-platform. Electronic platform, also *digital platform:* technology-enabled business model that facilitates the exchange of information, communication, or commercial transactions between groups. Examples of e-platforms include social media platforms such as Facebook, application stores such as Apple and Google Play, and crowdsourcing platforms such as Uber.

global navigation satellite system (GNSS). Integrated system of satellites providing signals from space that transmit timing data to receivers, providing global coverage. The information is then used to determine location. Examples include the US NAVSTAR Global Positioning System and Europe's Galileo.

information and communication technology (ICT). Technology that enable access, storage, transmission, and manipulation of information via telecommunications as well as necessary enterprise software, middleware, storage, and audiovisual systems. ICTs include the internet, wireless networks, cell phones, and other communication media.

internet of things (IoT). The interconnection via the internet of computing devices embedded in everyday objects and mechanical and digital machines provided with unique identifiers, enabling data transfer over a network without human-to-human or human-to-computer interaction.

mobile application. Software on a portable device (such as a mobile phone handset, personal digital assistant, or tablet computer) that enables a user to carry out one or more specific tasks not directly related to the operation of the device itself. Examples include the ability to access specific information (for instance, via a website), make payments and other transactions, play games, and send messages.

precision farming. Also *precision agriculture*, or *satellite farming*, the site-specific management of crop production inputs such as seed, fertilizer, lime, pesticides, and so on by observing, measuring, and responding to intra- and interfield crop variability. Precision farming aims to increase profits, reduce waste, and maintain environmental sustainability.

remote sensing. In contrast to on-site observation, acquiring information about an object or phenomenon without direct physical contact between the sensor and the object. Remote sensing is typically conducted by scanning the earth by a satellite or high-flying aircraft.

robotics. An interdisciplinary branch of technology that deals with the design, construction, and application of robots, as well as computing systems for their perception, control, sensory feedback, and information processing. Robotics makes use of disciplines such as dynamic system modeling and analysis, biology, mechanical engineering, electrical and electronic engineering, and computer science, among others.

satellite imagery. An image of Earth taken from satellites in orbit. Satellite imagery can be spatial (size of surface area), spectral (wavelength interval), temporal (amount of time), and radiometric (levels of brightness). Each type of image captures a variety of data about a given area that can vary in size. The resolution (in meters) of these images depends on the satellite system used and its distance from earth; weather can interfere mainly with satellite systems utilizing visible wavelengths of light.

sensor. Device that responds to a physical stimulus (such as heat, light, sound, pressure, magnetism, or a particular motion) and transmits a resulting impulse (as for measurement or operating a control).

unmanned aerial vehicle (UAV). Aircraft piloted by remote control or onboard computers without a human pilot. Commonly known as drones, UAVs may travel along a fixed flight path or can be controlled remotely. In agriculture, UAVs are frequently used to survey crops.